# REMEMBRANCE, COMMUNION, AND HOPE

Printed in the United States of America

ISBN-13: 978-1-950572-01-4
ISBN-10: 1-950572-01-3

Library of Congress Control Number: 2019938871

THE HISTORICAL SERIES OF THE REFORMED CHURCH IN AMERICA
NO. 96

# REMEMBRANCE, COMMUNION, AND HOPE

Essays in Honor of Allan J. Jansen

Matthew J. van Maastricht, editor

REFORMED CHURCH PRESS
Grand Rapids, Michigan

**The Historical Series of the Reformed Church in America**

The series was inaugurated in 1968 by the General Synod of the Reformed Church in America acting through the Commission on History to communicate the church's heritage and collective memory and to reflect on our identity and mission, encouraging historical scholarship which informs both church and academy.

www.rca.org/series

General Editor
   James Hart Brumm, MDiv, MPhil
   New Brunswick Theological Seminary

Associate Editor
   Andrew Klumpp, MDiv
   Southern Methodist University

Copy Editor
   Jordan Humm
   Grand Rapids, MI

Production Editor
   Russell L. Gasero
   Archives, Reformed Church in America

Cover Design
   Matthew Gasero
   Archives, Reformed Church in America

General Editor Emeritus
   Donald J. Bruggink, PhD, DD
   Van Raalte Institute, Hope College

Commission on History
   Alexander Arthurs, Western Theological Seminary
   Lynn Japinga, PhD, Hope College
   Andrew Klumpp, MDiv, Southern Methodist University
   Steven Pierce, DMin, Grand Rapids, MI
   David M. Tripold, PhD, Monmouth University
   Douglas Van Aartsen, MDiv, Ireton, Iowa

# Contents

# Donors

Pastor Dave Armstrong
Mary and Thomas Bartha
Rev. Charles and Debbie Bigelow
Erica & Joshua Bode
Rev. Dr. Michael S. Bos
Mary Jane and Ed Brown
Jim Brownson
The Rev. Dr. Donald J. Bruggink
James & Kathleen Hart Brumm
Daniel Carlson
Sally Ann M. Castle
Jaeseung Cha
Rev. Karen M. Chavis
Brian Clary
John and Margaret Coakley
Rev. Paige A. Convis
John & Glenda De Koster
Philip & Rosalyn De Koster
In Memory of Faith and Harry
    Dunlop
Stephen Eckert
Rev. E.J. Emerson
Rev. Timothy Espar
Reverend Barbara Felker
First Reformed Church of
    Bethlehem, NY
Rev. Donna Field
Rev. Peggy Funderburke
Matthew Gasero
Russell and Maria Gasero
Richard and Mary Glendening
Steve & Pat Goodman
David K. Groeneveld
Rev. Dr. Melva J. Hayden
Dr. Marvin D. Hoff
Steve and Judy Janssen

Rev. Dr. Jeffrey S. Japinga
Elizabeth Johnson and Peter
    Paulsen
Rev. Sharon D. Johnson
David Jones
Norm and Mary Kansfield
Susan Kerr
James Jinhong Kim
Norman and Joyce Kolenbrander
Charles & Beatrice Legere
Brad and Cathy Lewis
Ronald D. Lokhorst
Joan Marshall
Gregg and Vicki Mast
Rev. Micah L. McCreary, Ph.D
Rev. Dr. Ellen Canty McEachern
T. Patrick Milas, Ph.D.
Linda and Nickolas Miles
Rev. Charlie and Deb Morris
Gay Kersey Morris
Rev. Timothy Mulder
Carol Myers
New Baltimore Reformed
    Church, NY
Abigail Norton
John & Marilyn Paarlberg
Phyllis and Nolan Palsma
Demitra Tulla Pangburn
Rev. Carol Lynn Patterson, D. Min
Chad Pierce
Steven and Monica Pierce
Cathy Proctor
Harlan and Ellen Ratmeyer
Jim Reid
Won-Jong Rhee
Wilfredo Rodriguez

Fred and Claudette Schubert
Kerry Schubert
Revs. Douglas & Aleta Shepler
Sandra Sheppard
Kathleen S. Smith
Rev. Raynard Daniel Smith, Ph.D
Rev. Terry Ann Smith, Ph.D
Rev. Evans L. Spagner
Jill Stevenson
Rev. Beth Tanner, Ph.D
Nancy and Norman Tellier

Kenneth J. Termott
Rev. Dr. Lisa Vander Wal
Rev. Dr. Arthur "Bud" Van Eck
Timothy Van Heest
Rev. Matthew and Marie van
   Maastricht
Glenn and Eileen Van Oort
Maudelin Willock
Rett Zabriskie
John Zavacky

# Resolution
## Rev. Dr. Allan Janssen

WHEREAS the Rev. Allan Janssen, Ph.D. has served the Reformed Church in America as a General professor since 2012; and

WHEREAS Dr. Janssen, who was ordained as a minister of Word and sacrament in the Reformed Church in America in 1973 and served several congregations in the forty years that followed, has taught at New Brunswick Theological Seminary since 1999, becoming an affiliate faculty member in 2006 and, from that same year, has regularly taught courses through the Ministerial Formation Certification Agency; and

WHEREAS Dr. Janssen has served the Reformed Church in America faithfully on its boards, committees and commissions and in ecumenical bodies; and

WHEREAS through his teaching, his service on the Commission on Church Order, his publications, and his wise advice in settings formal and informal, Dr. Janssen has earned the church's deep appreciation for his insights into the Book of Church Order and its value for shaping our ministry and mission; and

WHEREAS Dr. Janssen through his teaching and writing, as well as through his leadership of New Brunswick Seminary's biennial International Summer School of Theology in the Netherlands, has introduced many students and others, both in and beyond the Reformed Church in America, to the rich traditions of Dutch theology;

THEREFORE, BE IT RESOLVED that the 212th regular session of the General Synod of the Reformed Church in America, meeting June 7 through 12, 2018, in Grand Rapids, Michigan, expresses its deepest gratitude to Dr. Janssen for his years of service, and offers its prayers for a fulfilling retirement along with his wife Colleen;

AND BE IT ALSO RESOLVED that Dr. Allan Janssen be declared a General Synod professor emeritus as of June 13, 2018.

# Acknowledgments

Literary works are always collaborative endeavors, particularly in essay collections as this one. I wish to express my gratitude to the authors for their excellent contributions to this volume and their patience with this editor as he was venturing into *terra incognita*. The ability to offer these volumes for retiring General Synod professors can be possible not only with the capable and willing authors but also the donors who give generously to financially support this volume and others that they might be offered to the church, to whom we all owe our thanks.

I am filled with gratitude to Russell Gasero, the Reformed Church in America (RCA) archivist and the committed and very capable production editor of the Historical Series of the RCA; Jordan Humm who copyedited this volume; and Daniel Meeter, one of the authors in this volume, who provided me some assistance with Dutch translation questions.

Finally, to James Hart Brumm, the new general editor of the Historical Series, for his steadfast commitment to continuing the great work that was put into motion by the General Synod of 1968 and stewarded over the past half-century by the general editor emeritus,

Donald Bruggink. James not only offered me this opportunity but also provided invaluable guidance and support along the way.

Matthew J. van Maastricht
Epiphanytide, 2019
Altamont, New York

# Contributors

**Carol M. Bechtel** is professor of Old Testament at Western Theological Seminary in Holland, Michigan, where she has taught since 1994. Dr. Bechtel studied at Hope College in Holland, Michigan, and Western Theological Seminary before receiving her PhD in Old Testament from Yale University in New Haven, Connecticut. Dr. Bechtel is a General Synod professor of theology in the Reformed Church in America (RCA) and has served as president of the RCA's General Synod. She currently serves as the executive director of the American Waldensian Society. Her publications include a commentary on Esther for the *Interpretation* series and several Bible study books and curricula.

**Abraham van de Beek** is professor emeritus of the Vrije Universiteit Amsterdam (Free University of Amsterdam) in Amsterdam, the Netherlands, and extraordinary professor at the University of Stellenbosch, South Africa.

**Karel Blei,** born 1932, studied theology at the University of Leiden in Leiden, the Netherlands, with K.H. Miskotte and earned a PhD in 1972 at Leiden under Hendrikus Berkhof. He served several parishes in the Netherlands Reformed Church before serving as the general secretary of the Netherlands Reformed Church from 1987 to 1997. He has published widely on church history and biblical and ecumenical theology, including most recently, *Karl Barth en zijn theologische weg door de tijd* (*Karl Barth and His Theological Way Through Time*).

**Leon van den Broeke** is associate professor of religion, law, society, and church polity and chairs the Centre for Religion and Law at Vrije Universiteit Amsterdam. He is also associate professor of church polity and director of the Deddens Church Polity Centre at the Theologische Universiteit (Theological University of the Reformed Churches) in Kampen, the Netherlands.

**John W. Coakley**, L. Russell Feakes Professor of Church History, emeritus, at New Brunswick Theological Seminary in New Brunswick, New Jersey, is a minister of Word and sacrament in the Reformed Church in America and a General Synod professor emeritus. Among his publications are *Women, Men, and Spiritual Power: Female Saints and Their Collaborators* (Columbia University Press, 2006); *New Brunswick Theological Seminary: An Illustrated History* (Eerdmans, 2014); and (as co-editor), *Readings in World Christian History: Earliest Christianity to 1453* (Orbis Books, 2004).

**Daniel M. Griswold** is the coordinator and clerk of the Classis of Holland (Michigan). Prior to that, he was the pastor of Trinity Reformed Church in Rochester, New York, for 15 years. He received a PhD in religious studies from Southern Methodist University in Dallas, Texas. While in Rochester, Daniel was a member of the Penfield Symphony Orchestra and of the Cordancia Chamber Orchestra, and his active string quartet, quintet, and sextet performed several chamber music concerts.

**Eugene P. Heideman** is retired secretary of world mission for the Reformed Church in America. Prior to that appointment, he served as a missionary in the Church of South India, as professor of Bible and religion at Central College in Pella, Iowa, and as academic dean at Western Theological Seminary.

**Paul Janssen**, a 1985 graduate of New Brunswick Theological Seminary and has served churches in Hackensack, Park Ridge, and Somerville, New Jersey. He is married to Annette, a teacher of teachers, and has two grown children, Samuel and Emma. He has served the Reformed Church in America and local classes on commissions, task forces, and committees dealing with the liturgical life of the church, polity, and ecumenical relationships.

**Leo J. Koffeman** is professor emeritus of church polity and ecumenism at Protestant Theological University in Amsterdam, the Netherlands. He also serves as an extraordinary professor in the respective theological faculties of Stellenbosch University in Stellenbosch, South Africa, and the University of Pretoria in Pretoria, South Africa. He is the author of *In Order to Serve: An Ecumenical Introduction to Church Polity* (2014).

**Christo Lombard** is currently teaching at the United Lutheran Seminary Paulinum in Windhoek, Namibia. He is a professor emeritus of the University of the Western Cape (UWC) where he lectured for 22 years and served as chair of the department of religion and theology for some time. He has been the Desmond Tutu Chair for Ecumenical Theology and Social Transformation. Previously, he taught at the University of Namibia as the founding chair of the department of religion and theology. During that period in Namibia, he was involved in the process of liberation of Namibia via the Namibia Peace Plan 435 movement and was later involved in the Breaking the Wall of Silence movement.

**Matthew J. van Maastricht** is the pastor of the Altamont Reformed Church in Altamont, New York, and an adjunct instructor at Western and New Brunswick Theological Seminaries, who serves as the general editor of the Congregational History Series of the Reformed Church in America.

**Gregg Mast** is retired after more than 40 years of ministry in the Reformed Church in America and is president emeritus of New Brunswick Theological Seminary. He served more than half of his career as a congregational pastor in Johannesburg, South Africa; Irvington, New Jersey; and Albany, New York. In addition, he served as the minister of social witness and the director of ministry services in the Reformed Church in America and was elected the president of the General Synod in 1999.

**Daniel J. Meeter** has been pastor of the Old First Dutch Reformed Church of Brooklyn, New York, since 2001. He began teaching at

New Brunswick Seminary in 1977, was ordained in 1980, and earned his PhD at Drew University in Madison, New Jersey, in 1989. He has published extensively on the RCA's Constitution: Doctrine, Liturgy, and Government.

**Micah L. McCreary** is president of New Brunswick Theological Seminary. Prior to coming to New Brunswick, Dr. McCreary served in the pastorate and as associate professor of psychology at Virginia Commonwealth University in Richmond, Virginia. He studied at the University of Michigan in Ann Arbor, Michigan, and at the Samuel DeWitt Proctor School of Theology at Virginia Union University in Richmond, Virginia. He received his PhD in counseling psychology from Virginia Commonwealth University.

# Laudatio

Matthew J. van Maastricht

It was a cold day in January, 2008, when I first encountered the Rev. Dr. Allan Janssen in room 106 at Western Theological Seminary in Holland, Michigan. I first encountered him not as a person but as an author. It was in this place and at this time that I took my first steps into church polity with two teachers. The course was taught by the late Rev. Dr. George Brown, Jr., and my second teacher was Allan, working through his book, *Constitutional Theology*. It was a world that opened to me, a world that I had not encountered before. It was in that room that I learned that church polity was not so much a matter of rules but a matter of theology.

Church polity operates at two major levels. First, there is the surface level, the one that includes the rules and regulations. Too often, this is the extent of one's entry into church polity. It sounds like law, and it makes us nervous. Or, we love legalism, and we spend all our time trying to ensure that we live by the letter of the law. But there is a deeper level, and this is the level that Allan invited us into, the level that is not just the "what" of the order but the "why." It is to understand the theology underneath the order: the logic and spirit of the order. This course, with these two teachers, quite literally changed the course of my life and ministry.

But my connection with Allan wasn't solely through his books. One of the wonderful things about a relatively small church communion is that there is a good chance there is only one or two degrees of separation between two people. It was not long before I started to get to know Allan as person. We would cross paths at General Synod and then later at commission meetings. He was the one who introduced me to a collection of church polity scholars and practitioners from around the globe, and he was the one who helped me to see and begin to think about how to connect with the (big and interesting) global Reformed community. My first steps in the Netherlands—literally; he met me in the airport—were guided by Allan, and through all of this I grew in my appreciation, not only for Allan the writer or Allan the scholar or even Allan the teacher, but for Allan the person. And it is this relational connection that has proven so valuable and meaningful to me.

The ministry was bred into his bones. His father was a minister, and Allan spent the formative years of his life in parsonages in the Midwest. The church was his contextual reality, it was the air that he breathed, and it is the blood that pulses through his veins. Growing up in Iowa, Allan studied at Central College in Pella, Iowa, before participating in the short-lived bi-level, multi-site formation and education process, which afforded him the opportunity to study at both Western and New Brunswick Theological Seminaries. Al received his first call not in the Midwest, but in Port Ewen, New York, a hamlet on the shores of the Hudson River in Ulster County, and it is in the eastern wing of the Reformed church that Allan would spend the rest of his ministry.

He labored there for five years until he received a call further north to the First Reformed Church of Bethlehem in Selkirk, New York. Selkirk was his longest pastorate and was a significant time in his ministry. During this pastorate he received a Master of Arts in Philosophy at the University at Albany. It was also during this pastorate that the struggle over the ordination of women to the ministry of Word and sacrament came to a head in the form of judicial proceedings, and Allan was in the midst of it, advocating for the inclusion of women in all the offices of the church.

In Selkirk, the first of Allan's books was published: *Gathered at Albany*. Researching the two hundred plus years of the Classis of Albany, Allan provided an accessible and winsome history of one of the oldest classes in the Reformed church. He cemented his role in Reformed church polity when he authored *Constitutional Theology*, a book which is to this day used in church polity courses for students of theology. And though he is no longer teaching at the seminary, his influence continues to reverberate through the seminaries and churches as they continue to learn from Allan as I did.

Shortly after this book was finished, Allan was called to Glen Rock, New Jersey, which would be his final pastorate. While in Glen Rock, he continued his academic pursuits, and, through his involvement with the International Reformed Theological Institute, he was introduced to Abraham van de Beek. Under Van de Beek's supervision (with Christo Lombard), he wrote his *proefschrift* (doctoral dissertation) at the Vrije Universiteit Amsterdam: *Kingdom, Office, and Church: A Study of A.A. van Ruler's Doctrine of Ecclesiastical Office*.

During his pastorate at Glen Rock, Allan was appointed as an affiliate professor of theological studies at the New Brunswick Theological Seminary and had a significant impact on a further generation of Reformed church ministers who studied at that esteemed institution. When the General Synod professorate was opened beyond tenured faculty at the seminaries, Allan was elected to the professorate— one of the very few professors of theology to serve concurrently under a pastoral charge.

This brief sketch covers some of the "about," but there is so much more to Allan and his contributions to the local church, the broader church, and to the academy.

For so many, Allan is the authority on Reformed church polity, and that is a well-founded view. He, quite literally, wrote the book on Reformed Church in America (RCA) polity and has dedicated himself to the church order as a matter of theology. Yet he is so much more than this: an ecumenist; a scholar of the Utrecht theologian A.A. van Ruler; a passionate advocate for justice whether it be in advocating against the Vietnam war, pushing for opening the ministry of Word and sacrament to women, or fighting against apartheid in South Africa. Al's presence and involvement in the international Reformed community is deep and rich.

Yet despite all of this work, Allan is not an "academic," at least in the way that is typically used. He has particular areas of scholarly expertise and interest, but he is not narrowly focused on one single area to the exclusion of others. He is a generalist in the long and noble tradition of the generations of ministers and professors who have gone before. While the term "generalist" in the scholarly world often lacks positive connotation, it does not necessarily imply a lack of academic or intellectual rigor and certainly does not in Allan's case. He is a true theologian in his own right. However, rather than spending his days in an academy, he spent his days below a steeple, in homes, beside hospital beds, and in his study. He was a both a scholar and the pastor of local churches who would write about A.A. van Ruler in the morning and talk about the color of the sanctuary carpet in the evening. While the recent trend generally has been to separate scholarship and pastoral practice, Allan lived out an old model of ministry which had been the oxygen of the church for so long: the pastor-scholar.

The pastor-scholar model is not the only model of ministry, nor is it necessarily the normative one. However, it is a model that has, all too often, gone the way of passenger pigeon. Changes in culture and changes in how we understand the church has led the pastor to function more like a manager: someone who can supervise staff, drive mission and vision statements, and run a programmatic organization. To be sure, these are all important giftings in a pastor and teacher of a local church. But notably absent is "theologian." Increasingly, it seems, pastors are less and less expected to be theological experts and more and more expected to be business and managerial experts.

While some may long for days gone by, Allan did not live in some imagined world before the professionalization of the ministry; he lived in the world that you and I inhabit, serving churches much like those with which you and I are familiar. Yet the truth is, we make time for those things which are important, and Allan made time for academic pursuits and accomplishments. He did this while faithfully continuing to serve his churches, "to preach and teach the good news of salvation in Christ, to build up and equip the church for mission in the world, to free the enslaved, to relieve the oppressed, to comfort the afflicted, and to walk humbly with God," as the Declaration for Ministers proclaims.

The separation of theology and the contextual role of a pastor has, in many ways, caused a disconnect in modern church life. On the one hand, theology can be done in isolation from the lived experience of the church. On the other hand, the lived experience of the church can de-theologize itself. Is the creation of a church budget a theological matter? Does the maintenance of a building have theological implications? Is there something theological about where a minister stands, or how announcements are handled in a worship service, or about the new light fixtures? Indeed, while many of these may seem simply organizational or functional, the pastor-scholar would say that these are also deeply theological. It is in the uniting of the head and the feet, of the lofty and the rooted, of the intellectual and affectual that a church exists differently from all other organizational entities.

The importance of pastor-scholars isn't simply so that they can help their churches understand theology, or so that they can have theologically rich and informed preaching and teaching, although these are all good things. The importance of pastor-scholars is that it is in the ministry of these individuals that the church and the academy come together. The church finds a footing and the academy finds life; head and heart join to perfect our love of God.

Al was the first real example that I had of the pastor-scholar. I always knew that there were theologically astute pastors who were well read, who thought deeply, and who tried to help convey the riches of the traditions to their congregations, all of which is laudable. But with Al there was something different: he was a scholar who engaged in significant research, writing, teaching, and lecturing. It was through Allan that I first glimpsed a vision of the church that was not simply a consumer of theological scholarship but could be a locus of theological scholarship itself.

With the increasing scarcity of the pastor-theologian and the pastor-scholar, we risk losing sight of the reality that these two roles influence one another. Pastoral work makes one a better scholar, and scholarship makes one a better pastor. It is in dealing with the realities of the church and pastoral ministry that one can bridge that gap that seems to have grown ever wider as the years progress between the church and the academy.

The title of this collection is *Remembrance, Communion, and Hope*. These three words are the outline of the "Meaning of the Sacrament" in the Liturgy for the Lord's Supper and a topic of an essay in this volume by Gregg Mast. This title reflects a couple of things. First, it reflects Allan's service not only behind the lectern of the seminary but behind the sacramental table as he ministered the holy mysteries to the people of God. Second, these three movements reflect the different temporal aspects of the Christian life. This is reflected in the ministry of Word and sacrament as we help God's people to remember the work of God in the past, to see the work of God in the present, and to look to the completion of the work of God in the future. This is not just a way of thinking; it is a way of being. Indeed, this can be seen in many of the contributions here.

The essays herein reflect Allan's commitments in the parish and in the academy. Daniel Griswold writes about the pastoral ministry in a

xxii    REMEMBRANCE, COMMUNION, AND HOPE

unique way, reflecting his additional identity as a musician, seeking to understand how we deal with the juggling of pastoral tasks, and putting it into the framework of musical lines which move interdependently with one another, creating something far more spectacular than just a single musical melody. Micah McCreary thinks about the need for the seminary to stay connected to the life of the local church and the essential role that the pastor-theologian has in bridging these two worlds which have grown further apart but, in doing so, have lost a significant part of their respective identities. Gregg Mast's contribution looks at the history of the 1966 Reformed Church Liturgy for the Lord's Supper, something that Allan has read and recited innumerable times in his own ministry of Word and sacrament. And John Coakley writes about John Henry Livingston, the first professor of theology in the Reformed church and one who balanced professorial duties and pastoral ministry. Coakley's contribution focuses on Livingston's thinking about missions—something that has risen to the forefront in the ecclesiastical life.

Daniel Meeter and Gene Heideman both offer essays on the Doctrinal Standards, a particular area of focus for Allan. This is fitting not only because he taught the Doctrinal Standards for several years but also because the "home" of the Standards are the church, not the academy. Most certainly it is used in academic settings, but the intentional locus of its use and the place where most people come into contact with it is the local church, the place where faith and life meet. And it is here where the Standards help to shape not only the doctrine of the church but also the lived faith of the church, and it is from here—from pews and chairs and stained glass windows, around pulpit, Table, and font—that churches develop their life. And this is greatly influenced by catechisms. Meeter writes about the Heidelberg and Westminster catechisms and shows how these two catechisms represent to distinct branches of the Reformed family. Heideman writes about the Canons of Dort (I,6 and I,7) and, in particular, examines the biblical passages that these articles cite as a way of understanding. Indeed, Heideman sees the Standards neither as something to be relegated to a shelf, never to see the light of day, nor as something to be treated as inerrant, as though they were dictated by God. But rather, we take them seriously within their context and look at the deeper thing to which they point.

A number of these essays arise from a Dutch context or have a focus on Dutch theology and ecclesiology. This has been a particular interest of Allan's; he may in fact be more well known on the other side of the Atlantic than on this one. He has long been involved in the International Reformed Theological Institute (IRTI), and he received his doctorate from the Vrije Universiteit Amsterdam where Van Ruler was the focus of his research. He has for many years directed and shepherded the International Summer School in the Netherlands through the New Brunswick Theological Seminary. Unfortunately, Dutch theologians tend not to receive as much focus in the Reformed Church in America, partly because comparably few of their writings are translated. It would be very beneficial and profitable for us and the church to become acquainted with their solid, rooted, and creative work. Karel Blei offers an essay on Oepke Noordmans, the subject of a book by Blei that Allan translated. Noordmans was a rather creative twentieth-century Dutch Reformed theologian and a significant voice in the Netherlands Reformed Church. Abraham van de Beek offers an essay on Van Ruler's theology of the sacraments. Van Ruler, of course, was the central theologian in Allan's doctoral research and is another very creative theologian in the Netherlands Reformed Church. Leon van den Broeke offers an additional essay on Van Ruler, this one on church polity and, in particular, Van Ruler's perspective of the boards, councils, and committees of the church that helped the church to live out its mission as a gestalt of the kingdom of God. Christo Lombard, a South African Van Ruler scholar, writes about Van Ruler's emphasis on joy, for God works not only in the future and or in the past but in the world that we inhabit right now. Leo Koffeman offers an essay on ordained office, particularly in light of the more recent discussions of missional ecclesiology. This is a conversation that is ongoing in the context of the Reformed Church in America as well. It would certainly benefit us to listen to our brothers and sisters in our motherchurch to learn from their work and experiences.

Finally, the volume concludes with essays of a more personal tone. Carol Bechtel offers some insight into future directions to which Al might turn, not only in his scholarship but also in life. And finally, though certainly not least, Paul Janssen offers us a rich dessert, allowing us an ear at the dining room table of a lifetime of conversations between two brothers who are both Reformed church ministers and care deeply about church polity.

As Bechtel mentions in her essay, theologians never stop be-coming theologians, and this is certainly the case with Allan. Truly, his retirement does not mark the completion of a vocation but only a point of transition. On a personal note, Allan and I share many of the same interests and pursuits, yet this makes me all the more aware that his shoes are ones that can never be filled, and I am grateful for his continuing mentorship, his colleagueship, and his friendship.

To be honest, Allan is far more of a gift than most people in the Reformed Church in America realize; perhaps familiarity leads to lack of appreciation. But as this volume reminds us, Allan is well respected around the world and broadly in the ecumenical movement. He is a gift to the church, and this is a small token of the great appreciation that not only I have for him but that the Reformed Church has for him.

It is a great privilege to offer these essays in honor of the Rev. Dr. Allan J. Janssen—to many of us, Al. These are offered to him, and to the church, and to the world.

CHAPTER 1

# The Calling of a Pastor

Daniel M. Griswold

I am a pastor.

I say that neither as a matter of pride nor of embarrassment. I say it like I would say my name. It is who I am. Others might not understand it or like it. Others might be too impressed by it or too intimidated. But there is little I can do about that. I am a pastor. It is what I do, and it is who I am.

As a pastor, I served a congregation in Rochester, New York—Trinity Reformed Church—for fifteen years. From August of 2003 to November of 2018, I ministered to and with the fine people of Trinity Reformed. I was blessed to be there. I hope that they were blessed too. It belongs, as do I, to a small yet historic Protestant denomination called the Reformed Church in America (RCA). The RCA has been home to me almost as long as I can remember, and it is within that communion that I hold (or does it hold me?) the office of minister of Word and sacrament. As a result, I know it very well, in a way that brings both joy and sorrow.

But I am not just a pastor. I am married for more than 30 years to Tammi, who is caring and strong in ways I do not deserve. And I have

1

children, three of them: Bethany, Jonathan, and Christopher, who are a continual source of joy and pride. Even there, it does not stop. I have parents and in-laws and aunts and uncles and cousins. I have friends. I have hobbies and interests.

Just as surely, I have not always been a pastor. There was a time when I was not one, and there will be a time when I am no longer. There is more to me than pastoral work, as there was a "me" before ordination. I am grateful for that. I have no desire to discard what came before or to preclude what is yet to come simply because it does not fit under a robe or in a pulpit.

This is all to say that I play many roles and wear many hats. I can name a number of them readily: friend, spouse, father, preacher, administrator, counselor, musician, academic, child of God, follower of Christ. Each of these (and more) are important to me. Even as I might find it difficult at times to live into all those roles, to give them all their due, I would not want to give up any of them. As I see it, they are all, somehow, part of the calling to be a pastor and yet more than that: to be a pastor with wholeness and integrity.

Martin Copenhaver puts it this way: "People rightly expect that the person they see in the pulpit will be the same person they run into at the grocery store or meet at the high school reunion. The pastoral life is an integrated life. There is another way to put it: being a pastor requires integrity."[1]

The integrity is the key here, not in a strictly moral sense but rather as a matter of unity and health (which of course does have ethical implications). By "integrity," I have in mind something more like "integration," implying unity and interconnection. It concerns questions such as these: How do I bring together all the things that make me who I am in a way that is healthy and whole? How do I give proper space to the things in and outside of me that require my attention?

What I have confessed here is by no means unique to me. It is, I expect, a story in which many will hear their own stories. Surely the struggle for integration of the self-in-ministry is a great challenge for most pastors today. We struggle to discern the integration of all our roles, all our "selves," finding the way of working and resting that gives coherence to the whole over which they usually seem to compete. We know, in ourselves or from our colleagues, the fatigue that comes from

---

[1]     Lilian Daniel and Martin B. Copenhaver, *This Odd and Wondrous Calling: The Public and Private Lives of Two Ministers* (Grand Rapids: Eerdmans, 2009), 62.

the struggle to give each of our several "parts" its own proper time and place.

Something like this is the case for most anybody in ministry. Of course, it is not just for those in ministry. This is a dominant feature of modern life in much of North America. We're all so busy as we struggle to earn a living and maintain relationships and raise families and volunteer for worthwhile causes and stay informed about the issues of the day.

Ministers sometimes act as if the challenge of integration is greater for those in ministry. They sometimes talk as if their challenges are unique to their profession. I want to be kind. But this is whining. Worse, it is an insult to non-pastors—those in other disciplines who likewise work hard—as those who thus whine overlook the real struggles of a similar nature that others surely have.

Even so, this is a significant aspect of the challenge of ministry. We juggle many responsibilities. We wear a lot of hats. With all those hats, it is tough to keep it all together. Yet keep it together we must, as our ongoing effectiveness as pastors depends on it. *Other people* depend on it. *How* do we keep it all together?

## Common Metaphors

Very often, people will respond to the challenge of life-ministry integrity with advice. It is well-meaning advice, offered at ordinations and after meetings and over lunch, advice that is wrapped up with particular metaphors, earnestly delivered with the intention of being helpful. I question whether they actually are. For me, the metaphors that come with the well-intended advice likewise come burdened with significant problems. I find that two metaphors in particular are especially common and commonly problematic.

The first of these metaphors is heard in the admonition frequently given to pastors and those training for ministry to be about "self-care." One must care for the self, we are told, as we likewise are told, in hushed tones and with sorrowful looks, about the ministers who did not exercise appropriate self-care, those who now serve as negative examples of the perils of insufficient care of the self.

Surely, there is something to this. After all, what would be the alternative to self-care? Self-hatred? Spiritual masochism? These, too, can be found among the church's servants, bringing harm to themselves and to those near them. So it might seem that self-care is not only good advice, but even obvious advice. Not so obvious is that "self-care" is also a metaphor, an imaginative and symbolic way of viewing reality, for it rests on a conception of the life-work and life-ministry struggle in therapeutic terms, and proposes the challenge of integration as an effort of the individual to achieve or maintain health.

I call this the "auto-therapeutic" metaphor. It is not necessarily a bad metaphor, nor is the advice given that derives from it. Yet the difficulty with this metaphor, in my observation, is that it rarely has any substantial positive content beyond the affirmation of the most obvious virtues and values. The practices of self-care seem to include days off and hobbies and time with family and friends. Did we not know this already?

Beyond that, I have seen at work a subtle yet disturbing tendency among some who are fond of this metaphor. Too often, some ministers (frankly, too many) who have been schooled in the metaphor of self-care will be so aggressive in their self-care, so vigilant in protecting their personal space and guarding their (barely discernible) boundaries, that they offend those to and with whom they minister. They come off as cold, mercenary, inflexible, or tone-deaf. The result, I have seen, can lead to unnecessary conflict, alienation, and even the early dismissal of pastors from ministries that had once seemed so promising.

Some might say that this is not a problem in the metaphor. One can care for the self without being a jerk about it. To be sure, I wish that more pastors would learn at least the simple power that comes from telling someone "yes" along with a needed "no" so that what is communicated is not merely what the pastor cannot or will not do but more positively what the pastor *will* do. Absent the latter, a parishioner will likely feel merely rebuffed and dismissed. But with it, feeling accepted and heard and even empowered is much more likely.

Even so, as important as self-care is, this auto-therapeutic metaphor is inadequate for providing a sufficiently broad and deep perspective on the challenge of authentic pastoral integrity. It is a blunt instrument for work requiring more subtlety, offering black-and-white prescriptions and yet precious few guidelines. There's no "there" there.

Moreover, I wonder about the *theological* integrity of this metaphor. Is there not at least some tension between an auto-therapeutic understanding of pastoral health and some core affirmations of the gospel? We are saved by grace through faith. We love because God first loved us. How can pastors affirm that and proclaim that yet also act as if achieving wholeness and integrity depends entirely upon one's own auto-therapeutic efforts? A principle of pastoral self-care too often comes wrapped in an auto-therapeutic metaphor. Consequently, I am inclined to continue looking.

A second metaphor, likewise used very frequently, is "balance." Yes, they say, it's all about balance. Balance is how to visualize and express the ideal relationship between the several aspects of our lives. We are encouraged to maintain balance, to keep things balanced. Health and wholeness for all busy people, and particularly for pastors, is understood by means of this one metaphor.

There is some wisdom expressed in the metaphor. Certainly, there are pastors who have become unbalanced, even spectacularly so. They lose themselves in their service to the church and to others. They neglect their families. They focus on one aspect of the ministry to the exclusion of other aspects likewise important. Out of whack within themselves, some even seek parasitically to meet their needs and satisfy their hungers from those they are called to serve. Pastors who have become unbalanced can be a danger to themselves and to their communities of faith.

Again, there is some truth to this, and balance does express something important about the proper integration of pastoral life and the rest of life. Yet I have come to regard "balance" as a singularly unhelpful metaphor. It is ultimately unhelpful for the challenges of having a well-integrated yet multiform life, and unhelpful specifically for the vocational challenges of a pastor. Why? What's my problem with balance? Actually, I have several.

First of all, the metaphor of balance is supposed to elucidate the dynamic reality we call "real life," which is always moving and never still. Yet "balance" seems to edge a bit toward the static, the unmoving, the carefully still. To be sure, proper balance is often best achieved when it is accompanied by forward motion, as when one rides a bicycle down the road, perfectly balanced on two wheels even if one at times lets go of the handle bars. That's probably the ideal implied in the metaphor. But practically speaking, I suspect that the ideal is rarely achieved and that a more typical response to the counsel to strive for balance is to hold on to the things to be balanced, grasping to hold them in check and in their appropriate spheres. As I see it, the metaphor of balance fails to drive toward the dynamic, and instead collapses into the static.

I believe I have seen this, often, in myself and in my colleagues. The pressure in ministry to have everything together is immense, and the advice to be in balance is easily internalized as an ever-nagging scold. So I desire balance, and from that desire I try to force this and that aspect of my life into their proper spheres and hold them there. And I cannot. Not for long.

There is a curious irony here, that those who yearn for balance seem so tense and rigid, as if the very desire for balance makes it impossible to attain. Yet "For those who want to save their life will lose it, and those who lose their life for my sake will find it."[2]

Another problem I have with the metaphor of balance is that it gives the impression that the things to be balanced are more or less of equal weight. When you want to be balanced, you must make sure that the weights on either side are about the same, otherwise the goal of balance will be difficult to achieve, if not impossible. But in the struggle with vocational integration, the objects that one is wishing to balance are often not of equal weight. How can one compare the weight or importance of a calling to ministry and the hobbies one enjoys? The obligations one owes to God and the promises one makes to oneself?

Yet this leads right away to another difficulty with the balance metaphor, for the different pressures, obligations, responsibilities, and joys we are urged to keep in balance are of such different types. How can they be compared, much less balanced? To subsume them all under a metaphor of balance suggests that they are comparable, of equal weight or import. But they are not. They cannot be. To suggest otherwise diminishes some and elevates others.

Of course, even in their differing kinds of meaning and levels of importance, all the aspects of life and vocation in their interaction and tension have meaning and importance to you. This brings us to another shortcoming of the balance metaphor. The activity of balancing is typically of objects outside of you, perhaps in your hands, or of one's body with reference to a "this side" and a "that side" as one walks balancingly along a ridge. The problem is that in the struggle for integration, the things to be balanced are *not* outside of you; rather, they are *inside* you, deeply a part of who you *are*. My spiritual commitments, my responsibilities to parishioners and family and friends, my avocations and simple pleasures, these are not just external objects to be kept in balance, but are somehow truly part of me. To some extent, they *are* me.

Yet the self that seeks balance is a broken self. And this is one of the subtlest and most serious problems with the balance metaphor, because it implies that arriving at wholeness is entirely by your own

[2]    Matthew 16:25.

efforts, and if you fail, then the results of failing to achieve or maintain will be that you "fall off," a catastrophe for the self that has sought to heal the self. In short, the balance metaphor contains within it a form of the auto-therapeutic, with a dash of dire consequences thrown in.

Both the self-healing and the catastrophism should raise problems for all those in the mainstream of the Christian faith. We are saved not by our own efforts but by God's love made flesh in Jesus Christ, which is extended even to the most unbalanced among us. The promise of the gospel, even for burdened and overwhelmed pastors, is redemption in spite of our messiah complexes and our catastrophism.

This desire to achieve and maintain balance is made even more problematic when we recall that this is supposedly advice for Christian pastors. Yet they should know that encounter with God is a profoundly unbalancing experience. To be in God's presence is *supposed* to be disorienting. From beginning to end, Scripture bears witness to God's tendency to disturb God's willing and unwilling servants and to disrupt the equanimity they had enjoyed.

Moses before the burning bush.
Isaiah in the temple.
Jonah in the belly of the fish, and then under the vine.
Mary meeting Gabriel.
The disciples in the boat, with Jesus fast asleep—until he wasn't.
John on the Island of Patmos, then lifted up in a vision into the throne room of God.

With these, the search for balance would have been, at the least, inappropriate. In some cases, it would have been a profound insult to God. God *meant* to disturb their balance. That was the whole point.

I have found this to be deeply true in preaching. As I try to discern what Scripture is saying, first in its original context and then to my own, I find (more times than I can possibly count) that the Word of God means to disturb me and those to whom I preach. If I were to go seeking for "balance" in what I say from Scripture, then I would run the danger of misunderstanding Scripture—of misrepresenting or misapplying it. Sure, subtlety and care are needed, as is sensitivity to the differing backgrounds and abilities and levels of maturity among those who are listening to me (as well as the reality that not all are listening). But when such proper attentiveness, grounded in right and good concern for rhetoric and pedagogy, gets turned into an attempt to make the proclamation of the living Word of God an exercise in seeking balance, then it is all over. The sermon will, and must be, a failure. And I, in that moment, have failed as a preacher.

For all these considerations and more, I find "balance" likewise to be an inadequate metaphor for guiding the integration of a pastor's identity.

## Musical Counterpoint

Are there better metaphors? I believe there are. For me, some of these come from the realm of music: its essence, its performance, and especially its composition.

I happen to be a violist. I have been deepening my knowledge of and skill with the viola for over 42 years. I love this instrument.

I say that in part as a lame attempt to elicit sympathy. The viola is the Rodney Dangerfield of the orchestra: it gets no respect. Nor do those who play the viola. Google "viola jokes" and you'll be entertained for hours. Or listen to Garrison Keillor, who, in his article "The Young Lutheran's Guide to the Orchestra," had this to say about violists:

> The *viola* section is not a place for a Lutheran and here you'll have to take my word for it. I know violists and they are fine people until, late at night, they start drinking a few bottles of cheap red wine and roasting chickens over a pit in a vacant lot and talk about going to Yucatan with a woman named Rita. Don't be part of this crowd.[3]

Of course, it is not (entirely) true that the viola gets *no* respect. But it is typically somewhat overlooked. In the orchestra, we violists are often assigned background parts, quite unlike the violinists and cellists and trumpeters (the orchestra's diva sopranos and helden tenors and soccer jocks). They get to shine far more often. But when we violists do, watch out. However, on the rare occasions when the viola section is given a solo, many violists (excluding professionals, of course) are known to be quite overcome with surprise. Cue the viola jokes.

Our culture tends to glorify the soloist, showering attention on the one who is center stage and carrying the melody. That, of course, is the heart of it. We love melody. In the West at least, our expectations of good music celebrate melody, just as we celebrate the soloists who carry the melody. Melody often seems to be widely understood as the most important thing in a well-loved piece of music, esteemed above all other components. Of course, it is not that simple.

---

[3]    *We Are Still Married: Stories and Letters* (Penguin Books: 1990), 32.

In some songs, the melody so much needs the other parts that it almost makes no sense without them.[4] Aretha Franklin is truly great in "Respect."[5] But her amazing performance, as fresh today as it was almost 50 years ago, requires her backup singers, especially but not only as they give their "sock-it-to-me" times four.

In some pieces, the melody and harmony are so close that it is hard at first hearing to say which is which, such as in the opening to "Long Distance Runaround" by the band Yes.[6]

In others, the melody is duplicated by repetition between a leader and the others in something known as call-and-response, found in the music of many different cultures and even in live hard rock performances, of which Joe Satriani's "Crowd Chant" is a great example.[7] Still other pieces are marked by collaboration, in which the melody is shared and the soloists change up, each one shaping and reshaping the melody so that by the end it is not one thing but many. This is particularly characteristic of jazz in its many forms. A classic example is "Take Five" by the Dave Brubeck Quartet.[8]

All of these, it must be said, reflect different ways of making music. But not only that, they show different ways of putting together a piece. For even as music is played and enjoyed, it is also constructed, or, rather, *composed*. Someone—a composer, with imagination, talent, and skill—makes decisions about the order of sounds—pitch, rhythm, tempo, phrases—so that something new (or perhaps merely somewhat new) results in the world of sound.

[4]    I encourage the reader to play recordings of the pieces named in this chapter, all of which can be readily found on the Internet.

[5]    Aretha Franklin, vocal performance of "Respect," by Otis Redding, on *I Never Loved a Man the Way I Love You*, compact disc, Atlantic Records, originally released 1967.

[6]    Yes, performance of "Long Distance Runaround," by Jon Anderson, on *Fragile*, Atlantic Records, originally released 1971/72.

[7]    Joe Satriani, performance of "Crowd Chant" on *Super Colossal*, Epic, originally released 2006.

[8]    Dave Brubeck Quartet, performance of "Take Five" by Paul Desmond, on *Time Out*, Columbia, originally released 1959.

There is not one way of composing music. In fact, musical composition has a history, reflecting the movements and changes of successive eras as well as their cultural biases and prejudices. Technology factors in as well, with some techniques of composition appearing on the scene when instruments could be made that would permit or inspire a composer to deploy them.

One technique of music composition is called counterpoint. Some explanation is needed because one might think that "counterpoint" is an objection or a contrary response you make to someone else's "point." Instead, musical counterpoint is a compositional technique, one widely used in the Baroque era (that is, in the seventeeth and eighteenth centuries) and only occasionally found in modern music. Here's a definition: "The practice of combining melodies, or adding a second melody to a first."[9]

An easy and lightweight example is the children's song "One Bottle of Pop." Some might think of this as a round, with which it is greatly similar, in that the three voices start not together but sequentially, or, one at a time. Yet a round will have the same melody for each voice. What makes "One Bottle of Pop" more characteristic of counterpoint is the distinct melodies for each of the three parts to the song.

First, one simple melody is sung:

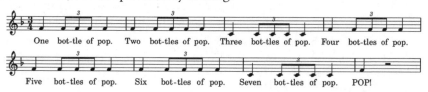

Then, as the first melody is repeated, another one is added, slightly more complex than the first:

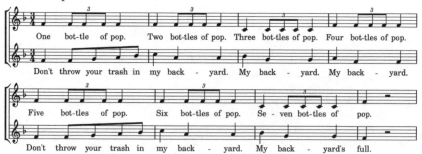

Finally, as parts one and two again sing their distinct lines together once more, a third melody joins, completing the song:

9     Alan Kendall, *The Chronicle of Classical Music: An Intimate Diary of the Lives and Music of the Great Composers* (Thames and Hudson, 1994), 273.

In the Baroque period, contrapuntal composition was raised to high art. Johann Sebastian Bach is among those high Baroque composers who used counterpoint, combining different melodies assigned to different instruments or even to the same instrument (as in the case of the fugues he wrote for organ and for violin).

One fine example of basic counterpoint in Bach's music is in the chorale "Zion Hört die Wächter Singen" ("Zion hears the watchmen singing")[10] from his cantata "Wachet Auf" (BWV 140). Here Bach combines a hymn tune, well known in his day (given to the tenors), with a theme of his own composition (played by the violins and violas). The upper strings, accompanied by continuo, begin the piece with a statement of the theme:

Then the theme repeats, with modifications, and the tenors soon enter with the hymn:

---

[10]  Johann Sebastian Bach, "Zion Hört die Wächter Singen" from *Wachet Auf, BWV 140,* Amsterdam Baroque Orchestra and Choir, Ton Koopman, conductor. From *J. S. Bach: Complete Cantatas Vol. 21,* Antonine Marchand, 2003.

Zi - on  hört  die  Wäch - ter  sing  -  en,
*Zi - on  hears  the  watch - men  sing  -  ing.*

Das  Herz  tut  ihr  vor  Freu - den spring  -  en,
*The  maid-ens'  hearts with  joy  are spring  -  ing.*

Sie  wach - et  und  steht  eil - end  auf.
*They  wake  and  quick - ly  to  Him  go.*

These two examples of counterpoint should suffice to illustrate the central point: musical counterpoint brings together multiple melodies into a greater whole. The music is given light or focus not simply by one melody. Rather, it is expressed in the combination and interaction of two or more melodies.

## Contrapuntal Identity

What does all this have to do with the difficulty I and many other ministers have in integrating ministry life with the rest of life? Quite a bit. It seems to me that the notion of counterpoint can be extended to help us with the challenge of vocation. In place of the metaphors of balance and self-care, I think that this musical notion can be used to shed light on the challenge of finding personal integration within ministry.

Surely, would it not help to look at our living and doing musically, even contrapuntally? For we carry multiple melodies, and they are meant to weave in and out, one being more prominent at one time, another next taking the lead, and at times the several blending together in a personal expression of polyphony.

I know this: the dominance of a single melody does not make life sing. It is in the *combining* of melodies that life's song is made a joy. Integration of identity is better understood neither as a striving for balance nor as an ongoing search for effective self-therapies but rather as an exercise in soulful counterpoint, in which we grapple with the lived reality of our multiform—even polyphonic—lives.

The blending is not always peacefully harmonious. Sometimes it is discordant. Some melodies at times seem to fight with each other.

Perhaps they are not meant to sound together, or maybe one must be silenced. Yet composers have often used discordant combinations intentionally and effectively. The tension is an essential part of the music. Without it, the musical experience would be less interesting and meaningful. So maybe we should expect, and even welcome, some tension between the melodies of one's life. Maybe the discord is not a sign that some melody should be silenced and removed from the score but rather is an opportunity to hear some more profoundly beautiful music being composed out of one's life.

*One Sunday in worship, I was close to tears. It does not happen often. That time it did.*

*Following the sermon and the offering, we took time to pray for those in need of healing. People seeking health in body, spirit, or mind came forward to receive anointing oil, to have hands laid on their heads, and to be prayed over. All at worship prayed for them, I by giving voice to what might be more typically known as prayers, and the rest of those there by singing some appropriate hymns and songs. That was their contribution to the prayer.*

*All was going well until the very end. Of course, I say "going well" in that I was doing my job in an appropriately pastoral way, as I applied the oil and prayed for each person in turn. But then I looked up and saw standing side by side in line these two people whom I and many in my congregation love very much. I had already seen them in line behind all the others coming forward. I had thought it was a little different that they were standing next to each other instead of first one then another behind. But I did not see what they had with them, and thus why they were standing side by side, until they were right in front of me.*

*They were together holding, between them, a finger looped through either end, a little plastic purple bracelet imprinted with the words "Kick it Kailee." And it was then clear to me why they were there. Four-year-old Kailee did not happen to be at worship that day. But Kailee was in need of healing—our dear Kailee, with the strong spirit and spunky attitude and beautiful smile and the recurrence of rhabdomyosarcoma in her young body. And her grandmother and aunt, weeping, were standing in front of me with her bracelet, for me to anoint that bracelet as proxy for Kailee and to pray for her healing.*

*As the congregation continued to sing, and then the organist continued with additional music, it took me a minute, a very long minute, to recover my voice, to push aside my tears, to withstand and continue standing in this collision of roles—pastor, friend, leader, weeper—so that I could utter the prayer and ask God, on behalf of her grandmother and aunt, and me, and the congregation, to heal her.*

*Eternal God, for Jesus"sake,*
*send your Holy Spirit upon your servant Kailee:*

*drive away all sickness of body and spirit;*
*make whole that which is broken.*
*Grant deliverance from the power of evil,*
*and true faith in Jesus Christ our Lord,*
*who suffered on our behalf*
*but also rose from death*
*so that we, too, could live.*
*In his name we pray. Amen.*[11]

*So, I was close to tears. Well, no: I was in tears. And yet my inability to hold it together seemed to be, although unintended, exactly the right response to a moment that had already been touched with holiness—all those dear holy ones, these saints in our midst, coming forward for anointing and prayer—but now a moment which had suddenly become drenched with the holy, and the tension between different melodic lines in my soul were stretched together for glory.*

As important to music as the blending of sounds surely is, at the same time, music is not merely an unrelenting sequence of sounds. Music also consists of rests. The rests in music—between notes, between phrases, between verses—are essential to its beauty. The temporal interaction of parts creatively set in place by the composer is essential to beautiful and intelligible counterpoint, and those creative choices by the composer will very often mean the sounding of one part and the silence of others, after which the sound texture will shift again as a formerly silent part will come to the fore and others will recede or rest.

Rest, we are told in the first creative narrative in the Bible, is built into the structure of creation. God worked on six days, creating the heavens and the earth and all that is in them. And then God rested. Later in the biblical narrative, God tells the children of Abraham gathered around Mount Sinai that they, too, are to rest. Rest is commanded of the people of God not because work is bad but because we are tempted to treat work as a god or to fancy ourselves as gods due to our unrelenting and (perhaps) impressive work. Pastors likewise need that command, as they are particularly tempted to such idolatries.

Understood musically and contrapuntally, personal identity needs the sounding and the silence, the notes and the rests of the different melodies that belong to the self. It should not be sounded all at once, nor can it be for long, not without damage to body and soul. The music of one's life also needs its rests, its sabbaths.

[11] "Order for Christian Healing in the Context of the Order of Worship," *Worship the Lord* (Grand Rapids: Reformed Church Press, 1991), 64.

Yet it must be said that rest is commanded of Abraham's children so that they may worship God. Rest becomes sabbath when it is focused on God and conducted in obedience to God. Otherwise rest is at most merely rest, at worst idolatrous sloth. In the same manner, if the metaphor of counterpoint is to be useful for understanding pastoral identity, it needs to be completed in relation to God.

We are always composing and performing the music that is our lives. We can make that music in isolation, without reference to any other song. Some do. Yet some are blessed with a desire to make that music in relation to a melody that is far greater than themselves: the song sung by God. Dietrich Bonhoeffer once spoke about this divine melody as a kind of holy *cantus firmus*, a deep song that invites, that demands, and that empowers our own music making in response and in harmony.

God wants us to love him eternally with our whole hearts, not in such a way as to injure or weaken earthly life, but to provide a kind of cantus firmus to which the other melodies of life provide the counterpoint. ... Where the cantus firmus is clear and plain, the counterpoint can be developed to its limits.[12]

In reflecting on these words from Bonhoeffer's letters, Jill Carattini offers the following:

As he penned these lines, Bonhoeffer, who was facing execution and the looming end of his life, confessed life to be an awe-inspiring symphony, a melody to behold with attention and appreciation for a great array of intricate choruses. In this intricacy, there is no better song composed than one that finds as its ground bass a wholehearted love of God. Where the enduring melody of life itself is a tune written and played for God, the composition can resound unto the heavens. It is this type of melody that endures even beyond the chorister who sang it.[13]

Yet such music-making before God requires that we listen. Listening, of course, is what musicians do. It is also what the obedient in Scripture's pages do.

---

[12]  Dietrich Bonhoeffer, *Letters and Papers from Prison* (New York: Simon and Schuster, 1997), 303.

[13]  Jill Carattini, "The Cantus Firmus" (February 14, 2011), RZIM: Ravi Zacharias International Ministries, http://rzim.org/a-slice-of-infinity/the-cantus-firmus.

"Listen for the Word of the Lord."
"Hear, O Israel, the Lord is one, the Lord alone."
"Those who have ears, let them hear."

Without listening, music-making falls apart. So does discipleship. To make music well, we must listen, especially to God.

The great masters of counterpoint take musical lines and weave them together into something greater, playing each off against the others, giving first one then another its time and space, yet always in interaction with the others. I believe that, likewise, my life—and the living and working of a pastor—may be better understood and lived as an exercise in *spiritual* counterpoint, in which my own several "melodies" find their true connection with each other only as they sing in relation to a more fundamental line, a cantus firmus, sung by the Triune God, who makes music in threefold yet one eternal relationship, into which other lesser musicians are invited.

CHAPTER 2

# The Pastor and Church in Modern Society

Micah L. McCreary

One morning while writing this book chapter, I received calls from two people involved in ministry. The first was from a pastor who at the time was completing a Master of Divinity degree at another seminary. He mentioned that his desire and goal in obtaining the degree was to become a better pastor. He mentioned that he had been pastoring for more than 15 years and that he did not want to study theology to "just study theology." He mentioned that he desired to make an impact on his community. When I queried him further about what he meant by impact, he said he was speaking about pastoring with integrity around issues of culture, poverty, disenfranchisement, and spirituality. He stated that he was very disturbed by the growing numbers of Americans and American churches choosing the label "none" or "non-denominational."

Soon after, I had a conversation with a gentleman who mentioned he had been struggling for some time with a call to preach and teach and would value a conversation about ministry and theological education. As we talked, it became evident that he did not see the necessity of theological education for his personal knowledge but as a "union card" for entrance into an established network of ministers. We then talked briefly about the advantages and disadvantages of a seminary education.

As a seminary president and former pastor, psychologist, and tenured professor of psychology, I am at peace with discernment discussions and conversations about pastoral and theological thought. According to Merriam-Webster, discernment is "the quality of being able to grasp and comprehend what is obscure ...."[1] In this current era, it seems that we American Christians are deeply in need of discernment. The year 2018 ended with a partial government shutdown and a seemingly very divided electorate. This raises the following questions:

- How do we lead in such a contentious environment?
- How do we know that we've arrived at the "correct" understandings and decisions in regard to what confronts us?
- How can we know with confidence that the actions we are taking are righteous?

To these questions I offer one answer: biblical discernment! In his article "Following Jesus as Discernment," author Jon Sobrino states that Christian discernment assists the believer not only in understanding the will of God but also in carrying out that will.[2] *The International Standard Bible Encyclopaedia* mentions the five Hebrew words for discern: *bin, yadha`, nakhar, ra'ah,* and *shama`*. It suggests based on certain biblical texts that (1) *bin* relates to "observation," (2) *yadha`* transmits "discriminating knowledge," (3) *nakhar* is associated with "discerning time and judgment," (4) *ra'ah* is used when the focus is on "discerning between the righteous and the wicked," and (5) *shama`* communicates "discerning good."[3]

In the New Testament, discernment is characterized as allowing us to exercise wisdom aided by the leading, prompting, and direction of the Holy Spirit. Furthermore, biblical discernment is commonly understood as the sound judgment that makes possible the distinguishing of good from evil and the recognition of God's right ways for his people. Practically speaking, here are six steps you can use to discern:

---

[1]   *Merriam-Webster's Collegiate Dictionary*, 11th ed. (2003), s.v. "Discernment."

[2]   Jon Sobrino, "Finding Jesus as Discrnment," in Casiano Floristán and Christian Duquoc, eds., *Discernment of the Spirit and of Spirits* (New York: The Seabury Press, 1979), 14-27.

[3]   *The International Standard Bible Encyclopaedia*, s.v. "Discern" (Grand Rapids: Eerdmans, 1939/1980).

1) Adhere to the Scripture and teachings of your faith tradition. This is more than just quoting Scripture; it is the continual searching and knowing of Scripture as a whole.
2) Nurture the fruit of the spirit (Galatians 5:22-23) and give priority to the virtue of love (1 Corinthians 13).
3) Offer inner authority and peace to yourself and others. Practice providing a sense of calm, serenity, and humility in divisive situations.
4) Promote community harmony through the Spirit, which is working toward reconciliation and harmony among people (John 17:23; Acts 4:32; 1 Corinthians 3:1-3).
5) Enhance rather than extinguish life (John 10:10). Move to promote vitality, heightened selfhood, and relational health in everything you do.
6) Arise with integrity in the discernment process with authentic pursuit of spiritual direction (through the spiritual practices of fasting, prayer, and personal Bible study).

Practical information, such as the above six steps to discernment, are readily available to pastors, theologians, teachers, and believers worldwide. However, as the apostle Paul states in Romans 10:14c, "How can they hear without a preacher?" Thus, I have come to be very appreciative of the seminary practitioner-teacher who guides, develops, and mentors existing pastors and called theologians through the process of pastoral formation and identity development. To use the title of Claudio Fernandez-Araoz's book, "It's not the how or the what but the who."[4] It is the "who" who faithfully accompanies ministers in their spiritual, personal, educational, theological, and vocational formation. That is, it is the Holy Spirit, and it is the Holy Spirit working in and through seminary faculty, staff, alumni, and friends, as well as through mentors and advisors.

I believe that the Rev. Dr. Allan Janssen is the epitome of the "who" of effective theological educators. I base this statement on my interactions, conversations, and observation of Dr. Janssen during my first year as president of New Brunswick Theological Seminary (NBTS), where he served as affiliate associate professor of theological studies.

For an amazing year, I have had the honor of interacting with Dr. Janssen as a faculty colleague and ecclesiastical associate at NBTS. Over this brief period of time, my admiration and appreciation has

---

[4]    C. Fernandez-Araoz, *It's Not the How or the What, but the Who: Succeed by Surrounding Yourself with the Best* (Boston, MA: Harvard Business Review Press, 2014).

increased, specifically as I traveled with Dr. Janssen during the 2018 Summer School of Theology course titled "The Church and Civil Society," held in Amsterdam, the Netherlands. It was in Amsterdam that I truly was given the opportunity to know Professor Janssen on a more in-depth level. For example, one of my fondest memories with Allan was accompanying him on an expedition as he went venturing around Amsterdam looking for rare books in vintage bookstores. I marveled at the humility of Dr. Janssen as, during our quest, we found copies of his published books at every—and I do mean every—bookstore we visited.

The course in Amsterdam examined the relationship of the church to the society in which it finds itself and raised such questions as: Is the relation of the church to the society simply to proclaim the gospel? Is the church built or designed to maintain the societal order and hence an arm of the state? Does it have a prophetic role to play, and, if so, how is that role executed? Dr. Janssen's excellent presentation during the conference was another example of his brilliance and his devotion to the church as a scholar.

Nevertheless, the powerful questions that framed the course are ones that I deeply reflect on from the perspective of leading the oldest seminary in the USA[5]—a seminary that must reinvent itself both from and within its foundational roots: the Reformed Church in America (RCA), traditional academic faculty, older diverse working student body, and two distinct alumni bases. New Brunswick Theological Seminary is at a crossroads as Dr. Janssen retires and I assume executive leadership. The seminary must also address the underlying questions of the gentlemen mentioned in the introduction: What is the relation of the church to society? And equally important, what role and relation must the seminary have to the church and to our society? My simple answer to these questions, which I will develop in the remainder of this chapter, is that the Pastoral Theologian as professor, mentor, and advisor is the vessel whom God has called, whom the seminary must employ, and whom the church must develop to fulfill the mission of connecting the church to our society in an effective manner.

The mission of New Brunswick Theological Seminary is "to educate persons and strengthen communities for transformational, public ministries in church and society. We fulfill this mission through creative,

[5]   New Brunswick Theological Seminary was started by the appointment of Dr. John Henry Livingston as professor of theology by the General Synod of the RCA in New York on October 5, 1784. See J.W. Coakley, *New Brunswick Theological Seminary: An Illustrated History, 1784–2014* (Grand Rapids: Eerdmans, 2014).

contextual, and critical engagement with texts, traditions, and practices." Our vision statement is to be "a light in God's cities, educating ministers and leaders to think critically, act justly, and lead faithfully."[6] We do this as one of three theological agents of the Reformed Church in America as well as by serving as an entity that has operated as a theological institution of higher education for over 234 years.

Dr. Cornelis Kors, director of the Reformed Church in America's Ministerial Formation Certification Agency (MFCA), suggested that the RCA theological agents would do well to focus our educational efforts on providing oversight of five key ministry formation functions.[7]

- Academic Preparation: successful completion of the fields of study as required by the *Book of Church Order*, normally fulfilled through the attainment of a Master of Divinity degree at an accredited seminary
- Spiritual Formation: manifest progress in the candidate's faith journey as a disciple of Jesus Christ
- Ministry Development: affirmation of gifts and calling, development of competencies for ministry in such areas as preaching, teaching, congregational care, evangelism, administration, and equipping church members for ministry
- Personal Wholeness: pursuit of reasonable health in all the significant aspects of life, including the physical, psychological, and social
- Denominational Identity: knowledge of the history, mission, worship, polity, and confessional statements of the RCA as well as demonstrated loyalty to the denomination and its program[8]

These five key ministry formation functions are similar to the "Four Formations" of the Roman Catholic church.[9] Pope John Paul II described these four formations as foundational for priestly development. Over time, I have come to understand these formations as follows:

---

6   "Mission & Values" *New Brunswick Theological Seminary,* https://www.nbts.edu/about-us/mission/.
7   The agents of the Reformed Church in America (New Brunswick Theological Seminary, Western Theological Seminary, and MFCA) are responsible for preparing and credentialing future RCA ministers of Word and sacrament.
8   "Our Specific Purpose," Ministerial Formation Certification Agency. 2018, https://rca.org/ministerial-formation-certification-agency-0.
9   John Paul II, "Pastores Dobo Vobis," 1992, w2.vatican.va/content/john-paul-ii/en/apost_exhortations/documents/hf_jp-ii_exh_25031992_pastores-dabo-vobis.html.

- Academic Formation: the deepening of faith, preaching, teaching, pastoral care, and Bible knowledge through the study of classics (Bible, theology, philosophy, and pastoral care) and other relevant subjects.
- Human Formation: the process of developing ministers with integrity, maturity, solid moral character, orientation to the truth, good social skills, emotional intelligence, and respect for every person, who exercise appropriate care for their physical well-being and are formed to be confident leaders.
- Spiritual Formation: the process of learning and mastering the spiritual disciplines of meditation, fasting, prayer, Bible study, and the revelation of how God moves in our lives.
- Pastoral Formation: the "hands-on" applied training in love, justice, mercy, Word, and sacrament that prepares ministers for effective leadership and ministry in parish, shelter, hospital, prison, jail, and hospice contexts.

These formation functions are integrated into the Reformed Church in America's Standards for Preparation for Ministry (standards).[10] The standards were created with the goal of being used

---

[10]   The General Synod of 2006 adopted the following standards:

#1 (Personal Faith and Evangelism)
    Demonstrate a mature personal faith in Jesus Christ and commitment and skill in nurturing others to embrace that faith.

#2 (Call)
    Demonstrate a life worthy of the gospel, a sense of call to the Office of Minister of Word and Sacrament, an understanding of that office in the Reformed tradition, and a commitment to its responsibilities.

#3 (Scripture)
    Demonstrate a thorough understanding of the Scripture (with sufficient Greek and Hebrew to understand nuances of the biblical text), commitment to its authority as Word of God, and insight into its interpretation.

#4 (History and Theology)
    Demonstrate a thorough understanding of the history and teachings of the Christian church, and insight into their interpretation.

#5 (Reformed Tradition)
    Demonstrate a thorough knowledge of and commitment to Reformed doctrine, government, and worship.

#6 (Leadership)
    Demonstrate the skill and understanding required to lead the people of God in faithfulness to their mission.

#7 (Pastoral Care)
    Demonstrate skill, understanding, and compassion in caring for persons and congregations.

by both the RCA classes and the RCA theological agents as markers in our assessment, evaluation, and development of ministers of Word and sacrament, as well as for ministerial formation among all of our constituents.

At NBTS, we are dedicated to helping seminarians, ministerial leaders, community activists, and social advocates respond to their individual spiritual and Christian callings through rigorous yet accessible theological education. We see ourselves as called to develop effective leaders who have a transformative effect in the places they live, work, and worship. Our innovative curriculum, which Dr. Janssen helped develop, is built upon our great diversity, resulting in an educative process that values each person's unique calling and gifts. As a result, our NBTS community is ecumenical, multicultural, and reflects the rich diversity of God's people.

As I assume leadership of the seminary Dr. Janssen attended, loves, and served as an educator for years, I understand the RCA's eight standards for preparation for ministry as critical to the development and assessment, including personal faith, of every student, minister, leader, and congregant we encounter.

As we develop ministers for service to God's Church, we must empower them to develop the faith, belief, and ability to trust God; and to commit to evangelism. We are dedicated to nurturing, developing, and being present in the lives of God's people and God's seminarians. This is our assignment! We are called to empower every student with the determination to cement their faith in God's ability to redeem and restore humankind.

I could elaborate on the role of any of the formations and Standards in seminary professors and students, but let's briefly explore how personal faith and ministry development might relate to the education, mentoring, and growth of a seminarian. I recall the personal impact that Erich Fromm, Henri Nouwen, Paulo Freire, and John Kinney had on my development as a pastoral psychotherapist. There were actually many biblical, theological, sociological, and psychological thinkers and practitioners that influenced my career, but the four mentioned have endured in my consciousness and ministry over the years.

I first encountered the writings of Erich Fromm in 1983 while in seminary. I was a youth pastor and was examining literature and

---

#8 (Worship and Preaching)
    Demonstrate skill and understanding to lead worship, preach the gospel, and administer the sacraments.

thinkers on the human condition. When I read *Escape from Freedom* by Dr. Fromm,[11] I perceived that he understood the issues of anxiety and fear in relation to power and losing one's core self. As a young minister whose brother was incarcerated and who perceived his father as a failure and victim of racial oppression, Fromm's book spoke to my soul. Fromm helped me develop a theology and philosophy of human nature that incorporates the human struggle between good and evil as an issue of human phenomena that is unsolvable and irreconcilable without God.

Henri Nouwen also influenced my personal faith and journey as a minister. In his book *The Wounded Healer: Ministry in Contemporary Society*,[12] I found great meaning in Nouwen's concepts. I still value and utilize the following metaphor Nouwen used to describe the Messiah as a wounded healer:

> I found an old legend in the Talmud which may suggest to us the beginning of an answer: Rabbi Yoshua ben Levi came upon Elijah the prophet while he was standing at the entrance of Rabbi Simeron ben Yohai's cave. ...
> He asked Elijah, "When will the Messiah come?"
> Elijah replied, "Go and ask him yourself."
> "Where is he?"
> "Sitting at the gates of the city."
> "How shall I know him?"
> "He is sitting among the poor covered with wounds. The others unbind all their wounds at the same time and then bind them up again. But he unbinds one at a time and binds it up again, saying to himself, 'Perhaps I shall be needed: if so I must always be ready so as not to delay for a moment.'" (Taken from the tractate Sanhedrin)[13]

This Messiah story helped me to frame my life and my experiences as one called to sit among those who are hurting while binding my wounds and waiting for the moment when God would utilize me in Christ's service. I am called as a wounded healer. I attend to my wounds and, at the same time, I know that my wounding has prepared me to

---

[11]     Erich Fromm, *Escape from Freedom* (New York: An Owl Book, Henry Holt and Company, [1941/1969]), xii–xiv.

[12]     Henri Nouwen, *The Wounded Healer: Ministry in Contemporary Society* (New York: Image/Doubleday, 1972/1990).

[13]     Nouwen, 81–82.

assist others in their healing process. Nouwen help me understand that I am both a wounded pastor and a healing pastor.

Yet, more than through his writings, my respect for him grew when I learned that Nouwen, who was also a prominent Catholic priest, requested a priestly placement with a parish that was overwhelmingly filled with members who were disabled and disenfranchised. He lived the remainder of his life among people with intellectual and physical disabilities. Nouwen became a wounded healer in practice and ministry. Thus, Nouwen taught me to be a man of virtue in my practices as well as in my language.

Paulo Freire and bell hooks have also greatly influenced my personal faith and ministry development.[14] Again, I was introduced to Dr. Freire, a South American sociologist, while attending seminary. Freire suggested that educators must not perpetuate the "Banking Concept of Education." From his writings I concluded that, as a pastor and teacher, I must not approach students from a hierarchical all-knowing educational perspective. Freire stressed that educators assume a problem-focused approach to education. This problem-focused approach is one in which the educator joins with the community to seek and strategically eliminate barriers to harmony and freedom. This resonated with my Luke 4:17-18 understanding of the ministry of Jesus. It motivated me to seek to empower the youth and families I was serving at that time.

This agency approach to education deeply impacted me as I completed my seminary education and began my doctoral studies in counseling psychology. I learned from Freire and his protégé, Gloria Watkins (a.k.a. bell hooks), to teach and reach out with a problem-posing pedagogy. This pedagogy is critical to my teaching, clinical, and service endeavors as a professor, psychologist, and, most importantly, as a pastor. It is also critical to my role as a parent, husband, son, and friend. Teaching others not to accept the status quo was only a part of the solution; I learned from Freire and hooks that you have to help humankind transform and become better.

My seminary experience relates directly to Dr. Janssen as an excellent seminary professor, pastor, and theologian. I see in Janssen what I saw in John Kinney. I enrolled in John Kinney's systematic theology class during my second year of seminary. I will never forget

---

14    See Paulo Freire, *Pedagogy of the Oppressed: 30th Anniversary Edition*, trans. Myra Bergman Ramos (New York: Continuum, 1970/2000) and bell hooks, *Teaching to Transgress: Education as the Practice of Freedom* (New York: Routledge, 1994).

our encounter surrounding the first exam in the course. While working on my examination, I noticed that several students in my classes were cheating. Outraged and alarmed, I approached the professor with my concerns. We talked and prayed, then he came into class the next day and gave a lecture/sermon/theological declaration on the parable of the fig tree from Luke 13:6-9. Kinney clearly identified his role in narrative: he was the vineyard keeper. He stated clearly that he was not the owner of the vineyard. He was a steward, and he interpreted the role of the steward as watching over, pruning, adding rich soil, and removing unproductive fruit. He stated that the vineyard keeper or minister was not the owner. Only the "owner" has the right to cut the tree down. I wanted to argue that to punish them for cheating was only removing unproductive fruit, but we agreed to disagree, and he made his point. Thirty-four years later, I still wrestle with his point. However, I learned that confrontation does not have to be antagonistic and that every offense does not have to be perceived as offensive. The encounter helped me to grow into a partner, parent, pastor, professor, pastoral psychologist, and, now, seminary president who focuses on healing as opposed to judging.

Consequently, I believe that without the literary, experiential, clinical, pastoral, and practical mentoring and development that I received from many, I would not be in the life position that I am in today. I perceive Dr. Allan Janssen as one among this "great cloud of witnesses."[15] He is one of the great examples of faith, pastoring, and theology that is critical to the nurture of the next generation of pastors, scholars, and pastoral practitioners. That is, through his writings, teaching, and mentoring, Dr. Janssen has shifted, and will continue to impact, the trajectory and the lives of many students, pastors, congregations, and the RCA denomination.

Indeed, I have witnessed the growth and development of an excellent young scholar, the Rev. Matthew J. van Maastricht, who has had the fortune of being mentored and taught by the Rev. Dr. Allan Janssen. Recently, the Rev. van Maastricht and I served together on a panel that discussed a community document that had been presented as a catechism to be considered by the RCA. I was delighted by the methodical, thoughtful, and historical accuracy of the Rev. van Maastricht's analysis of the document, and I realized then and there that his profound understanding of the process was due, in part, to his education and mentoring from Dr. Janssen.

---

[15]    Hebrews 12:1.

Further, as the twelfth president of NBTS, I needed to quickly develop a working understanding RCA governance and procedures. Thus, during my first year, I spent an exorbitant amount of time with Dr. Janssen's book *Constitutional Theology*.[16] I am so grateful for this book, which provided needed information and elaboration on the RCA's *Book of Church Order* in a very informative, insightful, and comprehensive manner. Furthermore, Janssen's writings, specifically on the Doctrinal Standards of the Belgic Confession of Faith, the Belhar Confession, the Heidelberg Catechism with its compendium, and the Canons of the Synod of Dort, were enlightening and allowed me to integrate, assimilate, and internalize important RCA information.

As *Flourishing for Ministry* states, pastoral ministry is a tough, demanding job that is not always understood or appreciated.[17] Over the years, I, like Dr. Janssen, have deepened my understanding of the seminary as a place and period of ministry life where seminarians and others can discern their gifts, graces, and vulnerabilities. The seminary and the seminary professor create a place of public shared community, consisting of the test of doing (preaching, teaching, counseling, gifts) and the test of being (courageous, character, bravery).[18]

As we celebrate the ministry of the Rev. Dr. Allan Janssen, it seems to me that he is the epitome of the answer to the problem facing seminaries and the church. That is, the church has a problem when it has a pastor only or theologian only. We conceptualize the pastor as authorized only to caretake the flock, and many overlook the fact that this caretaking must include careful speaking and thinking about God and the Christian gospel. This careful thinking and speaking must be reasoned and reasonable while conveying a sense of grace and mystery. Note that by speaking and thinking in such a way, the pastor is doing theology.[19] On the other hand, by definition, a theologian is a person who engages in or is an expert in theology—that is, the study of religious faith, practice, and experience, and, especially, the study of God and of God's relation to the world.

---

[16]  Allan J. Janssen, *Constitutional Theology: Notes on the Book of Church Order of the Reformed Church in America* (Grand Rapids: Eerdmans, 2000).

[17]  Flourishing in Ministry Project, *Flourishing in Ministry: Emerging Research Insights on the Well-Being of Pastors* (University of Notre Dame: Mendoza College of Business, 2013).

[18]  See H.R. Niebuhr, *The Purpose of the Church and Its Ministry* (New York: Harper and Brother, 1956).

[19]  A.C. Outler, "The Pastor as Theologian," in E. Shelp and R. Sunderland, eds., *The Pastor as Theologian* (New York: Pilgrim Press, 1988).

"Pastor" comes from a culture of pastoral society that is challenging for the twenty-first-century mind to remember. Pastoral society was a shepherd's society. The relationship between the shepherd and the sheep was crucial, rich, and nuanced. Shepherds were not to be hireling or mercenary (John 10:12-13). As stated earlier, the root meaning of "pastor" (shepherd) is caretaker with an unselfish devotion. I believe the meaning of pastoral greatness comes from the words attributed to Jesus in Matthew 20:25-28, Mark 10:42-44, and Luke 22:26-27. Jesus said clearly, "I am the good shepherd," or, the good pastor.

Changes in the pastoral image came about during the Catholic clerical privilege period, where the power of the "keys" in medieval times came into being. The pastor had the keys—the power—to absolve repentant sinners and to administer the sacraments of the church to the people. Only with the keys could the parish pastor's house and the Lord's house be unlocked. The pastor became a biblical exegete and a teacher of sound doctrine.

While the local pastor had the keys, the Bishop's power was passed to professor. "Professor" had been a term used for all professing Christians but now was passed to the Bishop as the keeper of knowledge, which was different from keeper of the keys. Pastors become caretakers of the soul, stewards of interpersonal matters, and very important to everyday parishioners. Pastors stood accountable to God alone. Pastors, inundated with care ministry, needed the expertise of scholars who understood what the controvertible texts in the Scriptures really meant. New confessions of faith, formulated by professors, became convenient and authoritative summaries of pure doctrine.

According to Outler, during the Reformation, the pastor's teaching function continued to be paramount, and academic training, especially in biblical languages and in Latin, became critical.[20] Five hundred years later, the status of clergy has been lowered. Additionally, the education of the general public has increased to an equal level, and the educational standards for the clergy have decreased. Furthermore, business management models, inflation of degrees, less basic education, and fancier titles have decreased prestige for the ordinary pastor, increased the attraction of specialization, and yielded the indirect consequence of undervalued caretakers becoming more mindful of their own self-interests, which has resulted in the church being run like a well-managed corporation.

[20]   Outler, 22–26.

The Rev. Dr. Jerry Carter, pastor of Calvary Baptist Church in Morristown, New Jersey, stated that the relationship of the seminary to the local church is similar to the friendship of the zebra and ostrich.[21] This symbiotic animal pair seems to be an unlikely match. However, they are crucial to each other's safety. While ostriches have poor senses of hearing and smell, zebras have bad eyesight. Ostriches and zebras often travel together because they can warn each other of possible dangers. The ostrich looks out for the zebra's enemies, and the zebra listens and smells for the ostrich's predators.

Reverend Carter also used the example of the symbiotic relationship between the oxpecker (an African bird) and large African animals like the rhino, hippo, or zebra to describe the relationship between the church and the seminary. The oxpecker does not merely ride the large animal; it is a dedicated cleaner.[22] That is, the oxpecker eats ticks, worms, and other parasites that can be found on zebras, rhinoceroses, impalas, giraffes, elephants, and hippos. While the oxpecker is helping these animals by eating parasites, it also aggravates their larger counterparts by picking at their open wounds and sipping their blood.

However, there is no business like soul business. Even as the needs of the caregiver appear ambiguous, exploitive, and diminished, and as the eighteenth-century model of the pastor is fading, the seminary needs to reinterpret its vision. This has been the work of Dr. Janssen. He embodies the perplexity faced by many who seek a distinction between the pastor's task as practical and people-oriented and the theologian's task as chiefly theological and idea-oriented.[23]

Faith in the church is diminishing and clergy's credibility is dwindling as a result of:

- Post-Enlightenment: Enlightenment thinkers believed that reason alone could solve our major social problems and give us true moral knowledge. They believed that faith obscures, while reason illuminates.[24]

---

[21] "Symbiotic Relationships of the Bird World," May 15, 2018, accessed August 13, 2018 https://www.sunnysports.com/blog/symbiotic-relationships-bird-world/.

[22] "The Oxpecker," accessed August 13, 208. http://smallscience.hbcse.tifr.res.in/oxpecker/.

[23] Outler, 12.

[24] Kevin Vallier, "Enlightenment vs. Post-Enlightenment Libertarianism," September 19, 2012, http://bleedingheartlibertarians.com/2012/09/enlightenment-vs-post-enlightenment-libertarianism/.

- <u>Postmodernism</u>: Postmodernism is generally defined by an attitude of skepticism, irony, or rejection of the meta-narratives and ideologies of modernism, often calling into question various assumptions of Enlightenment rationality.[25]
- <u>Postliberalism,</u> or narrative theology: This movement's proponents argue that the church's use of the Bible should focus on a narrative presentation of the Christian faith as regulative for the development of a coherent systematic theology. Thus, Christianity is to be viewed as an overarching story, with its own embedded culture, grammar, and practices that can be understood only with reference to Christianity's own internal logic.[26]

The question is not either pastor or theologian, but, rather, how does the pastor maintain theological skills, and how does the theologian maintain pastoral skills? The solution is the pastor as theologian and the theologian as pastor. The Pastoral Theologian must have a love of language and a lively sense of its mysterious power to convey meanings that reach further into the sacred mystery. The Pastoral Theologian also must be willing to gain an understanding of the problematic quality of all claimed knowledge of transcendent being.

My argument for the Pastoral Theologian grows out of my back-ground as a pastoral psychotherapist. Several years ago, my colleague, Dr. Jessica Young Brown, and I argued that the pastor and church were a non-traditional form of mental health care.[27] The church is a place where members of the community, in many instances, should be able to find mental health resources. However, in many instances, pastors and ministers can present a powerful distrust of the mental health profession while upholding a powerful trust in the spiritual healing art of the church.

This healing dichotomy has to be addressed. Pastors must be nurtured, taught, and developed in an ethos of the wounded healer. That is, pastors and ministers who have experienced brokenness and who have travailed through trauma should be taught to use this

---

[25]  Brian Duignan, "Postmodernism," in *Encyclopaedia Britannica*, last modified October 25, 2018, https://www.britannica.com/topic/postmodernism-philosophy.

[26]  Gary Dorrien, "A Third Way in Theology: The Origins of Postliberalism," *Christian Century* 118, no. 20 (July 2001): 16–21.

[27]  Jessica Young Brown and Micah L. McCreary, "Pastors' Counseling Practices and Perceptions of Mental Health Services: Implications for African American Mental Health." *Journal of Pastoral Care and Counseling* 68, no. 1 (2014): 1–14.

woundedness as a mechanism and passageway to healing others. Instead, many are solely taught that prayer changes things. We are taught that "Weeping may linger for the night, but joy comes with the morning."[28]

Yet even as the church struggles with its capacity to meet the needs of the congregation, research is showing that church members are more prone to use religious services as a source of help mental and emotional problems.[29] One of the models of pastoral care and counseling that has been easily digested by pastors is the biblical counseling model proposed by Jay Adams.[30] Adams conceptualized counseling as ministry. Heath Lambert suggests that counseling is synonymous with ministry. He states, "'Counseling' is the word used to describe what happens when people with questions, problems, and trouble have a conversation with someone they think has answers, solutions, and help."[31] Lambert argues that this counseling is the kind of conversations ministers have with congregants every day. He further suggests that because counseling is ministry, counseling is a theological task.

As a pragmatic president, pastor, professor, and psychologist, I am not going to engage in the contextual battle of the effectiveness or ineffectiveness of biblically-based counseling. What I am concerned about is the integration of pastor and pastoral counseling that leads to the pastoral psychotherapist. Unfortunately, as with pastoral practitioners and theological professors, we do not recognize the symbiotic partnership of these two disciplines. The bigger issue to address here is how to create more "Rev. Dr. Allen Janssens" who connect with congregants and live out the intersection between pastor and theologian. All pastors and theologians desire for their ministries to be informed by Scripture, practice, research, and reason. Every pastor or theologian must envision his or her pastoral ministry to be a ministry that responds with care and raises consciousness. The greater problem seems to be arming the Pastoral Theologian who wishes to provide effective ministry in the twenty-first century with the skills to navigate the inherent complexity of pastoral care and theological reflection.

---

[28]   Psalm 30:5b.
[29]   Charlotte Frazier, Laurie B. Mintz, and Michael Mobley. "A multidimensional look at religious involvement and psychological well-being among urban elderly African Americans." *Journal of Counseling Psychology* 52, no. 4 (2005): 583–590.
[30]   Jay E. Adams, *A Theology of Christian Counseling: More Than Redemption* (Grand Rapids: Zondervan, 1979).
[31]   Heath Lambert, *A Theology of Biblical Counseling* (Grand Rapids: Zondervan, 2016), 13–15.

I remember with deep affection walking the streets of Amsterdam, listening to Dr. Janssen share the history of the city, the Dutch Reformed Church, and New Brunswick Theological Seminary. I will never forget his encouragement to wander into the museums in Amsterdam and take in the rich legacy of church and society found in the artwork.

Dr. Janssen blessed me one Sunday, as we visited a Dutch church to observe and participate in a service, by revealing that the building next to the church was the place where John H. Livingston received his education. The Rev. Dr. John Henry Livingston was the first NBTS pastor, teacher, and president. According to Coakley, the RCA has always valued an educated clergy.[32] Initially, those called to the ministry of Word and sacrament returned to the Netherlands for theological training. Then, in 1784, the General Synod appointed John Henry Livingston professor of theology and charged him with the responsibility of preparing men for the ministry of Word and sacrament.

For a time, Dr. Livingston prepared and instructed candidates for the ministry from his study in New York. Eventually, Livingston went on to become the fourth president of Queen's College (later to become Rutgers College) in New Brunswick, New Jersey. He took his students with him from his pastorate-professorship in New York and established New Brunswick Theological Seminary in New Brunswick. Thus, for more than 234 years, NBTS has been preparing people for Christian ministry, not the least of whom is Allan Janssen.

Dr. Janssen's life is an example of a theological education that is more than theology and academic pursuits. He shows us that ministry begins and ends with belonging to and nurturing a congregation. The Rev. Dr. Allan Janssen lives, learns, worships, works, witnesses, and serves in a manner that forms and confirms the gifts of those who study under and benefit from his presence in our churches and society.

[32] Coakley, 2-3.

CHAPTER 3

# Lift Up Your Hearts: A History of the 1966 RCA Liturgy for the Lord's Supper

## Gregg Mast

It is a privilege and joy to share in this volume that honors the remarkable ministry of my colleague and friend, Dr. Allan Janssen. To many people, especially students, Al is known as Mr. BCO. This title is certainly deserved considering Al's long involvement in revising the *Book of Church Order* (BCO) with a deep commitment to keeping it relatively brief, always substantive and consistent with our creeds and confessions, and non-intrusive in the ways the Spirit works through the freedom of the church. But in addition, Al's foundational commitment to the Constitution of the Reformed Church in America (RCA) encourages this essay about the Liturgy for the Lord's Supper. The Communion liturgy was approved by the General Synod in 1966, published in 1968, and has lived on the shelves and in the hearts of many who have filled our pulpits and our pews since then.

In June of 1950, the General Synod of the Reformed Church in America appointed a committee to review the church's 1906 liturgy toward the goal of revising it. The committee had no idea that this committee, appointed in 1950, would serve for 16 years until *Liturgy and Psalter* was finally adopted by the General Synod and published two years later in 1968.[1] What made this 1950 action remarkable was that just four people were initially appointed to the committee: Dr. Stephen James, who was a professor at New Brunswick Theological Seminary and would become president of the institution in 1953; Dr. Richard Oudersluys, professor at Western Theological Seminary, where he served with distinction for 35 years; Dr. Gerrit Vander Lugt, who had been a professor, dean, and finally president at Carroll College in Wisconsin, and, at the time, was on the faculty of Central College; and the Rev. Howard G. Hageman, who was a 29-year-old pastor, just five years out of seminary and serving the North Reformed Church in Newark, New Jersey.[2]

I suspect that Hageman's surprising presence on the committee was the result of some quiet lobbying by his mentor, Stephen James, who was a seminary classmate of Hageman's father and who assumed a paternal role in Hageman's life following his father's sudden and tragic death on Lake Champlain in 1937. Providentially, the young Hageman resided in Albany, New York, where his father had been the pastor of Trinity Methodist Church and where Dr. James served as the senior minister of the First Church in Albany. In 1942, both Hageman and James moved to NBTS: Hageman as a first-year student and James as Professor of Homiletics.[3]

While the committee had been appointed at the General Synod in 1950, the Synod did not provide any funds for the group to meet. However, it did have an agenda item beyond its mandate as it left the Synod. The stated clerk of the Synod had received a communication

---

[1]   Gerrit T. Vander Lugt, editor. (New York: The Board of Education of the Reformed Church in America, 1968).

[2]   This chapter in the liturgical history of the RCA was inspired by a single sentence in Howard G. Hageman's article "The Eucharistic Prayer in the Reformed Church in America," published in the *Reformed Review* (Spring, 1977), in which he observed: "In composing this prayer the committee largely used as its resources the Liturgy of the Reformed Church in France and the Liturgy of South India."

[3]   I draw special attention to Hageman because the story of the work of the small committee will highlight Hageman's deep interest in and knowledge of the publication of new liturgical books having a profound impact on Reformed churches in Europe and beyond. Hageman utilized his classical education at Harvard and his knowledge of Latin to learn enough Dutch, German, and French to connect with Reformed and other ecclesial bodies in the Netherlands, France, Switzerland, and Scotland. We will discover that the 1950 committee will ultimately move well beyond the Reformed Church in America's rather narrow liturgical heritage to depend significantly on the liturgies of the French Reformed Church and the Church of South India in the creation of the Communion prayer that has inspired RCA congregations for more than 50 years.

from the General Synod of the Reformed (*Gereformeerde*) Churches in the Netherlands which had established a similar committee to revise its own liturgy. And so from the first day, the small but highly-experienced committee knew that the common work of liturgical renewal was being addressed across the Atlantic.[4]

Even though the committee did not have a budget in its inaugural year, it did manage to meet one time with all members present. In its report to the General Synod of 1951, the committee described its work:

> We conceived our concern therefore to be two-fold. First, to in-quire into the ways and means whereby deeper understanding of the Liturgy of our church may be promoted, and hence, a wider and more constant use of it encouraged throughout the church; and second, to propose such revision as will make that Liturgy a more adequate and living guide to our worship in all its forms and in all our churches.[5]

It is clear from the outset that all four committee members—three professors and one pastor—had a pedagogical purpose in mind. Indeed, there is almost a missionary zeal revealed in its words that would lead one to believe that their work was intended to change the worship and thus the culture of the Reformed Church in America. The committee had before it the last liturgy approved by the church in 1906. It had been nearly 50 years since the services of the church had been substantially reviewed, a time period that had included two world wars and an economic depression that had wounded the very soul of the American body politic. Despite, or perhaps because of, these global events, the committee intended to be cautious in its work which is reflected in the last sentence of its first report:

> The necessary revision, as contemplated by the committee, emphatically is not one looking away from our past teaching and emphasis but, to the contrary, it should look toward conserving and strengthening these positions and integrating them within the living worship of a living church.[6]

If there was any concern or worry within the church that the committee was ready to propose a dramatic change of the status quo,

[4]   *Acts and Proceedings of the General Synod of the Reformed Church in America* (hereafter referred to as *MGS*) *1950*, 298.
[5]   *MGS 1951*, 287.
[6]   *MGS 1951*, 288.

the professors and pastor could not have been more reassuring. It will, however, come as a great surprise that a decade later a liturgy for the Lord's Supper would be borrowed almost completely from a church quite distinct from their own context or the church's roots in the Netherlands.

Two meetings of three days each were held prior to the General Synod of 1952 with an approved budget of $500. Again, the report to the synod was reassuring in tone as it stated that it "sought to depart as little as possible from the established usages and practices of our Church."[7] The Committee for the Revision of the Liturgy had spent the year simply correcting mistakes in the installation liturgy, adding some rubrical directions consistent with the Constitution, and providing for inclusion of some fuller alternative usages as desired by the church but without straying from the Doctrinal Standards of the church.

In addressing the Liturgy for the Administration of the Lord's Supper, it assured the members of the 1952 Synod that "We have neither omitted, nor altered, in substance or form, any element now included." After the report, the committee made six recommendations to the synod which would set its direction and work for the next three years. The first recommendation summarizes a strategy seen in all six:

> That the Forms and Orders submitted herewith be authorized by General Synod for use in the Church for a period of three years. That General Synod urge as large use and study of these revised Forms as possible be made by Consistories and Classes during this period, and that Classes be urged by General Synod to promote such use and study.[8]

In order to implement this plan, the committee encouraged that the proposed forms be liberally distributed and that this distribution should not be limited to classes and clergy but also extend to consistories and the local congregations they served. The three professors and single pastor did not only need the professional evaluation of scholars and theologically trained ministers but wanted to encourage the use of the forms by people in the pews who could talk about what they both appreciated and missed in the proposed liturgy.

In a politically adroit move, the committee of four also recommended to the synod that it be enlarged to include one member

7     MGS 1952, 277.
8     MGS 1952, 279.

from each particular synod "to review the work and to prepare the final and complete draft of revision for the General Synod and the Church."[9] The synod approved all six recommendations from the committee but amended one of them by changing the number of copies of the proposed liturgy to be sent to each congregation from three to twelve!

The Reports to the General Synods of 1953 and 1954 describe a committee that was faithfully receiving the evaluations of the church in order to present a proposed liturgy that would be reviewed and hopefully approved by both General Synod and two-thirds of the classes. In its report in 1955, the Committee moved forward after three years of preparation:

> By the unanimous action of the Committee, we hereby present the draft of our recommended revised Forms and Orders of Worship on the Lord's Day, for the Administration of Baptism and Reception into Full Membership and Admission to Holy Communion, and orders to be used relative to the Celebration of the Sacrament of the Lord's Supper.[10]

At this point in the work of the Committee for the Revision of the Liturgy, we have another source to assist us. The archives of the Reformed Church in America holds most of the minutes of the Revision Committee beginning in 1956. In response to a decidedly split vote of the church, the General Synod of 1956 appointed a Special Committee on Reactions to Revision of the Liturgy, chaired by the Rev. Norman Thomas, who years later would serve as provost of New Brunswick Seminary when Hageman was called as president. In addition to Thomas, there were two other pastors and two elders. Following the Synod of 1955, 17 classes had voted to approve the Revised Liturgy, 17 had voted not to approve it, four took no action, and nine did not report at all. Obviously, the two-thirds vote required to change the Constitution was not achieved, and the committee as well as the RCA was challenged to consider next steps.

The committee chaired by Thomas observed within its written report: "The feeling was wide-spread that since the way we worship is so determinative for the life and future well-being of the church, the expenditure of a little more time on this project is not to be begrudged."[11]

9   *MSG 1952*, 279–80.
10  *MGS 1955*, 333.
11  *MGS 1956*, 291.

Further, the special committee recommended that the Revision Committee be continued, that the Revision Committee communicate with all classes, and that a "fresh revision be submitted by the Revision Committee to representative pastors, laymen and laywomen in each particular synod for their reaction" and that the fresh revision be presented to a future General Synod. In response to the adoption of these actions by the General Synod of 1956, the Revision Committee divided its members into working teams, and Stephen James and his protégé, Howard Hageman, were assigned the task of reviewing the Order for the Lord's Supper.

Since the Revision Committee had not yet accomplished the assigned task of the 1956 General Synod by the following year, it reported to the Synod of 1957 that it intended to present the completed revision in 1958. It did present the completed revision to the Synod of 1958 but only for the forms of worship required by the Constitution. Perhaps because the committee had become especially cautious due to its experience in the synod two years earlier, it recommended to the General Synod that the classes be given a period not to exceed *five* years to study and evaluate the revision. While it may have been careful and cautious, it should be noted that the revision presented to the Synod of 1958 was substantially the same as the one presented to the Synod of 1956.

Before we learn the response of the church to the committee's proposal, it is important to pause to notice an article that Hageman published in January of 1959 in *Theology Today*.[12] Titled "Three Reformed Liturgies," Hageman described the appearance of three Reformed liturgies—one in the Netherlands, one in France, and one in Switzerland—in 1955. The Dutch Liturgy, the *Dienstboek* (Service Book), was a provisional volume which Hageman described in some detail. The second liturgy was adopted in 1954 by churches in Berne, Switzerland. It is, however, the third volume that is of greatest interest to us. The French Reformed Church never had an official liturgy until it adopted one in 1955. Hageman observed that the French had made the normative Sunday service one that included the Lord's Supper, something that reflected its roots in John Calvin who argued for the organic unity of sermon and Supper in every service.

What makes Hageman's article intriguing is that he translated a portion of each of the Communion prayers into English. Since

---

[12]   Howard G. Hageman, "Three Reformed Liturgies," *Theology Today* 15 (January, 1959): 507–520.

the Dutch provisional liturgy offered five different Communion prayers, Hageman focused his attention on option three, which bore a resemblance to both the French and Bernese prayers. While Hageman did not include the entire Communion prayer for each church in his article, one can clearly see that the concluding paragraphs of the prayer from the French were a significant source of the RCA prayer not yet imagined.[13] It would be another couple of years before the Committee on the Revision of the Liturgy would untether itself from the Communion Prayer of the 1906 Approved Liturgy of the RCA. The 1955 French Order for Communion concluded with the following words:

> **Holy and Righteous Father, here recalling the unique and perfect sacrifice, offered once for all on the cross by our Lord Jesus Christ, in the joy of this resurrection and the expectation of his coming, we offer ourselves to thee, a holy and living sacrifice.**
>
> *Thou who knowest the heart, purify us and renew in us the assurance of thy pardon. Make us live by the life of the Risen One that he may in us and we in him.*
>
> **Send upon us thy Holy Spirit that in receiving this bread and this cup, we may be given to commune of the body and blood of our Lord Jesus Christ.** *For it is through him that thou dost create, sanctify, vivify, that thou dost bless and give us all good things.*
>
> **And as this grain once scattered in the fields and the grapes once spread on the hills have now been brought together on this Table in the bread and wine, Lord, grant that thy whole Church may soon be gathered from the ends of the earth into your thy kingdom. Even so, come, Lord Jesus. Amen.**[14]

I suspect that the committee had found its equilibrium again when it reported the following to the General Synod in 1960:

> Much as we would like to incorporate some of the suggestions already made, it is our considered judgement that this would be unwise for two reasons: (1) General Synod has approved a five-year period "for study and use within the church." We do not think that we are at liberty to make any changes until we are ready for the final draft. (2) To make changes in the Provisional Liturgy

[13]  *MGS 1959*, 514–515.
[14]  *MGS 1960*, 299. Sentences and phrases that appear in the 1966 liturgy for the Lord's Supper of the RCA are printed in **bold**.

each year would be confusing and hasty. Critical reflection upon the Provisional Liturgy should spring from honest, faithful use over the five-year period.[15]

At the November meeting of the Revision Committee, held in Sage Library at New Brunswick Seminary, Hageman, who had just concluded his service as President of the General Synod, reported that the committee had received a recording of a full service of worship, including Communion, from the Reformed Churches in the Netherlands. The minutes reflect that not only did the committee listen to the service but was also reminded that it had been instructed by the General Synod to initiate conversations with other denominations about liturgical renewal and revision in the Reformed family. To that end, the secretary of the committee was instructed to communicate with the liturgy committees of the United Presbyterian Church, the Canadian Presbyterian Church, the Reformed Churches in the Netherlands, and the Christian Reformed Church in North America.[16] Suddenly, what for a decade had been a process of liturgical revision exclusively within the Reformed Church in America now became a project open to what God was doing in Reformed churches around the world.

The General Synod report of 1961 made clear that the communications with other bodies had begun. Interestingly, the major focus of conversation in the 1960–1961 intervening year had been which translation of Scripture, the King James Version or the Revised Standard Version, should be used in the new liturgy. In the end, the Revised Standard Version was proposed to the Church.

At the fall meeting of the Revision Committee, held on November 14, 1961, a dramatic new development is reported in the minutes. Under the title "Correspondence," the following was recorded: "Reference was made to the letter sent by Dr. Hageman to members of the committee concerning the Eucharist of the French Reformed Church." This will be further considered in the revision of the Communion service.

A few paragraphs later the following appeared:

[15]   I am deeply indebted to Dr. Christopher Dorn, who, in his doctoral dissertation titled *The Lord's Supper in the Reformed Church in America* (Peter Lang International Academic Publishers, 2007), documented the RCA's dependence on the French liturgy in an excellent chapter on the development of the 1966 Eucharistic Prayer.
[16]   *Archives of the Reformed Church in America*, Gardner Sage Library, the minutes of the Committee on the Revision of the Liturgy, November 14, 1961.

The services in Part 2, the Sacrament of the Lord's Supper, were next discussed, and notation made of certain changes that can now be made. Dr. Hageman's letter was referred to as a possible model for a shorter form, which some ministers desire. A copy of the letter containing a translation of the Eucharistic Service of the French Reformed Church was ordered sent to all ministers in the denomination. This was referred to Dr. Hageman.[17]

What makes this direction from the committee's minutes so surprising is that the committee decided to send to all the ministers in the RCA a possible model that had not been presented to the General Synod through one of its reports. I suspect that more than a decade of regular correspondence between pastors, classes, consistories, and the committee had created a dynamic that nurtured the free flow of information and suggestions in both directions.

By sending out the French Communion prayer as a kind of trial balloon, the committee had looked well beyond its North American context, or even its roots in the Dutch Reformed Church, to identify a service that was biblical, brief, and deeply reflective of the theology of Communion shared in the RCA. We have seen the paragraphs that conclude the prayer in the 1959 article by Hageman. We now review the first paragraph of the prayer in order to again discover a primary source for the RCA Communion prayer.[18]

> *Holy and right it is and our joyful duty to give thanks unto Thee at all times and in all places, Almighty God, Holy and Eternal Father, through Jesus Christ our Lord. For thou didst create the heavens and all their hosts, and the earth with all of its plenty. Thou hast given us being and life and does preserve us by Thy providence. But Thou hast shown us the fullness of Thy love in sending into the world Thy Eternal Word, thy visible image, in thy well- beloved Son who stooped to us to lift us up to Thee. For the precious gift of this mighty Saviour and loving Mediator, who hast reconciled us to Thee, the living Bread given for the life of the world, we praise and bless Thee O God. Therefore with the whole Church, with all of the hosts of heaven, we adore Thy infinite majesty and praise Thy glory:*
>
> *HOLY, HOLY, HOLY, LORD GOD OF HOSTS, Heaven and earth are full of Thy glory.*

[17]  Minutes of the Committee on the Revision of the Liturgy, November 14, 1961.
[18]  *MGS 1963*, 245–246.

*HOSANNA IN THE HIGHEST!*
*Blessed is He that cometh in the Name of the Lord.*
HOSANNA IN THE HIGHEST! [19]

Remarkably, just a little more than a half year later in late June of 1962, the French Reformed prayer, slightly edited with one significant contribution from the Liturgy of the Church of South India, became the proposed Communion prayer for the Reformed Church in America. After more than a decade of moving carefully and cautiously, being delayed again and again, the committee took the dramatic step of placing the French prayer before the General Synod of 1963 and ultimately before the classes for a vote. When the smoke cleared, it would be Howard Hageman and his close colleagues who would convince a committee, and finally a church, to strike out in a whole new direction in its Communion form. Because of the adoption of the 1966 Communion liturgy, the RCA would move into the core eucharistic tradition of Western Christianity and finally commit to a trajectory of returning to the unity of sermon and Supper each time a worshiping congregation gathered. Before we turn to the last chapter of this surprising turn of events, let us pause for a moment to review what in 1962 was called "The Instruction" but later named "The Meaning of the Sacrament."

In the fall of 1974, I arrived at New Brunswick Seminary as a first-year seminary student just a year after Hageman had been installed as its president. For almost two decades following 1974 until his death in 1992, Howard became my mentor and colleague. He introduced me to a new Ph.D. program in liturgical studies at Drew University, served as one of my three dissertation advisors, and was there to congratulate me when I graduated as the first student from the program in 1985.

During my years at NBTS, Dr. Hageman was fond of sharing stories about his service on the Committee on the Revision of the Liturgy, a commitment that would require 16 years to fulfill! He often told the story of writing "The Instruction" in a single evening in response to the challenge of a colleague on the committee who could not imagine the whole theology of Communion shared in five brief paragraphs consuming less than a page. Hageman sat down with a portion of the long prayer that appeared in the abridged version of

---

[19]   *The Liturgy of the Reformed Church in America together with The Psalter* (New York: The Board of Publications, 1908), 42–43. Sentences and phrases that appear in the 1966 liturgy for the Lord's Supper of the RCA are printed in **bold**.

the Administration of the Lord's Supper of 1906 and crafted a brief and theologically fulsome instruction regarding the Supper. The genius of the Hageman "Instruction" is his commitment to envision the Supper as a place where past, present, and future came to nurture the congregation. He does this by identifying in the first paragraph that "we come in remembrance, communion and hope" and in the last paragraph that "through the death, resurrection and ascension of Christ" we receive the gift of God's Spirit who unites us in one body.

The 1906 abridged form of the Liturgy for the Administration for the Lord's Supper begins with a prayer that consumes almost five pages. The last portion of the prayer is printed in its entirety below, as phrases that found their way into Hageman's work are underlined and bolded in order to understand how Hageman dramatically edited the prayer for modern use. Interestingly, this portion of the prayer also appears in the 1966 liturgy as the first option under the title "The Meaning of the Sacrament." When the liturgy was reprinted for congregational use in 1987, it disappeared.

> *Beloved in the Lord, as we come to the holy Supper of our Lord and Savior, it is fitting that we consider to what end our Lord instituted it.*
>
> *"This do," he said, "in remembrance of me."*
>
> ***We are therefore, to remember that our Lord Jesus Christ****, according to the promises made in the Old Testament, **was sent of the Father into the world; that he assumed our flesh and blood**; that he bore for us the wrath of God, under which we should have perished everlastingly; **that he fulfilled for us all obedience to the divine law**; that he, although innocent, was condemned to death so that we might be acquitted at the judgement seat of God; that he took upon himself the curse due to us so that he might fill us with his blessings; that he humbled himself unto death, **even the bitter and shameful death of the cross**, when he cried out with a loud voice, "My God, my God, why has thou forsaken me?" **so that we might be accepted of God and never be forsaken of him** and finally, that he confirmed with shedding of his blood **the new and eternal covenant of grace and reconciliation**, when he said, "It is finished."*
>
> *"This do my body, broken for you," he said, "This cup if the new testament in my blood."*
>
> *We are therefore, to believe these promises which Jesus Christ, who is the truth, has himself given to us. It is his will that we be partakers of this body and blood and share in all his benefits, so that he may dwell in us and we*

*in him. We may not doubt that he will perform in our hearts and lives all that these outward signs signify and that he who is the **true heavenly bread will** nourish and **strengthen us to life eternal**. For in this Supper we share in the infinite goodness of our Savior and are made partakers of all of his blessings, of life eternal, righteousness, and glory.*

*But in this Supper of remembrance and communion we must also lift up our hearts in hope. For we do this, as he commanded, till he come. **As we eat this bread and drink this cup, he gives us a pledge and foretaste of that feast of love of which we shall partake when his kingdom has fully come.** Under the veil of earthly things we now have communion with him. **But with unveiled face we shall behold him**, rejoicing in his glory, **made like unto him in his glory**. Even so, come, Lord Jesus.*

***And as by his death, resurrection, and ascension he has obtained for us the life-giving Spirit**, who dwelling in him as the Head and in us as his members, **unites us all in one body, so are we to receive this Supper in brotherly love mindful of the communion of saint**s. As the holy Apostle says, "We being many are one body, for we are all partakers of the one bread." Hereto, assist us the almighty God and Father of our Lord Jesus Christ, through his Holy Spirit. Amen.* [20]

In order that the reader might fully appreciate the way in which Hageman wove together the words of the last portion of the 1906 prayer, here is the "Meaning of the Sacrament" as it appeared in the 1963 proposed liturgy.

*Beloved in the Lord Jesus Christ, the holy Supper we are about to celebrate is a feast of remembrance, of communion, and of hope.*

***We come in remembrance that our Lord Jesus Christ was sent of the Father into the world to assume our flesh and blood and to fulfill for us all obedience to the divine law, even to the bitter and shameful death of the cross. By his death, resurrection and ascension he established a new and eternal covenant of grace and reconciliation that we may be accepted by God and never be forsaken by him**.*

*We come to have communion with this same Christ who promised to be with always, even to the end of the world. In the breaking of the bread he makes himself known **to us as the true heavenly Bread that strengthens***

---

[20]    MGS 1963, 245. Sentences and phrases that will be utilized in the 1963 Meaning of the Sacrament are underlined and printed in **bold**.

*__us unto life eternal__. In the cup of blessing he comes to us as the Vine in whom we must abide if we are to bear fruit.*

*We come in hope, believing __that this bread and this cup are a pledge and foretaste of the feast of love of which we shall partake when his kingdom has fully come, when with unveiled face we shall behold him, made like unto him in his glory__.*

*__Since by his death, resurrection, and ascension he has obtained for us the life-giving Spirit who unites us all in one body, so are we to receive this Supper in true brotherly love, mindful of the communion of saints__.*

*Come, for all things are now ready.*[21]

The "Report of the Permanent Committee on Revision of the Liturgy" to the General Synod of 1963 began with some paragraphs that traced the committee's history from 1950 to the General Synod of 1963. One can sense in the words that the committee finally had a feeling that the end of its work may be in sight.

> Pursuant to your original instruction (1950), your Committee hereby submits it final revision of the Orders required by the Constitution of the Reformed Church in America. This final revision is truly a product of growth and cooperative effort.
>
> Since the year of its original appointment, the Committee has submitted from time to time provisional revisions, which you approved for use in the churches for a limited period of time. These have been extensively used during the permissive period.
>
> For a dozen years now there has been a most helpful exchange of thought between individuals, consistories, classes, Particular Synods, and your Committee. This profit has been mutual: a greater concern in the congregations with liturgical matters and enlightenment and inspiration for the Committee in its work of revision.
>
> The last exchange was during this past year when the Committee sent to all consistories its penultimate revisions ....[22]

---

[21]    *MGS 1963*, 218. Sentences and phrases taken from the 1906 liturgy are <u>underlined</u> and printed in **bold.**

[22]    *Archives of the Reformed Church in America,* in file 133.21 among the papers and minutes of the Revision committee.

Among the penultimate revisions was the Order for the Sacrament of the Lord's Supper, the edited version of the French prayer as promoted by Howard Hageman and distributed by him to all ministers in the RCA at the direction of the committee. The original committee of four that had been appointed in 1950 had grown to a committee of nine representing the particular synods. Gerrit Vander Lugt had chaired the committee since its inception with the names of both Hageman and Oudersluys appearing in all 13 reports. Perhaps to honor their faithfulness, the General Synod of 1963 approved a final three-year term for all three of them.

It is important to note that the Standing Committee on Overtures recommended to the Synod that it grant the church one additional year to study the most recent revisions of the liturgy. There would be no rush to judgement at the end of the long journey! Printed below is The Order for the Sacrament of the Lord's Supper as presented to the General Synod in 1963. We have already reviewed the Instruction for Meaning of the Sacrament and so we will proceed to the Communion prayer. As I have done previously, I have <u>underlined</u> and printed in **bold** the words and phrases that have come to the prayer from the French Communion prayer.

*Let us lift up our hearts unto the Lord!*

***Holy and right it Is and our joyful duty to give thanks to unto thee at all times and in all places, O Lord, Holy Father, Almighty and Everlasting God. Thou didst create the heaven with all its hosts and the earth with all its plenty. Thou hast given us life and being and dost preserve us by thy providence. But thou hast shown us the fullness of thy love in sending into the world thy eternal Word,*** *even Jesus Christ our Lord, who became man for us men and for our salvation.* ***For the precious gift of this mighty Savior who hast reconciled us to thee we praise and bless you, O God. Therefore, with thy whole Church on earth and with all the company of heaven we adore thy majesty and bless thy glory.***

***HOLY, HOLY, HOLY, LORD GOD OF HOSTS.***
***HEAVEN AND EARTH ARE FULL OF THY GLORY.***
***HOSANNA IN THE HIGHEST.***
***BLESSED IS HE WHO COMETH IN THE NAME OF THE LORD.***
***HOSANNA IN THE HIGHEST!***

*<u>Holy and righteous Father, as we commemorate in this Supper that</u>*
*<u>perfect sacrifice once offered on the cross by our Lord Jesus Christ</u>*
*<u>for the sin of the whole world, in the joy of his resurrection and</u>*
*<u>expectation of his coming again, we offer ourselves to thee ourselves</u>*
*<u>as holy and living sacrifices</u>*. *Send your Holy Spirit upon us, we beseech*
*thee, that the bread which we break may to be to us the communion of the*
*body of Christ and the cup which we bless the communion of his blood.*
*Grant that being joined together in him we may attain to the unity of the*
*faith and grow up in all things into him who is the Head, even Christ our*
*Lord.*

*<u>And as this grain has been gathered from many fields into one loaf</u>*
*<u>and these grapes from many hills into one cup, grant, O Lord, that</u>*
*<u>thy whole church may soon be gathered from the ends of the earth</u>*
*<u>into thy kingdom. Even so, come, Lord Jesus!</u>*[23]

It is immediately apparent that the prayer is an almost exact
translation of the French Communion prayer except for one significant
portion that is often called the epiclesis. Within the archives of the RCA,
which holds the minutes of the Revision Committee from 1956 onward,
there is a file of liturgies which the committee had at its disposal during
its work. Among them is The Service of the Lord's Supper or the Holy
Eucharist from the Church of South India. The epiclesis in this liturgy
reads the following:

*And we most humbly beseech thee, O merciful Father, to sanctify with thy*
*Holy Spirit, us and these thine own gifts of bread and wine, **<u>that the bread</u>***
***<u>which we break may be the communion of the body of Christ, and the</u>***
***<u>cup which we bless the communion of the blood of Christ. Grant that</u>***
***<u>being joined together in him, we may all attain to the unity of the</u>***
***<u>faith and grow up in all things unto him who is the Head, even Christ</u>***
***<u>our Lord</u>*** ....[24]

With this last section of the prayer identified we can see that
the Communion prayer recommended at the General Synod of 1963

[23]   *MGS 1963*, Reports and Overtures, 71.
[24]   The liturgy in the RCA Archives box identified as 133.21 is titled "The Service
of the Lord's Supper or The Holy Eucharist." The information at the end of the
liturgy indicates that it was first published in June of 1950 with a second edition in
December of 1950 and reprints in July of 1951, August of 1952, and May of 1953.
The Order of Service for the Church of South India was printed and published by
Oxford University Press, Oxford House, Apollo Bunder, Bombay. The underlined
words are found in the 1966 Communion Prayer above.

and adopted in 1966 consists of a significant portion of the French Reformed prayer of 1955 and the epiclesis from the Church of South India. It should be noted that the mission of the Reformed Church in India focused its work in South India and that when the Church of South India was formed in 1947, our missions and congregations became a part of this new indigenous denomination.

The move toward the finish line for the liturgy was not without some conflict. The minutes of the Revision Committee dated March 30–31, 1964, contained a paragraph which highlighted the charges of those who believed that the new Communion service lacked an emphasis on "substitutionary atonement." It was at this point that the committee decided to include the "Instruction" that Hageman had used to craft the new Meaning of the Sacrament. Indeed, the 1958 "Introduction," which is based on the 1906 Abridged Communion Service, was to be offered to the General Synod and the classes as the first option with Hageman's "The Meaning of the Sacrament" as the second option.

In response to the proposal of the committee, the General Synod of 1964 recommended that each classis call a meeting to review the Provisional Liturgy and that a member of the Revision Committee be invited to be a resource person at the classis meeting, with each inviting classis underwriting the expense.

The critique and affirmation of the church came to bear on the proposed liturgy which was presented to the General Synod of 1965. There were 26 overtures that year, some of them addressed the liturgy and many of them recommended specific changes. The committee met for three days in Holland, Michigan, in February of 1965 to prepare for the synod. It should be noted that it appears that a significant number of concerns focused on the liturgy for baptism rather than Communion. The committee held fast in response to most suggestions, compromising when it was wise.

The Synod of 1965 approved the Provisional Liturgy and sent it to the classes for a vote. Interestingly, the liturgy was not sent as a single document and a single amendment to the Constitution but was sent to the classes as 12 orders of worship. The orders, which required a vote of each of the 46 classes, included Morning Worship, Alternate Order, Evening Worship, Baptism, Adult Baptism, Admission to the Lord's Table, Admission from Other Churches, Preparation for the Lord's Supper, the Lord's Supper, the Ordination and Installation of Ministers or Missionaries, the Ordination of Elders and Deacons, and the Installation of a Minister. Since some of the orders were not constitutionally required, it remains a mystery why all of them were sent for vote.

The vote totals for each of the orders is instructive. In order to be approved by two-thirds of the classes, a vote of at least 31 classes was required. The Order of Baptism was the only liturgy that received the minimum number of votes. The ordination and installation orders were passed overwhelmingly, the Order of the Lord's Supper received thirty-eight positive votes and six negative votes with one classis not voting and one classis not reporting.

With a two-thirds vote for approval for all 12 orders, the General Synod of 1966 passed the declarative act which would bring the work of the Revision Committee mandated in 1950 to an end. It is noted, however, that in 1960, the General Synod changed the name of the committee to the Permanent Committee on Revision of the Liturgy, which meant that the revising of liturgies was affirmed as a constant labor of a faithful church.

The Liturgy of the Lord's Supper approved in 1966 set the whole church on a new road.

1. The 1906 liturgy, which remained in effect, was eclipsed by a service that was far briefer—half the length—and thus far easier to integrate into a Sunday morning service.
2. The 1966 service had as its foundation Calvin's strong belief that every congregational service should include the New Testament model of both sermon and Supper.
3. The pattern of New Testament eucharistic practice, which can be seen in the four actions of taking, blessing, breaking, and giving, is clear in the 1966 service and returned the Reformed church to the normative pattern of Western Christianity.
4. This implicit understanding was made clear when the liturgy was modestly revised and republished 20 years later in 1987 when the Supper was fully integrated into a normative Sunday morning service.
5. Surveys of worship practices in the Reformed church conducted in 1987, 1994, and 2004 clearly reveal that the required liturgy of the RCA is followed by an overwhelming portion of the church and the frequency of Communion has grown dramatically since the days of the required quarterly celebration.
6. The presence not only of the Crucified Christ but also the Resurrected One can be seen clearly in both the Meaning of the Sacrament and the Communion Prayer.

It may be helpful to revisit the important role Hageman played in the writing of the new Communion service. In 1959, he published an article that introduced readers to the new liturgy of the French Reformed Church, especially the Communion prayer which became the primary source of the provisional liturgy of 1963. In 1959/1960, Hageman served as the president of the General Synod, and in 1960, he delivered the Stone Lectures at Princeton Seminary, which were published in 1962 as his seminal work, *Pulpit and Table*. The premise of the lectures was that, while Calvin provided the theological foundation to the church, it was Zwingli and his theology of Communion—which Hageman playfully described as the celebration of the "real absence of Christ"—that had taken root in the minds and hearts of many. To this end, witness the number of Communion tables that are engraved with the words "Do This in Remembrance of Me," which formed pastors and parishioners in Zwingli's theology of memorialism. Hageman was among those who promoted Calvin's theology of the Table, which celebrated that the risen Christ was present with the communing congregation through the power of the Holy Spirit. Hageman suggested that a far more felicitous translation of Jesus's words should be: as often as you do this, you *re-call* me into your midst. It was also during this time that Hageman purportedly authored the "Meaning of the Sacrament," which was built on the past, present, and future presence of Christ and would appear first in the 1963 proposed liturgy. Hageman was the person who brought the French Reformed Liturgy to the Revision Committee in late 1962, which inspired the group to distribute it to all RCA ministers before the 1963 General Synod. It was finally at the 1963 Synod that the Communion prayer woven together from the Communion prayers of the Reformed Church in France and the Church of South India would suddenly appear and three years later receive the approval of the church.

As we conclude this brief but important chapter in the Liturgy of the Reformed Church in America, it also may be helpful to recognize that the ecumenical world had grown and deepened since the initial mandate to the Revision Committee in 1950. This is seen most clearly with the gathering of Vatican II, which met from 1963 to 1965. It cannot be overemphasized the important role this gathering had among Catholics but also among Protestants, who sensed that their neighbors were followers of Jesus and committed to his work in a world hungry for hope and thirsty for grace.

CHAPTER 4

# John Henry Livingston on Mission and the Millennium

John W. Coakley

The New-York Missionary Society came into being in 1796, announcing its existence in a published "Address and Constitution" dated November 1 of that year. It conceived of itself as an organization whose efforts would be "exclusively directed to the propagation of the glorious gospel of Christ, in places which are destitute of it."[1] As such, it was one of the earliest of the voluntary American missionary societies that, following the example of their recent counterparts in Britain, were laying the groundwork for the great Protestant world mission movement that would flourish in the decades to follow.[2]

---

[1]  In citing manuscript sources, I have used the following abbreviations: SB: Bound manuscript sermons, Livingston collection, Seminary Archives, Sage Library, New Brunswick Theological Seminary, New Brunswick, New Jersey. Cited by volume number and page numbers (e.g., "SB 1:37–41"). CC: Livingston Papers, Collegiate Church Corporation Archives, New York. Cited by document number and, where applicable, page number (e.g., "CC doc. 35:1–2"). *Address and Constitution of the New-York Missionary Society* (New York: T. and J. Swords, 1796), 13.

[2]  *Address and Constitution*, 3–4; Oliver W. Elsbree, *The Rise of the Missionary Spirit in America, 1790–1815* (Philadelphia: Porcupine Press, 1928/1980), 47–54.

In the list of officers that appears at the end of the "Address and Constitution," we find the name of John Henry Livingston as vice president. Livingston was then the senior minister of the so-called Collegiate Reformed Dutch Church in New York City. He had been called to that church in 1770 while he was completing his theological studies in the Netherlands and had served it continuously since September of that year, with the exception of a seven-year period during the Revolutionary War when he had ministered to various Dutch congregations in the Hudson Valley. Over most of the years of his ministry until this point, he had had a leading role in the process of establishing the Reformed Dutch Church as a self-determining American institution even as it retained and valued its Dutch heritage.[3] He was then 50 years old, and that process had been largely completed since the publication of the Church's Constitution in 1793 in which he had taken the lead; and though his duties as the Reformed Dutch Church's official professor of theology still also occupied him beyond his pastoral responsibilities,[4] he took his new involvement in the missionary cause seriously and was able to invest significant intellectual energy in it. This becomes clear (as will be seen) in a sermon he delivered to his colleagues in the Society in 1799 and especially in a second sermon he gave them five years later.

In this essay—offered in honor of Allan Janssen who, like Livingston, has made important contributions to theology through his writing even as he remained a faithful pastor—I consider Livingston's thinking about missions in terms of its place in the development of his thought and with particular reference to the two sermons he gave to the New-York Missionary Society. Key to that thinking was his concept of history in the light of the millennium, that future period of time in which, according to Scripture (most explicitly in the book of Revelation but by implication elsewhere as well, above all in the Prophets), the kingdom of Christ will be significantly extended throughout the world. This is unsurprising in itself; millennial themes abounded in American

---

3    John W. Coakley, "John Henry Livingston (1746–1825): Interpreter of the Dutch Reformed Tradition in the Early American Republic," in Leon van den Broeke, Hans Krabbendam, and Dirk Mouw, eds., *Transatlantic Pieties: Dutch Clergy in Colonial America* (Grand Rapids: Eerdmans, 2012), 295–313.

4    Indeed at the moment of the founding of the Missionary Society, he was engaged in working out an arrangement with his consistory to reduce his pastoral responsibilities so that he could devote more time to what would ultimately be an unsuccessful effort—because of (as Livingston saw it) a lack of financial support from the General Synod of the Reformed Dutch Church—to establish a theological school in Flatbush on Long Island. Coakley, 309–10.

public discourse, both religious and secular, throughout his lifetime, and had played an important role in most Anglo-American Protestant theological writing about the spread of the gospel for more than a century beforehand.[5] What Livingston's case offers us is a detailed look at how a mature vision of world mission in relation to the millennium could emerge in the mind of a Reformed preacher of his place and time, namely New York in the years surrounding the American Revolution. As the connection of the millennium with world mission became clear to him, his view of it and, by implication, of the course of history became more precise and detailed in a way that had some demonstrable influence on the movement itself.

## Millennial Themes in Livingston's Thought before 1796

In the early years of his ministry in New York City, Livingston already showed an interest in the prospect of the millennium but without attempting to establish its relation to current events or otherwise to foretell the circumstances of its arrival. In a sermon preached in New York on May 2, 1773, when he was 27 years old, he cited the prophecy from Daniel 2, of a stone "hewn out of the mountain without hands" destroying a great statue before filling the world, as foretelling the fall of Islam, the "Eastern AntiChrist." His intent then, however, was not to picture that event as foreshadowing the last days so much as to contrast Islam—a movement that would come to an end—with the kingdom of Christ, which will be eternal.[6] Later that same year on August 8, he preached from Philippians 2:9, that the name of Jesus will be lifted "above every name" at the last judgment so that even his enemies would be obliged to confess his lordship, but that even before that "solemn period arises," many more people than now will make that confession. But all of this served him only as a cautionary contrast to the present moment, when, as he said, believers struggled to know even what it meant to "lift" the name of Jesus.[7]

During the Revolutionary War, we find him still considering the millennium but now beginning to place it in the same historical frame as the present moment. In a sermon that he preached in Albany during

5    Ruth H. Bloch, *Visionary Republic: Millennial Themes in American Thought, 1756–1800* (Cambridge: Cambridge University Press, 1985); James De Jong, *As the Waters Cover the Sea: Millennial Expectations in the Rise of Anglo-American Missions 1640–1810* (Laurel, MS: Audubon Press, 2006; orig. 1970).
6    SB 1:97–106.
7    SB 2:25–35.

his self-imposed exile from British-occupied New York, probably in late 1778 or early 1779, he envisioned the time when "God will establish his Church in all parts of the Earth—there shall be his worship, the preaching of the gospel, the sacraments and ordinances," in fulfillment of the promise that "All the Ends of the world shall remember and turn unto the Lord and all the kindreds of the nations shall worship before thee [Ps. 22:27]."[8] Here his focus had shifted to the future, and he was mainly concerned with envisioning the spread of the gospel, which he imagined happening in "all the world within its extensive limits, and [involving] kindreds or families of the nations, not all at one time, but in succession, some families of all nations." And he added that the proof of the promise was "seen at large" in his hearers'"own lifetimes, for "who can tell what providence designs to bring to pass in America by the present grand revolution!"[9] This is to be sure only a passing comment, without explanation, but shows Livingston incorporating a present event—not insignificantly the American Revolution itself[10]— into his scenario of the future conversion of the world.

By the 1790s, Livingston was more explicitly assigning current events—not only the American Revolution now but also the revolution in France—a direct role in the approach of the millennium.[11] Thus, in a sermon that probably dates from March 1791, he returned to the prophecy from Daniel of the stone that filled the world as foreshadowing the time when "the truths of the gospel will be understood and acknowledged" universally, and he suggested that Christ will particularly work to "overturn, overturn, overturn" other empires as the moment nears when he himself will reign. He added: "in

[8]     SB 6:41. The sermon, on Psalm 22:27-28, is undated, though the one that follows it in the manuscript volume, which likely was its sequel, since the text is the next verses of the same Psalm, was also preached in Albany and dated January 1779 (42–44). Livingston's period of ministry at Albany, as colleague of his brother-in-law Eilardus Westerlo, extended from 1776 to 1779. Alexander Gunn, *Memoirs of the Rev. John H. Livingston* (New York: Rutgers Press, 1829), 252–54.

[9]     SB 6:39, 41.

[10]    On theological significance, for Livingston, of the American republic, see Earl William Kennedy, "From Providence to Civil Religion: Some 'Dutch' Reformed Interpretations of America in the Revolutionary Era," *Reformed Review* 29 (Winter, 1976): 117, and John W. Coakley, "John Henry Livingston and the Liberty of the Conscience," *Reformed Review* 46, no. 2 (Winter 1992): 125–28.

[11]    On the widespread approbation of the French Revolution by American writers on millennial themes in the early 1790s (Livingston's view of the matter being a common one), see R. Pierce Beaver, "Eschatology in American Missions," in Jan Hermelink and Hans Jochen Margull, eds., *Basileia: Walter Freytag zum 60. Geburtstag* (Stuttgart: Evangelische Missionsverlag, 1959), 68–69, and especially Bloch, *Visionary Republic*, 154–63, 168–79.

this view we may safely consider the revolution in America ... and in the same view the astonishing revolution in France," both of which he sees as undermining the authority of the Antichrist, which he identifies with the Roman papacy. "Believers have an eye to providence, and with the Word for their guide can discern events as connected with something great respecting the Church—they look to the end."[12]

Then two years later in the "Preface" to the Constitution of the Reformed Protestant Dutch Church, in what has become one of the best-known passages in his writings,[13] Livingston accorded a role, by implication anyway, to the new Constitution of the American republic in the millennial conversion of the world to Christianity. For referring to the major change that the Dutch Americans were then making in the Dutch church order—namely, to renounce any vestige of their church's heritage as a "national establishment" with government support, thus embracing their new nation's freedom of religion—he remarked with evident reference to the millennium that "all who love the truth will rejoice in the prospect which such a happy situation affords for the triumph of the Gospel, and the reign of peace and love."[14]

As for the French Revolution, Livingston continued to see it, too, as sign of the coming millennium. As late as New Year's Day of 1795 in a sermon on Romans 13:11 ("now is our salvation nearer than when we believed"[15]) in the wake of the Reign of Terror in Paris, he was still referring positively to the French Revolution, if more tentatively now, praying "that the revolutions abroad may prove subservient to the gospel."[16]

---

[12]  SB 10:11.

[13]  On the significance of the passage for the history of the Reformed Church in America, see Eugene Heideman, "Theology," in James W. Van Hoeven, ed., *Piety and Patriotism: Bicentennial Studies of the Reformed Church in America, 1776–1976* (Grand Rapids: Eerdmans, 1976), 98-105. The "Preface" is not signed, but both its content and the fact that the publication of the Constitution had been entrusted to Livingston (see Coakley, "John Henry Livingston: Interpreter," 305-6), argue for his authorshi

[14]  "Preface to the Entire Constitution," in E. T. Corwin, ed., *A Digest of Constitutional and Synodical Legislation of the Reformed Church in America* (New York: RCA Board of Publication, 1906), vi. Theologically, as John Beardslee has observed, Livingston's crucial affirmation here is of "the fullness of Christian living as residing in the life of every individual, not in some sacred group or in 'authorities'"to whom the good Christian is subject." John W. Beardslee III, "John Henry Livingston and the Rise of the American Mission Movement," *Historical Highlights* [Journal of the RCA Historical Society] 8 (1989): 7-8.

[15]  KJV.

[16]  CC doc. 7. Even two years later, in a sermon dated March 5, 1797, he still makes positive reference to the French Revolution, at least obliquely, when he affirms

In all these instances, Livingston did not explicitly mention the sending of missionaries or the establishment of mission societies as events that mark or foreshadow the coming of the millennium. But we do find him in a sermon of March 20, 1796, on Isaiah 59:19 ("So shall they fear the name of the Lord from the west, and his glory from the rising of the sun."[17]) commenting on the geography of mission history. There he noted that the proper course of the gospel's progress had been from east to west and so had not yet gotten to Asia, which was still "in the darkness of paganism, or under the illusion of the imposter Mahomet"—but that in the great events to come, the gospel will triumph there as well, as it encircles the world to "come round to the place from whence it commenced."[18] Very possibly he was already then in conversation with his co-founders of the New-York Missionary Society, which would be formed later that year and would provide him a context for the full development of his ideas about mission.

### The Glory of the Redeemer (1799)

As mentioned above, Livingston was vice president of the New-York Missionary Society at the time of its founding. In the annual reports of the directors of the Society, he continued to be listed as holding that office at least through the year 1804 with the exception of one year (1797).[19] On April 23, 1799, he preached a sermon to the

---

"what God is now doing in the world ...[and] the principles friendly to man which are prevailing—which actually proceed from revealed religion, however disposed many are to oppose and contradict this!" CC doc. 33:4. Livingston in any event appears, for all his opposition to Deism, to stop short of the "Francophobic reaction" that Ruth Bloch has seen to characterize much American millennialist writing in the late 1790s in contrast to the tendency to Francophilism earlier in the decade, and which was motivated by alarm at infidelity. Bloch, *Missionary Republic*, 202–31.

17    Isaiah 59:19, KJV.
18    CC doc. 11:33–44.
19    The fact that Livingston was on partial leave from his pastoral ministry in New York in 1797 probably explains his absence from the list of officers that year; see Coakley, "John Henry Livingston: Interpreter," 310. I have not been able to examine the annual report for the years 1804–1810. In the report for 1811, by which time he had moved from New York to New Brunswick, his name is no longer on the officers' list. *Annual Report of the Board of Directors of the New-York Missionary Society, Presented and Approved March 25, 1811* (New York, 1811), 7.
    That he remained in the leadership cadre of the Society as late as 1807 is suggested by an entry in the journal of the pioneer British missionary to China, Robert Morrison. relating a meeting with a "committee of the Missionary Society," including Livingston by name as well as the names of others who had served with

Society, which was then published under the title "The Glory of the Redeemer" along with the group's annual report of that year.[20] In this sermon, we see him for the first time bringing those millennial themes that had been part of his thinking for years into his consideration of what, for him, was the new topic of the prospect of world mission.

By April of 1799, when Livingston first preached to the Society, its work was well under way. Already in the "Address" of 1796, the Society had made clear that their organization, like the British societies that were their models, would work for the conversion of the "heathen," but instead of sending missionaries abroad would focus both on the native people of "our own land" and on the settlers of European extraction on the American frontiers who had no access to preaching or Christian ordinances or "religious instruction" and are thus "Heathen in reality." Perhaps curiously to our mind, but significantly for Livingston (as will be seen), the address also declared it to be part of the Society's task to oppose the "infidelity"— that is, apparently, the influence of free-thinkers, Deists, and other "enemies of the gospel"—of their own place and time, specifically by demonstrating through their zealous actions that "the Spirit of Christ continues to animate his body,"[21] i.e., the ongoing vitality of the Christian faith. In the following two years, the directors had established a standing monthly prayer meeting held in rotation in "all the churches of which the Ministers are members of the Society," had contributed funds to existing Native American missions in Massachusetts and Long Island, had formulated a "set of instructions for Missionaries," and had opened correspondence with other societies. But they had begun only one major mission project, namely to send a missionary, the Rev. Joseph Bullen of Vermont, to the Chickasaw nation in Georgia. Bullen, having been commissioned, had begun his journey south from New York on March 26, 1799.[22] When Livingston delivered his sermon, Bullen would have still been in transit.

---

him as officers when Morrison passed through New York in 1807. Eliza A. Morrison, *Memoirs of the Life and Labours of Robert Morrison*, vol. 1 (London: Longman, 1839), 129.

[20] John H. Livingston, *The Glory of the Redeemer. A Sermon, Preached before the New-York Missionary Society in the Scots Presbyterian Church, 23rd of April, 1799*, in *Two Sermons Delivered before the New-York Missionary Society ...* (New York: Isaac Collins, 1799), 3–48.

[21] *Address and Constitution*, 3–10.

[22] "Directors' Annual Report," in John M. Mason, *Hope for the Heathen: A Sermon, Preached in the Old Presbyterian Church, before the New-York Missionary Society, at their Annual Meeting, Nov. 7, 1797* (New York: T. and J. Swords, 1797), 98.

In the sermon, Livingston made reference to the Society's efforts that were then beginning, after bringing some of his previous reflections on millennial themes to bear on the broader task of world mission. Thus he alluded, as he had done already many years before, to Daniel's image of the stone from the mountain, as a prophecy of the end time when the kingdom of Christ "shall triumph over all its adversaries, extend its boundaries and spread throughout the world"[23]—but now, as in those earlier sermons in the 1790s, he placed that triumph in specific historical context, as coming eventually on the heels of the tumultuous events of his own time, which he again interpreted as signs of God's preparation for it. Thus, obliquely referring to the papacy and the revolutionary events in Europe, he commented that "that wicked power which has so long resisted the progress of the gospel but which for some time has been gradually consuming, will soon be destroyed by the brightness of the Redeemer's coming. ... The desolations of war, the revolutions, terrors and convulsions, unrecorded before in history, announce the approach of some period, new and interesting. The redeemer is shaking the nations, and his people hope, it is to prepare the way for his coming."[24] And now he took the momentous step of adding the recent work of the British societies to that list of events to be seen as preparatory of the end time: "In the Indies, in the islands of the Pacific Ocean, and in Africa, the precious name of JESUS is now proclaimed by their heralds."[25] Then he made specific reference to his society's work: "Our feeble efforts," he said, "although late, have not been disowned by our LORD. We have succeeded in obtaining one missionary, and he is now on his way to a tribe of savages [sic] upon our frontiers. The LORD direct the steps of his servant, and render this beginning of our labours as 'the handful of corn upon the top of the mountain, the fruit whereof shall shake like Lebanon!' [Ps. 72:16]."[26] And though he rested the matter in God's hands (an important point for him), at the very end of the sermon, he made at least an effort to connect these missionary "labours," i.e., the human efforts involved in the work of the Society, to the eventual triumph of Christ's kingdom: "Whatever may be the immediate consequence of your efforts, it will be accepted of the Lord, that it was in your hearts to build him an house. Whatever may be the issue of the individual or joint exertions in this good work; it will not

[23]    Livingston, 33.
[24]    Livingston, 45.
[25]    Livingston, 43.
[26]    Livingston, 47.

be long before the morning will break, and with its rising lustre dispel the shades of night. Another season of refreshing is at hand. Another Pentecost will awaken the churches and amaze the world."[27]

Here then we see Livingston placing the nascent world mission movement, to which he himself had begun to lend his voice, in historical relationship with the coming millennial kingdom of Christ that he had long envisioned. This would not be his last word on this topic, as we shall see, and before we proceed to examine his considerable elaboration of it five years later, it is worth mentioning that much of the 1796 sermon is not focused on millennial expectations at all but on another topic close to Livingston's heart. In fact, the passages that I have just cited come toward the end of the sermon, in approximately the last quarter of it. The first three-quarters are taken up with that other theme that had appeared in the Society's explanation of its purposes in 1796, namely its opposition to "infidelity," i.e., to Deism and other unbelief that constituted an evil precisely among European peoples like themselves. The stated text for the sermon is Colossians 3:11, "Christ is all and in all." The statement—construed to mean that the person of Christ the redeemer represented "everything essential in the salvation of sinners"—does not apply, said Livingston, to *natural* religion, that is, to religion based on reason and nature alone (such as the Deists promoted), in which it is not the redeemer but the creator who is "all in all in all."[28] Rather, the text applies to *revealed* religion, that is, to religion based on the revelation contained in Scripture, which, taken as a whole, witnesses to the sinfulness of human beings and their need for a redeemer and thus to the inadequacy of natural religion for human salvation, which has "no room for the sinner."[29]

This train of thought expresses the "supernatural rationalist" approach to religious authority—i.e., affirming the power of reason to achieve some religious truths but not adequate to save sinners, for which purpose supernatural revelation was necessary—was an approach that was common in eighteenth-century academic Protestant theology, which Livingston absorbed from his teachers at the University of Utrecht. His own inaugural discourse as the Reformed Dutch Church's professor of theology in 1785 consisted precisely of an extended explanation of these principles, in which he listed the truths of natural religion essentially as the Deists had named them—that God exists and

---

[27]   Livingston, 47.
[28]   Livingston, 4.
[29]   Livingston, 14.

is to be worshiped through virtue and piety, that sins are to be avoided, and that there will be an afterlife of rewards and punishments—and acknowledged them to be valid but of insufficient value for the saving of sinners, and thus he presented Deism, which declared natural religion as sufficient in itself, as the mortal enemy of the Christian faith. And supernatural rationalism had been a recurrent theme in his preaching, used almost reflexively as a tool to frame a variety of assertions in a variety of contexts.[30]

What then was the connection for Livingston between the theme of the necessity of revealed rather than natural religion for salvation and that of millennial expectations as motivation for the missionary enterprise? The answer appears to rest in the notion of the lordship of Christ, and by implication, in the affirmation of the agency involved in mission as being divine not human. For in the process of explaining how it is that Christ is "all in all" in revealed religion, he quoted Scripture that "the Father has committed all judgment to the Son [John 5:22]" and has "given all things into his hands [John 13:3]," and he declared accordingly that the Christ who is "all in all" has oversight of world history in its present dispensation, that is, until the "kingdoms of this world shall become the kingdoms of our LORD and of his CHRIST [Rev. 11:15]"[31]—a point which, having been made, allowed him to proceed to his explanation of Daniel's prophecy of the stone and thus speak of the evangelization of the whole world, including "souls of savages [sic] [which] are as precious as your own" and in turn to arrive at his comments on the current mission movement.[32]

Livingston would not make a major point of the theme of the relationship between revealed rational religion in his second sermon to the New-York Missionary Society, to which I will turn next; nor was this the central theme of any of the other sermons given at the annual

---

[30]    John H. Livingston, *Oratio inauguralis de veritate religionis Christianae* (New York: Samuel and Johannes Loudon, 1785). The contrasting distinction between the power of the gospel to change lives and the limited power of natural reason to do, even as the consistency of the gospel with reason is affirmed at the same time, is not just *a* theme in his thought but a sort of *basso continuo,* a strain that underlies its various melodies. Three examples among many: SB 4: 45–51 (sermon of March 14, 1784); SB 5: 17–30 (sermon of Nov. 12, 1786); SB 8: 37–43 (sermon of March 28, 1790). The distinction also structured the "System of Didactic Theology" of his lectures as Professor of Theology. Ava Neal, *Analysis of a System of Theology Composed Chiefly from Lectures Delivered by the Late John H. Livingston* (New York: J.F. Sibell, 1832), 26–29.

[31]    Livingston, *The Glory of the Redeemer,* 25, 32.

[32]    Livingston, 33, 43, 46.

meetings of the Society through 1803.[33] Yet especially insofar as this theme bore upon the question of divine versus human agency in the project of mission—never an incidental question for him—he surely continued to think it germane to the work of the Society and of the missionary movement.

### The Triumph of the Gospel, 1804

In 1804, Livingston preached a second sermon to the New-York Missionary Society, which was also published along with the Society's annual report of that year.[34] Here again, he places the missionary movement in the context of the prospect of the millennium as a basis on which to exhort his hearers to support of the Society—for their mission to the Chickasaws in Georgia had in the meantime begun to fail, and their attention had shifted to the Tuscaroras and Senecas of western New York, where they would continue their efforts[35]—and of the world mission movement generally. But in its approach to that topic of the millennial significance of missions, this second sermon stands in some contrast to the first, and indeed, to the other annual meeting sermons given by his Society colleagues in the meantime. For here the historical role of the missionary movement as anticipation or

---

[33]  Those published sermons were as follows (titles abbreviated): Alexander McWhorter, *The Blessedness of the Liberal: A Sermon Preached … before the New-York Missionary Society at Their First Institution, November 1, 1796* (New York: T. and J. Swords, 1796); John M. Mason. *Hope for the Heathen: A Sermon, Preached … Nov. 7, 1797* (New York: T. and J. Swords, 1797); John McKnight, *Life To The Dead. A Sermon Preached … the 24th of April, 1799 …* in *Two Sermons* (see note 18), 49–73; William Linn, *A Discourse, Delivered April 1ˢᵗ, 1800 …* (New York: Isaac Collins, 1800); John N. Abeel, *A Discourse, Delivered April 6ᵗʰ, 1801 …* (New York: Collins, 1801); Samuel Miller, *A Sermon Delivered … April 6ᵗʰ* (New York: TandJ Swords, 1802); John Williams, *A Discourse Delivered April 5, 1803* (New-York: Isaac Collins and Son, 1803). After 1804, the Society ceased publication of the annual sermons.

[34]  John H. Livingston, *The Triumph of the Gospel. A Sermon, Delivered before the New-York Missionary Society, at Their Annual Meeting, April 3, 1804* (New York: T. and J. Swords, 1804).

[35]  The New-York Missionary Society would then continue to exist as a discrete entity until 1820 when it was folded into the United Foreign Missionary Society, a likewise predominantly Presbyterian and Reformed organization, which had been founded the year before and which was itself in turn absorbed by the American Board of Commissioners for Foreign Missions in 1826. Elsbree, *Rise of the Missionary Spirit*, 114; Robert F. Berkhofer, Jr., *Salvation and the Savage: An Analysis of Protestant Missions and American Indian Response, 1787–1862* (Lexington: University of Kentucky Press, 1965), 172; Clifton J. Phillips, *Protestant America and the Pagan World: The First Half Century of the American Board of Commissioners for Foreign Missions, 1810–1860* (Cambridge, MA: Harvard East Asian Research Center, 1969), 75.

sign of the future millennium is no longer primarily a rhetorical means to frame an encouragement of interest in missions, as had been the case with the previous sermons[36]; rather, though the encouragement remained, the placing of the movement in its proper historical position in the sequence of events leading toward the end time has itself become Livingston's major interest. The sermon presents itself as a thorough, painstaking, and, as it were, a scientific attempt to establish that placement precisely.

What is new about the 1804 sermon is on display already in its published length and presentation. Though the preached text, at 36 pages, is of comparable length to the previously published annual-meeting sermons by others as well as Livingston, it differs from them all in including an extended appendix, which contains 12 discursive end notes in a smaller typeface, which add 38 additional pages to the publication. The text itself refers the reader to these notes at the appropriate places in its argument. The notes are titled, respectively: "Former Missions" (a long-term history of Christian missions), "Present Missions" (a survey), "Isaiah xxvi. 17, 21" (as an example of Old Testament prophecy about the future church), "The Apocalypse" (on, i.e., the Book of Revelation), "The Reformation," "The Fall of Babylon" (see below), "The Millennium" (a concise overview of how the term was generally understood), "The Martyrs Avenged" (on the French Revolution as God's vengeance for the "suffering of the Huguenots"), "Delays Compensated" (citing Jonathan Edwards's speculations about the increase in human population during the millennium), "Persecutions" (an estimate of the number of Christian martyrs ancient and modern), "Missionary Societies," and "The Church hath seen her worst Days" (an excursus arguing this thesis).[37] The overall effect is to present the sermon as an annotated and erudite scholarly treatise on Christian mission in the broad perspective of salvation history.

Indeed, the substance of the sermon consists, treatise-like, of a learned attempt to formulate and answer a particular question. He

---

[36]   It is true that most of the preachers (see note 33) cited their turbulent times as evidence of the coming of the end time. But none attempted to construct a detailed exegetically-based timeline of coming events to include the great world mission movement that was then in its infancy, as Livingston does here – although Mason in 1797 anticipated Livingston in identifying the prophecy of the angel with the "everlasting gospel" in Revelation 14 as a prophecy of the evangelization of the world. Mason, *Hope for the Heathen*, 23.

[37]   Livingston, 41–78.

prefaced the attempt by noting that there have been "constraining motives for propagating the Gospel," and that moreover Christ commanded to "teach all nations [Matt. 28:19-20]," yet that, historically, Christians have been weak in their efforts. It was clear enough to him why Christians neglected Christ's command "in the dark period of ignorance and oppression" before the Reformation, but he lamented that there has been so little "zeal" for it in the three centuries since the Reformation, which have been "more prosperous times [for the Church]"—until, ironically, it had suddenly caught fire in the present, which was seemingly not a favorable time at all, but "a season the most unpromising, when wars, revolutions, and confusion prevail ... [and] infidelity assumes a formidable aspect... ." So here is his question: "What is God doing? Why are the intricate wheels, which, with respect to this important object, have so long seemed stationary, now put in motion?"[38]

Livingston then introduced the Scripture text, not in his usual way, as an ostensible given from which the sermon's theme was derived, but rather as a choice of the most promising source material in which to find an answer to the question he had posed. He found Old Testament prophecies (such as we know to have been common in mission sermons) to be of no help, since they generally refer either to the time of Jesus and the apostles or to the end time itself, whereas his question pertained to the present moment and thus not to the end time, only marking its "approach." The Gospels and Epistles also offered little assistance, he remarked. Rather, it was the book of Revelation that provided the most explicit information, and so Livingston chose as his text Revelation 14:6-7, in which John of Patmos describes a vision of an angel flying "in the midst of heaven," with "the everlasting gospel to preach unto them that dwell on the earth, and to every nation, and kindred, and tongue, and people ...."[39] Livingston promised that this text would answer his question—would explain why the missionary movement had arisen at the present moment—and furthermore would provide "a NEW MOTIVE for strenuous and persevering exertions in your missionary engagements."[40]

Livingston proceeded then to describe the event described in the vision of Revelation 14:6-7 in terms that make clear that he finds it to refer to the present moment, that is, to the emergence of a world

[38]    Livingston, 5–7.
[39]    Revelation 14:6, KJV.
[40]    Livingston, 7.

mission movement. The vision was to be seen as partially symbolic and partly literal. The symbols are "heaven," which refers to "the Church under the New Testament dispensation," and "angel," which refers to "the Gospel ministry in the aggregate." "Flying" symbolizes "speed." So the symbols showed John foreseeing "a period when a zealous ministry would arise in the midst of the Churches; a ministry singular in its views and exertions and remarkable for its plans and success; a ministry which would arrest the public attention, and be a prelude to momentous changes in the Church and in the world."[41] And the "literal" parts of the text made the symbols"meaning even clearer. The "treasure the angel bears" was literally the gospel, which was "called EVERLASTING [v. 6]" to show that the message now to be spread around the world was the "*same* Gospel which had always been maintained by the faithful followers of the Redeemer."[42] Finally, the *content* of the gospel as the angel proclaims it is the exhortation "Fear God; give glory to him ... and worship him that made Heaven and Earth ... [v. 7]" that refers "the whole of true religion, as it respects principles and practice," which signifies the "truth, that revealed religion adopts, confirms and enjoins the religion of nature"[43]—thus implying the distinction and relationship between revealed and natural religion, which, as we know, Livingston regarded as de rigueur in his own preaching. The angel preaches moreover with urgency, since "the hour of God's Judgment is come" in fact is already begun. And the message is for everyone on earth: "EVERY NATION, AND KINDRED, AND TONGUE, AND PEOPLE."[44] He summarized the event that the vision is speaking of: it is "a singular movement ... not in a solitary corner, but in the very midst of the Churches—That [i.e., whereby?] the Gospel, in its purity, would be sent to the most distant lands, and success crown the benevolent work."[45]

Having found in his text, in effect, a description of the mission movement he was witnessing in his own time, Livingston then proceeded to investigate what context, and therefore what significance, the book of Revelation assigned to it. He began by asserting the event was "something vastly beyond what was realized at the Reformation," but that on the other hand it was not to be identified with the millennium since it was "only the appointed means for introducing

---

[41]   Livingston, 8–9.
[42]   Livingston, 9–10.
[43]   Livingston, 12.
[44]   Livingston, 12–13.
[45]   Livingston, 13–14.

that state; ... it must, in the nature of things begin its operation some considerable time before the Millennium can commence." He argued this from the textual placement of the vision itself in its chapter of the book of Revelation. He noted that in the text, the vision that precedes this vision of the preaching angel is a vision of the Lamb [i.e., Christ] on Mount Zion with the elect gathered around him. Mount Zion symbolizes the Church, and the assembly of the elect there to sing a song "known only to themselves" (cf. v. 3) signifies that they are a group safely preserved from the Antichrist though as yet "unacknowledged by the world"—a scene which, he added in the appendix, could only refer to the Reformation, which occurred "about three hundred years ago."[46] And the vision that follows the vision of the preaching angel is of "the fall of great Babylon [v. 8]," understood to the demise of the papacy, the "duration" of whose power "is limited to twelve hundred and sixty prophetic years," according to what Livingston assumed, along with a long tradition of Protestant interpreters, to be meant by the reference to that number of "days." The dating of the end of the reign of this "Babylon" will depend on when the corruption of the papacy is thought to have begun (i.e., at what point in the early Middle Ages popes began to be despotic), and this, he says, is controverted, but "the latest date which has been, or, indeed, can be, fixed for his rise, extends his continuance to the year 1999" and so his fall must be "at farthest, immediately before the year 2000, when the Millennium will be finally introduced." So the beginning of the Angel's "flight must be "after the year 1500, and before the year 2000."[47] And since this was only happening now, it must be beginning only now. Thus the period of its "accomplishment" would be in "the short remaining space of two hundred years" from the moment of his sermon.[48] So Livingston concludes that the mission movement currently taking shape marks the beginning of a period of no more than two hundred years, which is not the millennium but rather will lead up to it. That, he is saying, is our particular place in history.

What was left for him to explain, then, was what was to happen in this two-century period then beginning. Here he named four events that appear in Scripture to happen before the millennium can occur. Two of these he had already mentioned, namely the judgment of God—with attendant tribulations—which marks the period's beginning and

[46]  Livingston, 16, 56.
[47]  Livingston, 16, 58.
[48]  Livingston, 17.

the fall of the Antichrist, which signals its end. The other two events are the conversion of the Jews and the bringing of the "fullness of the Gentiles ... into the Church." These two events, presumably—though here he elaborates mostly on the Gentiles, in effect the "heathen"—will, extending over time, be the concern of the missionary movement.[49]

So what Livingston has done is to assign to the nascent world mission movement, which he and his hearers are witnessing, a place within—or rather, at the beginning of—a sequence of works that have been revealed already as leading, over a 200 year period, to the final establishment of Christ's kingdom. Thus he has placed himself and his hearers more or less precisely within the course of salvation history.[50] He has explained to them what they are doing, and when it is, in cosmic terms, that they are doing it—all as a "NEW MOTIVE" for getting on with the task.

When, however, at the end of the sermon, Livingston came to his obligatory list of applications, or as he (unusually) called them here, "reflections," he also explained to his hearers—and here we are most reminded of his earlier sermon to the Society—that in an important sense, *they* were really not doing anything. The events he had described, consistently with the traditions of Reformed doctrine, would be the work of God, since "the truth of God is pledged to accomplish his word. Nothing can possibly intervene to change his plan," and by implication therefore, God is not dependent on us to carry it out.[51] In this sense, Livingston would have considered any argument that we must accept mission as a responsibility rather than leave it all to God to be misplaced; for him, orthodox Calvinist that he was, the point was not to accept a responsibility but to feel a passion for what God was doing and to wish to be a part of it: "While we are musing upon the prediction before us, *our hearts are hot within us; the fire burns;* zeal kindles to a flame; we glow

---

49     Livingston, 17–24.
50     Livingston developed a theology of mission "not simply as an obligation to redeemed individuals but as an aspect of the total movement of history." John W. Beardslee III, "John Henry Livingston and the Rise of American Mission Theology." *Reformed Review* 29, no. 2 (1976): 106. (The publication is not to be confused with Beardslee's similarly titled study published in 1989 (see notes 14 and 51)
51     Livingston, 28. As Beardslee has noted, for Livingston the "emphasis" in the Scripture text is on something "happening in heaven," and thus is "God's work" not ultimately ours, and that this "clearly links the missionary call to the deepest springs of Reformed theology." John W. Beardslee III. "John Henry Livingston and the Rise of the American Mission Movement," 11.

with ardour to perform our part, and assist the flight of the preaching angel. We live to see the dawn; we long to see the day."[52]

## Contribution and Influence

In its broad expression of millennial expectation as well as in many of its particulars, Livingston's thinking about mission was not original. Certainly the impulse, evident in Livingston as much as in his New-York Missionary Society colleagues, to understand mission in terms of the millennium—to connect the missionary mandate with millennial expectations—had been a major theme in Anglo-American evangelical Protestantism as far back as the seventeenth century and was in particular vogue in the 1790s.[53] Likewise, the calculation of the beginning of the millennium on the basis of Old Testament prophecy that appeared to predict the length of rule of Antichrist had been a well-worn exercise among theologians of the previous two centuries, several of whom Livingston cited in his Appendix.[54]

Still, coming at the moment it did, Livingston's second missionary sermon made a contribution to the great world mission movement then emerging—namely by his use of the well-honed concepts of millennial thinking just then to construct a compelling historical and theological explanation for the fact of that movement's sudden appearance. In De Jong's words, he "ascribed a missionary essence to the period between his day and the millennium and contended that the latter would be the product of faithful mission efforts during the next two hundred years,"[55] thereby providing an aid to the movement's self-understanding and to its sense of its own significance.

There is, as it happens, some anecdotal evidence of the impact of his thinking upon the missionary movement in its formative moments beyond the bounds of the New-York Missionary Society. Samuel J. Mills, one of the four Andover Seminary students who catalyzed the formation of the American Board of Commissioners for Foreign Missions (ABCFM) when they presented themselves to the General Association of Congregational ministers in Bradford, Massachusetts in 1810,[56] had first encountered Livingston's second missionary sermon

---

[52]   Livingston, 34.
[53]   Bloch, *Visionary Republic*, 215–31; De Jong, *As the Waters Cover the Sea*, 204–27.
[54]   Livingston, 58.
[55]   De Jong, 219.
[56]   Elsbree, *Rise of the Missionary Spirit*, 109–13; Phillips, *Protestant America and the Pagan World*, 20–31.

as a freshman at Union College in 1805. After a term at Union, he had then transferred to Williams College, where he was one of the founders of the secret "Brotherhood" of young men committed to foreign mission, which continued in existence for several decades as a seed-bed for missionary vocations; and it was at Williams that he and some other students republished Livingston's sermon in 1809.[57] As Mills told his friend John Schermerhorn not long afterward when they were both students at Andover, at Williams, the sermon had (in Schermerhorn's words) "produced a wonderful effect in favor of missions among the students, and particularly in enlisting in favor of this cause, Gordon Hall, James Richards, [Edward] Warren, and others who have since spent their days [as missionaries of the ABCFM] in heathen lands."[58]

## Postscript

If Livingston's advocacy of missions thus had some influence outside the Reformed Dutch Church, it had greater impact within that church. It was doubtless under his guidance that, in 1811, shortly after his arrival in New Brunswick to teach at the church's infant seminary at New Brunswick, his students formed the mission society called the Berean Society, later to be called the Society of Inquiry on Missions and to survive under that name well into the twentieth century.[59] He also mentored the first missionary that the seminary produced, David Abeel.[60] And Reformed Church in America denominational historians have routinely paid tribute to him as the initiator of the denomination's venerable tradition of world mission service that has continued to the present day.[61]

A caveat is also important as we consider his legacy. For Livingston, mission was certainly one imperative for the church. But it was also, as we might say, one of many. Even after he had preached and published his missionary sermons, his preaching did not (according to my reading

57   Greenfield [Massachusetts]: John Denio, 1809. The cover lacks the phrase "The Triumph of the Gospel."

58   John F. Schermerhorn, Letter to the Editor, *Christian Intelligencer,* October 6, 1838. The letter itself is dated September 27, 1838.

59   Luman Shafer, *History of the Society of Inquiry, 1811–1911* (New Brunswick: Laidlie Fund, 1912); John W. Coakley, *New Brunswick Theological Seminary: An Illustrated History* (Grand Rapids: Eerdmans, 2014), 19–20.

60   G. R. Williamson, *Memoir of the Rev. David Abeel, D.D.* (New York: Robert Carter, 1848), 11–14.

61   Most recently: Eugene Heideman, *A People in Mission: The Surprising Harvest* (New York: Reformed Church Press, 1980), 2–3.

of his manuscripts) routinely focus on missions in either concept or particulars. For him, as for most of his contemporary Protestant mission advocates, world mission was a *function* of the Christian church, a means whereby to expand the bounds of that church as they understood it, and, therefore it constituted but one theme among many for the preacher. By contrast, over the course of the twentieth and now twenty-first centuries, mission thought has increasingly attempted to conceive of mission not merely as a function of the church, however deeply valued a function, but rather as its very essence—to conceive, that is, of "church *as* mission" and thus to view all of its life and work as expressions of its missionary identity.[62] Livingston, as a person of his own time, did not consider the matter of mission in those terms. In this, we may feel his historical distance from us, even as we admire the passion and integrity of his writings and acknowledge our debt to him as ancestor in the faith.

---

[62]    David Bosch, *Transforming Mission: Paradigm Shifts in the Theology of Mission* (Maryknoll: Orbis, 1991), 368–73.

CHAPTER 5

# Heidelberg and Westminster, Especially on Worship

Daniel J. Meeter

It is my privilege to honor Allan Janssen with this article, not least because he has been its champion. I presented this first as a lecture to the Mercersburg Society 15 years ago, and since then, despite Al's efforts, its publication has been frustrated. I am pleased to offer it also because of Al's evident love of the Heidelberg Catechism, a particular love that is an example of his more general esteem for the theology of the church—that the church itself makes theology precisely to do its mission. And one of the chief ways the church makes theology is by means of catechisms. Finally, I offer this not as an academic theologian but as a Reformed pastor for whom theology is of first importance—a pastor is a local theologian! My public ministry, like Al's, has been formed by the Heidelberg Catechism as has my own devotion and faith.

Although the Heidelberg Catechism and the Westminster Shorter Catechism were written 80 enormous years apart and for slightly different purposes, they deserve comparison because of their similar influence and ubiquity. They are the epitomes of the two divisions of the Reformed movement—the Continental and the British. By the nature of the case, I will stress the differences between them, but we do well to remember that many of our Reformed ancestors took them as harmonious.

First, a word about catechisms in general. The literary genre of the catechism predates the Reformation. Already in the ninth century some German dioceses had primitive catechisms. Later the Waldensians and the Bohemian Brethren had one in common. But the genre was invigorated by the Reformation, and a golden age of catechisms extended from 1529 to 1647, from Luther to Westminster. In this flourishing of catechisms, the genre was developed and enriched. Even Rome and Constantinople produced their first authorized catechisms at this time. All these catechisms were written by the best and busiest theologians who regarded this task among their prior obligations.

The genre is not a simple one—a number of interests are to be served. There is the obvious interest of children and the most basic instruction in the Christian faith. But there is also the interest of pastors and teachers. And it was for this reason that some catechisms were issued in pairs. Luther published a Small and a Long. Westminster published a Shorter and a Larger. The Heidelberg is not a children's catechism—it was designed for preachers and teachers. Churches that used the Heidelberg also had specific children's catechisms, such as the one my father, a pastor, used in his ministry within the Reformed Church in America. But the remarkable thing about the Heidelberg is that it's the only one of the longer catechisms that has come to be loved by ordinary church members.

The genre often had also to deal with political interests. Both Heidelberg and Westminster first appeared as parts of larger legal documents. The Heidelberg was published within the Church Order of the Palatinate, which itself was part of the law of the land. The Westminster Standards were presented to Parliament as the official Advice of the Westminster Assembly. Parliament ratified the whole set of standards, but they could hardly take effect before the Restoration of Charles the Second. The Standards did hold their legal force in Scotland, of course.

In this regard, the great difference between the Heidelberg and the Westminster is that the respective rulers were the patron of one and the enemy of the other. Elector Frederick, if not the father of the Heidelberg, was certainly its godfather, while King Charles Stuart bitterly opposed the whole Westminster project, and the Standards were written against the royal interests. The polemic purpose lies just beneath the surface of Westminster. It was meant to push the nation along in its further reformation, and its system was conceived as an ideal. By contrast, the Heidelberg was as practical as it was pacific, for it was intended to consolidate religion and to keep the peace. Furthermore, the Palatinate, unlike Great Britain, was a principality where the ordinary pastor knew somebody who knew the Elector.

Let me frame the political dynamic in the words of a well-informed parish pastor who spoke at a church conference in Ontario, Canada a few decades ago:

> Now you know that the Heidelberg Catechism was part of the Palatinate Church Order of 1563, and that included rules for church government and administration, and worship too. Why did they do this? You to have to understand that the Reformation spread quickly in the universities, where they could all read Latin, and it spread quickly in the cities, where they could all read German, but when it got to the countryside, the people couldn't read, and it ground to a halt. And so in the Palatinate, as late as the 1560s, you had Ursinus in the university, and Olevianus in the city, but when you got out to the countryside you still had Father Schultz and Father Schmidt [*sic*: more likely Father Franz and Father Hans]. Now these were good men, but they weren't scholars. They were loyal enough to their prince, and they didn't mind doing what they were told to do. So the Heidelberg Catechism is basically a "How-to-be-a-Protestant-minister Kit" for Father Schultz and Father Schmidt.[1]

Let me compare the outlines of the two. The first answer of the Heidelberg is that much-loved overture which establishes the key, sets the tone, and states all the themes. The second answer provides the outline, the triple knowledge of Guilt, Grace, and Gratitude. There is movement implicit in this structure—from guilt through grace to gratitude—and this movement is built into many of the answers, with their threefold pattern of past, present, and future, such as in Answer 1: "he has fully paid" and "set me free"; "he also watches over me" and "assures me"; he "makes me wholeheartedly willing and ready from now on to live for him." The answers of the Heidelberg often tell a story, the whole thing's got a plot, and I think that's part of its appeal.

The first answer of the Westminster is also justly famous, but for its precision and clarity. Its second answer does not provide the outline,

---

[1]    Daniel James Meeter, *Meeting Each Other in Doctrine, Liturgy, and Government: The Bicentennial Celebration of the Constitution of the Reformed Church in America,* number 24 in the *Historical Series of the Reformed Church in America* (Grand Rapids: Eerdmans, 1993), 203, n. 14.

however. It deals with the sufficiency of Scripture. You might consider this a sidetrack, but think of the context. The enemy was not modernism or liberalism but the pretensions of the crown, the prerogatives of Canterbury and York, the preferments of the bishops in Parliament, and the ancient patterns of English common law. It was a strong statement to make, and we ought not to underestimate its daring.

The third answer gives Westminster's outline, and it's a very simple one: first, what we are to believe concerning God? And second, what duty does God requires of us? The first part (Questions 4–38) takes us through the doctrine of God, the decrees, creation, providence, sin, election, Christology, redemption, effectual calling, justification, adoption, and sanctification. The second part (Questions 39–107), on the duty which God requires, takes us through the Ten Commandments, faith, repentance, the Word, the sacraments, prayer, and the Lord's Prayer. The Apostles' Creed is included only as an appendix. The section on the Ten Commandments takes up 41 answers, which is quite more than a third of the whole document, and this brings out the strongly ethical tone of the whole catechism.

The Westminster Standards are admirable. The first question of the Shorter Catechism is brilliant, and it is a question that people are asking every day. My wife has a book by Wendell Berry with the title, *What Are People For?* This is another way of asking, "What is the chief end of man?" The answer: People are for glorifying God and enjoying God forever. I use that answer all the time in my ministry, and it is better than the first answer in Calvin's catechism, "to know God," which is an answer that is open to new age gnosticism. There is a transcendent vision to the Westminster Shorter that goes beyond the Heidelberg. And the Westminster system speaks beyond the church to human society as a whole.

And yet, while we admire the Westminster, it is not lovable in the way that the Heidelberg is loved. The Westminster earns more passionate loyalty than love. You do not see answers from the Westminster Shorter on Presbyterian funeral bulletins as you do with the Heidelberg in the Reformed churches. You often see Heidelberg Answer 1, but occasionally you will even see Answer 54 on the holy catholic church. What accounts for this difference in affection?

The reasons are many, and Philip Schaff is quite good on this in the relevant chapters of *The Creeds of Christendom.*[2] His trenchant

---

[2]     Philip Schaff, *The Creeds of Christendom in Three Volumes* (New York: Harper and Row, 1931; Grand Rapids: Baker, 1983), Vol. I, 787.

observation is that the Westminster deals in dogmas rather than in facts: "It addresses the disciple as an interested outsider rather than as a church-member growing up in the nurture of the Lord." The virtue of this is that it can speak to non-churched seekers. But, in doing so, "it substitutes a logical scheme for the historical order of the Apostles' Creed."[3] And this is because the Westminster is the harvest of Calvinist scholasticism, while the Heidelberg was written at the seedtime. The Heidelberg takes the standpoint of the *"ich"*; it is an I-statement from one end to the other, while the Westminster was written in the third person.

The Heidelberg is historical, while the Westminster is philosophical. The Heidelberg is narrative, while the Westminster is logical. The Heidelberg stresses the actions of God on our behalf, while the Westminster stresses the obligations of humanity toward God. The latter is about what we should do, and the former is about what God has done, does now, and will yet do. The appeal of the Heidelberg is that it's more about God and less about us, which makes sense if Westminster is correct that we were designed to enjoy God (and not ourselves).

The scholastic character of the Westminster is most obvious in the emphasis it places on the two related doctrines of the "decrees" and "effectual calling," which are terms used throughout the document. God has decreed, before the foundation of the world, everything that will come to pass.[4] Some of these eternal decrees are for the salvation of the elect.[5] This is timeless and unchangeable. God brings these decrees to reality in the individual by means of effectual calling:

> The Spirit applieth to us the redemption purchased by Christ by working faith in us, and thereby uniting us to Christ in our effectual calling. / Effectual calling is the work of God's Spirit, whereby, convincing us of our sin and misery, enlightening our minds in the knowledge of Christ, and renewing our wills, he doth persuade and enable us to embrace Jesus Christ, freely offered to us in the gospel.[6]

There are two problems with this scheme of the decrees and effectual calling. The material problem is that salvation is removed from

---

[3]   Schaff, Vol. I. 787.
[4]   The Westminster Shorter Catechism, in *The Confession of Faith; the Larger and Shorter Catechisms, etc.* (Edinburgh: Johnstone, Hunter, and Co., 1876), Questions 7 and 8.
[5]   Westminster Shorter, 20.
[6]   Westminster Shorter, 30 and 31.

history and located in eternity, which is unreachable and unknowable. The formal problem is that Westminster, in a shorter catechism, raises to first importance a pair of theological terms that are derivative and extra-biblical.

Like Westminster, the Heidelberg teaches in human participation within the scheme of salvation. But its categories are biblical and dynamic. Q & A 88 is telling:

> *Jn wieuiel stücken stehet die warhafftige buß oder bekerung des menschen? Jn zweyen stücken: Jn absterbung des alten vnd aufferstehung des newen menschen.* / In how many parts is the true repentance or conversion of man? In two parts: in the dying-off of the old man and the resurrection of the new.[7]

Right upon this, Answer 89 defines the dying-off of the old self, and 90 defines the resurrection of the new. These three answers locate our human obligation in the death and resurrection of Christ. Answer 88 is thoroughly Lutheran. It goes back even to the "Ninety-five Theses," which state that the whole life of Christians is repentance. This Lutheran element in the Heidelberg is not just the result of what some later Calvinist scholars have regarded as an unfortunate Melanchthonian political compromise between the Lutherans and the Calvinists in the Palatinate but is actually the proper inheritance of original Calvinism at its evangelical heart.

The differing emphases in soteriology are magnified in their respective ecclesiologies. Here is Heidelberg 54 in a recent translation:

> **What do you believe concerning the "holy catholic church"?**
> I believe that the Son of God, by his Spirit and his Word, out of the entire human race, from the beginning of the world to its end, gathers, protects, and preserves for himself a community chosen for eternal life and united in true faith. And of that community I am and always will be a living member.[8]

Notice, first, the personal and experiential emphasis; and second, the threefold past-present-future pattern of "gathers, protects, and preserves." This is an example of what Schaff means by calling it

---

[7]   Wilhelm Niesel, ed. *Kirchenordnung der Kurpfalz* (1563) in *Bekenntnisschriften und Kirchenordnungen der nach Gottes Wort reformierten Kirche,* 3rd ed. (Zürich: Evangelischer Verlag, 1938) 171; my translation.

[8]   *Our Faith: Ecumenical Creeds, Reformed Confessions, and Other Resources* (Grand Rapids: Faith Alive, 2013).

historical. Third, the church is defined as an activity of the Son of God. It is within God's activity that we find ourselves and our identity.

The Westminster, by contrast, has no equivalent answer about the church. Indeed, the only mention of the church is in the answer on the administration of baptism, number 95, where the word appears twice but is coupled with "visible," as in "visible church." The visible church in scholastic Calvinism is by definition a relativized church. Indeed, it can be said that the Westminster lacks a positive ecclesiology. The community that it addresses is not the church but the whole Christian commonwealth of the British crown. One could say that its church is England and England is its church.

This represents the full secularization of the church—a statement that is not entirely negative. In fact, it is the ideal vision of Revelation 21. It is a fully realized eschatology. It is the full Calvinist vision of the total reformation of Christendom. (One thinks of Bucer's *De Regno Christi*, a comprehensive plan for the total Reformation of England politically and economically no less than theologically.) But what if God's economy is not there yet? Or, what if Christendom is over? We know from history that Heidelberg had an immediate appeal to the refugee and the persecuted congregations of the Dutch and the Hungarians. Perhaps this means that it can survive the end of Christendom better than Westminster can.

In the same way, the Westminster lacks a positive doctrine of worship. This is in spite of the fact that it is all about worship, from one end to the other. The whole life of Christians is worship, all day, every day, at work, at rest. Again, it is an ideal, almost a heavenly one. But something so general is bound to be diffuse and therefore weakened in reality. Worship is always assumed, but never defined, and this is a huge lack in a document that trades in precise definitions.

Neither does the Heidelberg offer a definition of worship as such. But one can easily deduce it. We find in Q & A 65:

> *Dieweil denn allein der glaub vns Christi vund aller seiner wolthaten theilhafftig macht woher kompt solcher glaube? Der heilig Geist würckt denselben in vnsern hertzen durch die predig des heiligen Euangelions vnd bestätiget den durch den brauch der heiligen Sacramenten.* **Since then only faith makes us partakers of Christ and all his benefits, whence comes such faith?** The Holy Ghost fashions (works, creates) this faith in our hearts through the preaching of the holy gospel and strengthens it through the use of the holy sacraments.[9]

---

[9]  Niesel, 164; my translation.

The point here is that the ordinary worship service is God's chosen workshop for creating and strengthening faith. God's activity in the worship service is paramount. God uses preaching and the sacraments for the creation and sustenance of faith. Preaching is the constant presentation and rehearsal of the gospel promises, which are the object of our faith. The sacraments point us to and sustain us in the passion of Christ, by which he won the benefits that the Holy Spirit applies to us. Worship is at the very center of God's saving work. One goes to church to get saved.

Westminster does give the worship service a role in effectual calling. Answers 88 and 89:

> The outward and ordinary means whereby Christ communicateth to us the benefits of redemption are his ordinances, especially the Word, sacraments, and prayer, all of which are made effectual to the elect for salvation. / The Spirit of God maketh the reading, but especially the preaching, of the Word an effectual means of convincing and converting sinners, and of building them up in holiness and comfort, through faith unto salvation.[10]

The difference is subtle but significant. First, the ordinances of worship are qualified as the outward means and are therefore relativized. Second, faith is presupposed in order for the believer to get the benefit of the ordinances, not understood as being generated by the ordinances themselves. This is more apparent in Answer 91:

> The sacraments become effectual means of salvation, not from any virtue in them, or in him that doth administer them, but only by the blessing of Christ, and the working of his Spirit in them that by faith receive them.[11]

What does it mean that the sacraments have no virtue in them? The long-range effect of this was to remove Reformed and Presbyterian worship from the table of Emmaus and back into the Second Temple, which was empty of the presence of the glory-cloud.

If you combine such statements with Answer 60, on the Sabbath Day, the picture is complete:

> The Sabbath is to be sanctified by a holy resting all that day, even from such worldly employments and recreations as are lawful on

---

[10]  Westminster Shorter.
[11]  Westminster Shorter.

other days; and spending the whole time in the public and private exercises of God's worship, except so much as is to be taken up in the works of necessity and mercy.[12]

Notice this phrase, "the public and private exercises of God's worship." Worship is a human exercise, and it can be either public or private. It is no less in these private exercises that effectual calling can take place. This is a natural conclusion that can be drawn from the fact that, after effectual calling is defined in Answers 30 and 31, the subsequent answers treat it in a most general way, as something that God just freely and mysteriously does in us, without any reference to either the worship service or the church.

My thesis here is that, in the Heidelberg, the service of Word and sacrament is the essential means by which God makes faith in us. In the Westminster Shorter, the worship service is an outward human exercise, the ordinances of which may be used by God, along with other things, for effectual calling among those persons who have saving faith. Here *in vitro* is the difference between Mercersburg and Princeton, between Nevin and Hodge. There are two interpretations of Calvinism here: according to its Lutheran core, or leaning toward scholastic speculation. It was toward the latter that the energy of the world was moving.

Schaff regards both Heidelberg and Westminster as each reflecting the genius of their native nationalities. That may be. More to the point is that these catechisms, once wrought, gave shape and formation to centuries of spiritual culture. Over time, in some places, their subtleties will have been magnified in effect, and in other places, they will have conditioned each other. In what proportion the Westminster either reflected or determined the kind of worship that became typical of the Calvinist tradition is difficult to determine, but there is no doubt what happened. And it happened even to the lovers of Heidelberg in spite of Heidelberg, because, in a real sense, Westminster was closer to where the mind of Protestant Europe was going.

Evidence for this in my own denomination, the Reformed Church in America, is the loss of the Flood Prayer from the Liturgy for Baptism. The original of this prayer was probably written by Martin Luther, and then Leo Jud, the successor of Zwingli, introduced a revision of the prayer to Zürich. It was taken into many subsequent church orders and liturgies, including the Palatinate Liturgy that accompanied the catechism, and from there it passed into the Dutch Reformed Liturgy.

---

[12]　Westminster Shorter, Answer 60.

In North America, beginning in the 1760s, the Flood Prayer began to be omitted by some preachers, and by 1815, it had been deleted from our official Liturgy altogether. And this happened without any approval or even notice of our synods.

It is not coincidental that the deletion of the Flood Prayer happened in the same era in which the Dutch Reformed Church was introducing English preaching by importing Presbyterian ministers. The Westminster is not congenial to the Flood Prayer's strong emphasis on baptism as foremost a miraculous activity of God. In the Netherlands, it was a century later that the Flood Prayer was disused, and it is no surprise that Herman Kohlbrügge defended it, that champion of Heidelberg.

It is well known that American revivalism was born in backwoods Presbyterianism. The original camp meetings were held in Scotland. They were called "sacramental seasons" and were always tied to the Lord's Supper. They were the preparation meetings, and they could sometimes last a week. The people had to get themselves ready for eating and drinking worthily, and they did this through many exercises of penitence and self-examination. The Supper was not taken lightly, and God's presence was not denied, but the sacrament was regarded first as duty and obedience, and one had to be converted first in order to profit from it. In 1801, at the Presbyterian Church of Cane Ridge, Kentucky, the crowd of Scotch-Irish believers had gathered for such a sacramental season, and it was here that the first revival broke out, with all the physical manifestations. In the words of Barton Stone himself, "Many things transpired there, which were so much like miracles ...."[13]

I submit that what you have here is the result of a hunger for some experience of worship in which the action of God is paramount. When the sacraments are emptied of miracle, then people will come up with substitute sacraments that have miracle in them. If the worship service itself neither converts them nor makes faith in them, then they will get converted and get their faith outside of church. And eventually they will turn all their worship services into such exercises, once they have shaken off the firm authority of Westminster. Nevin was right to make the connection between Puritanism and revivalism. Horton Davies and Charles Hambrick-Stowe were right to have taught us to be fair to the Puritans themselves, but the issue we all face is the nature of God's activity in worship. Does God work saving miracles in church?

---

[13]   Sydney E. Ahlstrom, *A Religious History of the American People* (New Haven and London: Yale University Press, 1972), 433.

In 1986, the Reformed Church in America added to its Constitution the following definition of worship: "Worship is the action
of acknowledging God's worth."[14] This is a rather shallow exercise
in etymology, but worse, it approaches worship as primarily human
obligation. Yes, of course, when doing the scientific study of religion,
we will have a phenomenological definition that will define worship as
a human cultural activity. But a church's definition of worship must be
theological, and a Reformed church's definition ought to harmonize
with Heidelberg. To introduce a definition like that of Westminster is
to condemn our congregations to the constant cycle of rationalism—
revivalism, rationalism, revivalism—and the constant invention of
substitute sacraments that finally do not satisfy.

Let me propose a definition of worship that I derive from
Heidelberg 32, 54, 65, 66, 67, and 88. *Christian worship is when God comes
to have a meeting with us in Christ.* And then we may define liturgy as the
form which the church has given to these meetings which God has with
us. These meetings are business meetings, for God is busy with us, by
means of Word and Sacrament, saving us, gathering us, and converting
us into a kingdom of priests and a holy nation. (I use the word "convert"
according to Heidelberg 88.) In the very act of our embracing the work
of God in us, we offer praise to God.

The sacramental question was framed for Nevin as the question
of the real presence of Christ. The corollary question is the real action
of Christ. The presence and action of Christ in the sacraments, and
in the whole service, is to be distinguished from the general presence
and action of God in the world. There are sound biblical reasons to
make this distinction, reasons which may be drawn from a new and
better understanding of the covenants. The covenant theology we
have inherited is the federal theology of Westminster, which doesn't
hold up, and which, together with the decrees, suggests an incipient
Unitarianism. We need to do better with covenant, and we need to do
better with the Trinity as well. We need to move beyond Nevin to a
more fully Trinitarian theology of the sacraments and of the church,
especially with an enriched Pneumatology, and there are signposts in
the Heidelberg for this. (I may mention the Pneumatologies of A. A. van
Ruler and Eugene F. Rogers, Jr.)[15]

---

[14]   "The Directory for Worship," in James R. Esther and Donald J. Bruggink, eds.,
*Worship the Lord* (Grand Rapids: The Reformed Church in America and Eerdmans,
1987).

[15]   A. A. van Ruler, *Calvinist Trinitarianism and Theocentric Politics,* trans. John Bolt,
Toronto Studies in Theology (Lewiston NY: Edwin Mellen Press, 1989), and Eugene

The Heidelberg closes with Thanksgiving. Thanksgiving—eucharist—is the main theme of the Lord's Supper. In the Palatinate Lord's Supper Form, the prayer of consecration is not a proper eucharistic prayer. But the note of thanksgiving is triumphant in the Supper by means of it ending on Psalm 103, "Bless the Lord, O my soul." This will have formed anyone growing up in the Reformed Church in America to expect to come to the end of Holy Communion by blessing God. The worship service stages the same drama, liturgically, that the Heidelberg does catechetically, from Guilt, to Grace, to Gratitude. The kind of praise here is not just a general praise, as in Westminster, but the particular sort of praise which is thanksgiving. In a real sense, therefore, the Heidelberg is a eucharistic catechism.

If the Heidelberg is not as transcendent as Westminster in its vision for humanity, it is deeper in its feeling for the heart of God. The book of Revelation tells us that the saints in heaven will be singing the songs of Moses and the Lamb. Both of these songs are eucharistic songs in that they are songs of thanksgiving for rescue and reconciliation. So then, may I ask again, what are people for? To glorify God and enjoy God forever, yes, but what this will look like is a great feast of thanksgiving.

F. Rogers, Jr. *After the Spirit: A Constructive Pneumatology from Resources outside the Modern West* (Grand Rapids: Eerdmans, 2005).

CHAPTER 6

# Biblical Citations in the Canons of Dort, Articles I,6 and I,7

Eugene P. Heideman

As an ordained minister and professor of theology in the Reformed Church in America, Allan J. Janssen is a signatory to its "Declaration for Ministers," according to which he affirms: "I accept the Standards as historic and faithful witness to the Word of God." The Standards are the sixteenth- and seventeenth-century Reformed confessions: the Heidelberg Catechism, composed at the request of Elector Frederick III in the Palatinate in 1563; the Belgic Confession, prepared by Guido de Bres in 1561 and sent to King Philip II of Spain in 1562; along with the Canons of Dort, the judgment of the Synod of Dort rejecting the "Errors" of the Remonstrant in the Netherlands in 1618-1619. The Belhar Confession, first drafted in the Republic of South Africa by the Dutch Reformed Mission Church in 1986, was adopted to be a Standard in the Reformed Church in America in 2010. These four confessional statements were not only true contemporary witnesses in their own time and context, but "to the extent that we still live within that age, they are so for us."[1]

---

[1]  Allan J. Janssen, *Confessing the Faith Today: A Fresh Look at The Belgic Confession* (Eugene: Wipf and Stock, 2016).

Throughout his ministerial career, Allan Janssen has sought to remain a faithful signatory to the Declaration for Ministers. He is persistent in his personal engagement with the Standards and in helping his students and members of his congregation to appreciate them in their historical context and their contemporary significance. However, in the Preface to his book, titled *Confessing the Faith Today: A Fresh Look at the Belgic Confession,* the Canons of Dort are not mentioned by name. According to Janssen, the Heidelberg Catechism is "still beloved," and the Belgic Confession is "the only comprehensive confession," and the Belhar Confession has been recently adopted. He points out that the confessional testimony, "Our Song of Hope," was adopted as "a statement of the church's faith for use in its ministry of witness, teaching, and worship."[2]

The avoidance of specific mention of the Canons of Dort in his Preface is the first hint that Janssen may hesitate about its function today as a Standard. That hesitation becomes even more apparent in his discussion of the Belgic Confession, Article 16, on election. There he indicates two specific points of criticism of the Canons of Dort, Articles I,6 and I,7. He is critical of the notion in Article I,7 that "God has chosen the precise number of the saved, even before their birth" and of versions of the doctrine "that are difficult to accept, let alone defend. I do not intend to engage in such false attempts."[3] I believe it is possible to accept Janssen's criticism of the Canons at this crucial point and still refuse to go on to deny recognition of the Canons of Dort today as part of the Standards.

## The Synod of Dort (1618–1619) as a Defender of The Protestant Reformation (1517)

The Canons of Dort were drafted in an era of intense religious and political controversy in western Europe, almost exactly 100 years after Luther posted his "Ninety-five Theses" in Wittenberg. Wars of religion were going on in Western Europe. Protestant memories of the Saint Bartholomew's Day Massacre (1585) in France and of the Guy Fawkes attempt to blow up Parliament in London (1605) were still fresh in the minds of Reformed delegates at the synod meeting in the city of Dordrecht. Moreover, the Netherlands States General believed that the unity of the Dutch Republic was at stake, so it paid the costs

---

[2]   *MGS 1978,* 37, as quoted in Janssen, viii.
[3]   Janssen, *Confessing the Faith,* 66.

of the synod, amounting to more than 1.5 million Dutch guilders. The Reformed Church feared that the Arminian theologians, allied with the Advocate General Johan van Oldenbarnevelt, were too ready to compromise with Philip II, king of Spain, and thereby open the door to Spanish rule and a return to Roman Catholic dominance.

The Synod of Dort was called to end the threat to the Reformed faith and the unity of the Republic by rejecting the "errors" in the five points of "The Remonstrance of 1610" submitted by the Remontrant ministers in the Reformed Church. The Remonstrants claimed to be as orthodox in the Reformed faith as were the delegates to the synod. Both sides in the controversy agreed in accepting the ancient Nicene Creed and accepted the Athanasian Creed, the doctrine of the Trinity, the Heidelberg Catechism (1563), and the Belgic Confession (1561). They agreed that God has issued a decree or decrees from before the foundation of the world that God elects some individuals to salvation and reprobates the rest (probably the majority), condemning them to eternal punishment in misery for their wickedness. Both taught that God's justice "demands that sin, committed against his supreme majesty, be punished with supreme penalty—eternal punishment of body and soul."[4] Both also believed the Jews who reject Jesus Christ as their savior are heretics and therefore to be reprobates who are not loved by God.

The sharp difference between the synod and the Remonstrants is precisely stated in the Canons' Rejection of Errors where it refutes the Remonstrant doctrine that it is "the will of God to save *those who would believe and persevere in faith and the obedience of faith* that is the whole and entire decision of election to salvation and that nothing else has been revealed in God's Word."[5] The synod declared this opinion to be heresy: "For they deceive the simple and plainly contradict Holy Scripture in its testimony that God does only wish to save those who would believe, but that he has also from eternity chosen certain particular people to whom, rather than to others, he would within time grant faith in Christ and perseverance."[6] The Canons of Dort continue to be important in its rejection of the threat posed by the Remonstrants who taught

---

[4] Heidelberg Catechism, Q & A 11.

[5] Canons of Dort (Canons), Rejection of Errors, I,i.. (Citations of the Canons of Dort use the translation of the Reformed Standards in *Our Faith: Ecumenical Creeds, Reformed Confessions, and Other Resources* (Grand Rapids: Faith Alive Christian Resources, 2013).

[6] Canons of Dort, Rejection of Errors, I,i.

that election is based on God's foreknowledge of who would believe and who would not believe. It is crucial to respect the judgment of our forefathers who rejected the Pelagian teaching of the Remonstrants that in election "to faith a prerequisite condition is that humans should rightly use the light of nature, be upright, unassuming, humble, and disposed to eternal life, as though election depended to some extent on these factors."[7] The synod correctly recognized danger smacking of the heresy of Pelagianism in what the Remonstrants were teaching. That constituted not only a threat to the Reformation doctrine of justification by grace through faith alone but also a threat to the unity of the Dutch Republic. The error had to be rejected in the seventeenth century but also in all following centuries. Karl Barth in the twentieth century, who was often critical of the Synod of Dort, was even more opposed to the Remonstrants when he wrote, "The basic decision which the [Remonstrants] made was this—that in the understanding of God and His relationship with man, in the question of the formulation of Christian doctrine, the criterion of measure of all things must always be man, i.e., man's conception of which is right, and rational, and worthy, therefore of God and man."[8] In election, it was actually man who made the decision; not God. "Above and beyond that, there is no more than a foreknowledge of what individuals will become as measured by this order of salvation and on the basis of the use which they make of their creaturely freedom."[9] "[I]n the mouth of the Remonstrants it should not be a more accurate or Christian definition of the mystery of the election of grace, but an attempt to deny it altogether; an attempt to make of divine predestination something more akin to a religious world-order."[10]

While in full agreement with the basic judgment of the synod that the Remonstrants were guilty of serious errors, even Pelagian, in their doctrine of election, my purpose in this essay is to examine the extent to which the Synod's own teaching of the doctrine of election is in accord with Scripture. Due to lack of space in this festschrift, I focus my attention on the Canons of Dort, Articles I,6 and I,7 that cite Acts 15:18, Ephesians 1:11, Ephesians 1:4-6, and Romans 8:30 in support of its doctrine of election and reprobation. It will be suggested that the Synod of Dort cited the appropriate passages of Scripture

---

[7]   Canons of Dort, Rejection of Errors I,iv.
[8]   Karl Barth, *Church Dogmatics* (*CD*), 2/2 (Edinburgh: T&T Clark, 1956–1975), 66.
[9]   Barth, *CD*, 2/2, 68.
[10]  Barth, 68.

but misinterpreted them because the Synod operated with a serious blind spot that inhibited it from appreciating the relation of Jews and Gentiles in God's plan of salvation.

### Acts 15:18, Ephesians 1:11, Ephesians 1:4-6, and Romans 8:30, Cited in the Articles I,6 and 1, 7, Do Not Support the Doctrine of Election and Reprobation as Taught by the Synod of Dort.

The synod ignored the first-century A.D. biblical and historical context of the four passages that are cited in Article I,6 and I,7. The Acts and Epistles were composed in the time when the Gentiles were entering the church. The early church was struggling with the integration of Gentile Christians into the covenant community of descendants of Abraham. In their first-century context, each of these passages says that the gospel is not for the Jews only but also for the Gentiles. The Synod of Dort was called to defend the sixteenth-century "orthodox" Reformed doctrine of election and reprobation of individuals that ignored the issue of God's covenant with Abraham and his seed in Old Testament and in the early New Testament church. [11]

Acts 15 reports on the recognition by the apostolic council in Jerusalem that "God first looked favorably on the Gentiles, to take from among them a people for his name," in agreement "with the words of the prophets" that from the ruins of the house of David, God would rebuild it "so that all other peoples may seek the Lord—even all the Gentiles over whom my name has been called. Thus says the Lord, who has been making these things known from long ago" (Acts 15:14-18). This pervasive theme that Christ's salvation is first for the Jews but also for the Gentiles flows through the whole New Testament. Ephesians 1:3-14 says that it was God's plan from the foundation of the world that Jews and Gentiles would be worshiping together in Ephesus in the unity of the Spirit. Romans 8:30, in the context of the whole book of Romans, says that God will certainly bring to full fruition the plan of salvation for the Jews as well as the Gentiles, "for those whom [God] predestined he also called; and those whom he called he also justified; and those whom he justified he also glorified."

---

[11]   By "orthodox" here I am thinking of the doctrine as taught by Theodora Beza (1519-1612) in Geneva, William Perkins (1558-1612) in England, and Franciscus Gomarus (1563-1641) in Leiden; see H. Heppe, *Reformed Dogmatics*, trans. GT Thompson, 1950 (Eugene: Wipf and Stock, 2007), 146-148. All three men were "supralapsarian," but the Canons of Dort are "infralapsarian" in nature.

These verses are used in I,6 and I,7 to support the doctrine of election and reprobation as depicted in the Canons of Dort. I suggest that: (A) None of the passages propose a *decree* of eternal reprobation alongside a decree of election. (B) It is an error to interpret Ephesians 1:11 ("who accomplishes all things according to his counsel and will") in terms of God's general providence while ignoring the Christological emphasis of the whole chapter. (C) They do not suggest that "God chose in Christ to salvation *a definite number of particular people out of the entire human race*"[12] while leaving the rest "in their common misery"[13] and "finally condemn and eternally punish those who have been left in their own ways and under God's just judgment."[14]

Acts 15:18, quoted in Article 1,6, should not be translated "all his works are known to God from eternity" as if God determined every event in time from the foundation of the world. New Testament scholars now agree that the text should be translated, "Thus says the Lord, who has been making these things known from long ago."[15] James, the brother of Jesus, quoted Amos 9:11-12 as ancient prophecy that Gentiles are included along with Jews in God's plan of salvation. In the events of the resurrection of Jesus Christ and the outpouring of the Holy Spirit, God's ancient covenant with Abraham and his seed was opened up to include people of all nations. Acts 15:18 provides no support for the idea that "The fact that some receive from God the gift of faith within time, and that others do not, stems from his eternal decree. For 'all his works are known to God from eternity'" (Acts 15:18; Ephesians 1:11).[16] In affirming the inclusion of the Gentiles, Acts 15:18 points in the opposite direction from Article I,6, which teaches a radical separation between the elect who receive eternal life and the reprobates who enter into eternal damnation.

The Synod also made a wrong turn when it used Ephesians 1:11 to support the doctrine of a double decree of election and reprobation in Article I,6. It narrowed the clause "who accomplishes all things according to his counsel and will" to refer to God's decree to "soften the hearts, however hard, of the elect and incline them to believe, but by a just judgment God leaves in their wickedness and hardness of hearts those who have not been chosen." However, Ephesians 1:11 does not say anything about God's judgment on those who have not been chosen.

---

[12]   Canons, Article 1,6.
[13]   Canons, Article 1,6.
[14]   Canons, Article 1.15.
[15]   NRSV.
[16]   Article I,6.

## God's Plan of Election in Christ (Acts 15:18; Ephesians 1:13-14)

When we read in Article I,6 that in God's decree "all his works are known to God from eternity," (Acts 15:18; Ephesians 1:11) we should not conclude that God's decree for the world is an exercise of absolute sovereignty whereby God "from all eternity, did by the most wise and holy counsel of his will, freely and unchangeably ordain whatever comes to pass."[17] Loraine Boettner expanded Westminster's doctrine in the twentieth century to say:

> God would have an exact plan for the world, would foreknow the actions of all the creatures He proposed to create, and through his all-inclusive providence would control the whole system. If he foreordained only certain isolated events, confusion both in the natural world and in human affairs would be introduced into the system and He would need to be constantly developing new plans to accomplish what he desires. His government of the world would then be a capricious patchwork of new expedients.[18]

In opposition to the Canons of Dort, Article I,6 and Westminster Confession, 3,1, we must not interpret Ephesians 1:9-11 as a proposition about God's system of providence in general, but we should read it as God's particular plan of redemption in Christ.

> With all wisdom and insight he has made known to us the mystery of his will, according to his good pleasure that he set forth in Christ, as a plan for the fullness of time, to gather up all things, things in heaven and things on earth. In Christ we have also obtained an inheritance, having been destined according to the purpose of him who accomplishes all things according to his counsel and will, so also that we, who were the first to set our hope on Christ, might live for the praise of his glory.[19]

## God's Plan for the Fullness of Time

The broad scope of God's decree in Christ comes into full view in Ephesians 1:9-11. In contrast to the Synod of Dort that concentrates its

---

[17]   The Westminster Confession, Chapter 3, 1.

[18]   Loraine Boettner, *The Reformed Doctrine of Predestination*, (Grand Rapids: Eerdmans, 1957), 24. See also Louis Berkhof, *Systematic Theology* (Grand Rapids: Eerdmans, 1976), 100.

[19]   Ephesians 1:8b-12.

sole attention on God's decree to elect a definite number of particular individuals and to reprobate others in the course of history,[20] God's plan in Christ from before the foundation of the world is a "plan for the fullness of time" when all things are gathered up in Christ in the culmination of time. With the plan to gather up all things in Christ firmly in place, it is not necessary for God to determine from the beginning every event and every detail in the history of the world. God's plan does not need a precise blueprint for every event that takes place in history. The Holy Spirit is free to blow "where it chooses, and you hear the sound of it, but you do not know where it comes from and where it goes. So it is with everyone who is born of the Spirit" (John 3:8). In theological terms, eschatology is not trumped by predestination; predestination anticipates eschatology. Gerhardus Vos points out that eschatology antedates redemption: "Creation was but the origin. The destination was the tree of life, with humanity conformed to everlasting glory, immortality and righteousness."[21]

Markus Barth translates the word *oikonomia* in Ephesians 1:10 as "administer" rather than "plan," writing that "he should administer the days of fulfillment" (NRSV: "as a plan for the fullness of time").[22] The word *oikonomos* indicates a "steward" or an administrator of a household, a private estate, or a city (1 Corinthians 4:2; Luke 16:1-8; Galatians 4:21).[23] As God's Son is designated God's manager over all things, "Christ is entrusted not only with the care of God's people, but with the responsibility to rule in God's name over all times, spaces, powers."[24] As a wise manager of God's plan, Christ does not have to micromanage every detail. God's plan to gather up all things in Christ must not be understood to apply only to those things that are in existence on the Last Day at the end of time. The gathering up of all things reaches back to the beginning of time as well as to the end of time. That is why God can exercise patience in dealing with the sin of the world (Romans 8:25-26). The past is not absolutely fixed forever; the past is not yet beyond redemption. The events and fragments of human history are not consigned to eternal oblivion or meaninglessness, but somehow, in a way we cannot yet understand, are gathered up and woven together

---

[20]    Canons, II,9.
[21]    Quoted in Michael S. Horton. *The Christian Faith: A Systematic Theology for Pilgrims on the Way* (Grand Rapids: Zondervan, 2011), 437.
[22]    Markus Barth, *Ephesians: Introduction, Translation, and Commentary on Chapters 1–3* (Garden City: Doubleday, 1974), xxvii.
[23]    Barth, 86.
[24]    Barth, 88.

in Christ. Even those things that human beings intended for evil can be used by God for good, as Joseph told his brothers many centuries ago (Genesis 50:20).

### Article I,7 in the Light of Ephesians 1:4-14; Jews and Gentiles Elect in Christ

As we turn to look in more detail at Article I,7, its quotation of Ephesians 1:4-6 and Romans 8:30, we should first take note of two blind spots in the Canons of Dort. One is the lack of awareness of the pervasive anti-Semitism that left the papal church, the Remonstrants, and the Synod of Dort free to ignore the biblical references to Jews in the doctrine of election. Second, the emerging individualism in the post-Reformation modern world was already encouraging the synod to ignore the fact that election in the New Testament always has a covenantal setting inherited from the Old Testament Israelitic tradition, beginning with God's election of Abraham and his seed. Participating in the emerging individualism in the opening decades of the seventeenth century, the Synod of Dort constantly kept to a narrow vision of election on the salvation or reprobation of the individual soul while ignoring the fact that in the biblical passages it cites (Ephesians 1:4-6; Romans 8:30; 9-11), it is not isolated individuals but believers in covenantal contexts who are elect.

Both blind spots play a role in Article I,7. By amending Ephesians 1:4 to say, "God chose in Christ to salvation *a definite number of particular people out of the entire human race*," the synod screened out recognition of God's particular election of Israel and also narrowed the doctrine of election to God's action of electing one individual and reprobating another according to the good pleasure of his will. This amendment to the text of Ephesians 1:4 leads in the opposite direction from what Paul wrote.[25] Article I,7 encourages us to conclude that, since the majority of people in the world do not believe the gospel, the majority of humankind are not elect but are reprobate. The amendment of Ephesians 1:4 improperly shifts attention from Paul's concern about the division between Jew and Gentile to Dort's focus on the gulf between the elect and the reprobate.

---

[25] The authorship of Ephesians is disputed. It is not necessary for our purpose to decide whether Ephesians was written by Paul or a person who may have been a follower of Paul. For a very brief discussion of the matter, see James D. G. Dunn, *The Theology of Paul the Apostle* (Grand Rapids: Eerdmans, 1998), 729-733.

Ephesians 1:4-6 is part of the opening hymn of blessing in praise of God who "has blessed us in Christ with every spiritual blessing in the heavenly places." The epistle is addressed to a congregation or congregations having Jews and Gentiles in their membership. One of the themes running through the epistle is that in Christ the Jews and the Gentiles are being united in one body. Paul writes that by the Spirit it has now been revealed that the the Gentiles have become fellow heirs, members of the same body, and Jews and Gentiles are no longer strangers to each other. In Christ, they are members of the household of God, joined together in one structure, a holy temple in the Lord (Ephesians 2:19; 3:6). Their unity in Christ is not an accident of history. God chose us in Christ before the foundation of the world so that we should be holy and blameless before him with love (Ephesians 1:3-4). They were not elected to individual piety, but were called to live in unity, "with all humility and gentleness, with patience, bearing with one another in love, making every effort to maintain the unity of the Spirit in the bond of peace" (Ephesians 4:2-3).

The elect in Ephesus did not come together as an accident of history or as an aggregate of individuals elected according to an abstract eternal decree. Paul is saying that as Jews and Gentiles worshiping as one in the first century, they are brought together as the elect community in Christ in fulfillment of God's promise to Abraham. They were taking part in God's plan to unite all things in Christ, beginning with the healing of the breach between the Jews and the Gentiles (Ephesians 1:11).

The Synod of Dort severely distorted the point of Ephesians 1:4-6 when it amended *"us"* to read, *"a definite number of particular people out of the entire human race."* The whole passage, 1:3-14, is open to the unveiling of the mystery of God's plan "for the fullness of time, to gather up all things in him, things in heaven and things on earth." There is nothing in this passage to indicate that the number of elect is limited in this plan of God. In 1:4-6, Paul is urging the Jews and Gentiles who worship together in Ephesus to recognize that they have not only been chosen in Christ from the foundation of the world, but also that their election is part of God's plan "for the fullness of time, to gather up all things" in Christ (1:9-11). The "us" or "we" in Ephesus "who were the first to set our hope on Christ" are chosen to "live for the praise of his glory" (1:12). But this is true not only for us, but our being "marked with the seal of the promised Holy Spirit" is "the pledge of our inheritance toward redemption of God's own people, to the praise of his glory"

(1:13-14). We should conclude that the Synod of Dort made a serious error when it amended the text of 1:4 to include the words "*a definite number of particular people out of the entire human race*" and thereby avoided reference to the Jews in God's plan of salvation in Christ. Instead of teaching that God decreed from the foundation of the world that the number of elect is limited, Ephesians opens up God's plan of election for Israel to include Gentiles in the gathering of all things, things in heaven and things on earth.

When Paul writes that "God chose us in Christ before the foundation of the world to be holy and blameless before him in love" (Ephesians 1:4-5), we need not to conclude that God decided before the creation of the world the precise number of individual human beings who would come into existence. We can understand Paul to be saying that before the foundation of the world, God chose to love in Christ each person who would come into existence. Although this interpretation of Ephesians 1:4-5 would at first sight seem to imply that every human being will ultimately inherit eternal life, that conclusion does not necessarily follow. In fact, Jesus's warning to the "righteous" (Matthew 25:31-45), the scribes and Pharisees (23:1-3, 9), and those who put a stumbling block before the "little ones who believe in me" (Mark 9:42) provides evidence that it is precisely those leaders within the covenant community who are in most danger of eternal punishment. In Jesus's words of warning to those saying "Lord, Lord"—that God never knew them (Matthew 7:21)—we come to know that in spite of God's eternal faithfulness, there are some who could become reprobates in time if they insist upon rejecting God by refusing to show mercy to their neighbors, however illogical and perverse that may be.

**Article I,7 in the Light of Romans 8:30; 9:1–11:36**

Article I,7 ends by quoting Romans 8:30 to say that God will not forsake those who are elect in Christ. It is important to read the verse as the conclusion to the paragraph, 8:28-30, that reads,

> We know that all things work together for good for those who love God, who are called according to his purpose. For those whom he foreknew he also predestined to be conformed to the image of his Son, in order that he might be the firstborn within a large family. And those whom he predestined he also called; and those whom he called he also justified; and those whom he justified he also glorified.

Most Protestant biblical scholars from the time of the Reformation to the present have interpreted 8:28-39 to bring to its culmination Paul's central teaching that we are justified by grace through faith alone, followed by Paul's excursus in chapters 9–11 on a topic of intense personal interest to Paul. However, the Synod of Dort was not interested in the Jews. It believed that 8:28-30 applies only to the elect, "to those who love God," but not to unbelieving Jews and Gentiles. It applies to Jacob but not to Esau. The synod focused on God's purpose according to which "there is a single good pleasure, purpose, and plan of God's will, by which he chose us [as individuals] from eternity both to grace and glory, both to salvation and to the way of salvation, which God prepared in advance for us to walk in."[26] God's purpose to adopt "certain particular persons from among the common mass of sinners as God's own possession" has been fulfilled. "As Scripture says, 'When the children were not yet born, and had done nothing either good or bad ... [Rebecca] was told, "The older will serve the younger." As it is written, "Jacob I have loved, but Esau I hated"' (Rom. 9:11-13)."[27] According to Article I,10, God's election of Jacob from before the foundation of the world was an eternal, unchangeable decision; God's decision to hate Esau was equally unchangeable.

Ignoring the argument in chapters 9–11, the Canons of Dort Article I,18 admonishes us not to complain about "this grace of an undeserved election and about the severity of a just reprobation ... 'Who are you, O man, to talk back to God?' (Rom. 9:20)." Romans 11:33-36 is quoted to marvel at the "secret things" [the decree] of God, reminding us of God's wisdom in executing the decree of election and reprobation in the words, "'Oh the depths of the riches both of the wisdom and the knowledge of God! How unsearchable are his judgments, and his ways beyond searching out ....'"[28] However, the Synod of Dort made a grave error when it urged Reformed believers to praise God for his wisdom in executing the unchangeable double decree. In 11:33-36, Paul is praising God for God's wisdom in showing mercy to all, both Jews and Gentiles; he is not praising God for God's wisdom in showing mercy to the elect and eternal judgment to the reprobates.

Immediately following his joyful exclamation that nothing can separate us from the love of God in Christ Jesus our Lord (Romans 8:39), Paul's mood shifts to the great sorrow and anguish in his heart

---

26   Canons, I,8.
27   Canons, I,10.
28   Canons, I,18.

(9:2) because his own people, the Israelites, are not coming to faith in Jesus Christ the Messiah. The people of Israel were God's chosen people, to whom the law, true worship in the Temple, and the promises given to Abraham and his seed belonged (9:4-5). Paul's anguish is about Israel's failure to believe in Christ as the Messiah but even more because it left the appearance that God was failing to keep God's covenantal promises to Abraham and Israel. When we hear Paul's cry of anguish and willingness to be accursed "for the sake of my own people" (9:3), we should immediately determine that Paul could not conclude the book of Romans at 8:30-39 because it leaves him with despair over the destiny of his own people. Because readers of Paul since the time of the Reformation have read 8:30 as Paul's last word on the subject of election, all too many of them come to share Paul's anguish about their own election. Reading 8:30 through the eyes of the Canons of Dort, they ask themselves, "Am I really one of the elect? Am I like the seed that fell on the hard path, or like the seed that soon eaten by birds, or like the seed that is choked out by "the thorns of life's cares and with the pleasures of the world"?[29] In spite of the canon's word of reassurance that we should not doubt our election,[30] the anguished question cannot be put down. In Paul's mind, 8:30 finally becomes a word of comfort and assurance only when it is read it in the light of 11:33-36.

C. E. B. Cranfield writes that Romans 8:28-30 and 9–11 must be read together if we are to know the certainty of Paul's hope in Christ and the anguish in his heart over the failure of the Jews to accept God's gift of faith in Christ. According to Cranfield,

> In 8:28-30 Paul referred to God's purpose as the ground of our certainty. But, according to the OT, the nation of Israel had a special place within God's purpose. The end of this section was therefore a natural point at which to introduce a discussion of the relation of Israel to the divine purpose. We may, in fact, go further and say that at this point the need for such a discussion has become urgent, since the very reliability of God's purpose as the ground of Christian hope is called in question by the exclusion of the majority of the Jews. If the truth is that God's purpose with Israel has been frustrated, then what sort of basis for Christian hope is God's purpose?[31]

---

[29]  Matthew 13; Canons, Article III/IV,9.
[30]  Articles I,12–13; R. E. I,vii; Articles IV,3,5–11; R. E. V,vi.
[31]  C. E. B. Cranfield, *The Epistle to the Romans* (Edinburgh: T and T Clark, 1986), 446-7.

N. T. Wright rightly contends that Romans should not be read "as a book about individual salvation rather than as a treatise on the nature of the people of God."[32] If we cannot be sure that Paul's promises to his covenant people Israel are carried out, then can we trust God to be faithful to us in our election in Christ? Wright says that

> The whole of Romans 9–11 is, in one sense, an exposition of how the one God has been faithful, in Jesus Christ, to the promises he made to Abraham: and this exposition must of necessity reach its climax in the historical survey of how these promises have worked out (note the way in which Romans 9:66 ff. begins with Abraham and works through to the prophets, in typically Jewish style), before then moving forward to Christ (10:4) and the mission of the church (10:9ff.).[33]

It is important at this point to pause to see also the covenantal context of the election of Israel as described in Exodus 34:1-27, when Yahweh proclaimed to Moses:

> The LORD, the LORD, a God merciful and gracious, slow to anger, and abounding in steadfast love and faithfulness, keeping steadfast love for the thousandth generation, forgiving iniquity and transgression and sin, but by no means clearing the guilty, but visiting the iniquity of the parents upon the children and the children's children to the third and fourth generation. (Exodus 34:6-7)

According to these words, God is righteous in being faithful to an endless number of generations, while, in his being slow to anger, divine wrath endures for three or four (the Babylonian captivity was for 70 years!).

God's proclamation to Israel through Moses also established the radical separation between Israel (Jacob) and the other nations (Esau), with whom Israel was forbidden to make a covenant (Exodus 34:12) or intermarry (34:9-10). They were not to live in the same land with other peoples. This point was so crucial for Yahweh that God promised to "drive out before you the Amorites, the Canaanites, the Perizzites, the Hivites, and the Jebusites" (34:11). God commanded Moses to write

---

[32]    N. T. Wright, *The Climax of the Covenant: Christ and the Law in Pauline Theology* (Edinburgh: T and T Clark, 1991), 252.
[33]    Wright, 252.

these words on stone tablets as God's permanent promise to Israel. In reading Romans 9-11, we must remember that Paul surely had these words in mind when he agonized about his people who were rejecting Jesus the Messiah and experience anguish when it could appear that God was no longer "righteous" by failing his people (9:1-5).

N. T. Wright suggests that the failure of the Jews to believe the gospel does not have to do merely with Israel but with God's covenant righteousness. The section 9:6-14 as a whole

> has to do with the character and purposes of God and particularly his faithfulness to his promises, and hence the justice of his dealing with Israel and the world. Thus the opening claim in 9:6 has to do with the unfailing character and purposes of God's word; 9:14 raises the question of whether God is unrighteous; 9:19, that of why he still finds fault; 9:19-23, of the rights of the potter over the clay, a metaphor taken directly from the discussions in Isaiah and Jeremiah of God's covenant behavior with Israel.[34]

The words, "I have loved Jacob, but I have hated Esau" (Romans 9:13) were written by Paul in the context of his exposition of God's plan of salvation, not in the context of Article I,6 of the Canons of Dort. Paul was saying that God chose not to use every single descendant of Abraham in the plan of redemption. God passed by Ishmael and Esau in carrying out the line of redemption, but in chapter 11 we discover that Ishmael and Esau are ultimately included among those who receive mercy (11:25-32). In the course of executing the plan of salvation, God remains free to choose Israel and then to exercise his wrath over Israel, calling them "not my people," yet saving "a remnant" of Israel (9:22-33).

In Romans 9:30–10:21, Paul writes that God's promises to Abraham now apply to the Gentiles as well. The breach between Israel and the Gentile nations is overcome in the resurrection of Jesus the Messiah. Righteousness is not based on fulfilling the law but is on the basis of faith as Abraham had faith (9:31-32). The New Testament scholar James Dunn writes, "Paul took it for granted that God's righteousness was to be understood as God's activity in drawing individuals into and sustaining them within the relationship, as 'the power of God for salvation.'"[35] God would be unjust (or, "unrighteous") if God failed to keep the covenant promises God given Abraham. If Paul had brought

[34]  Wright 234.
[35]  Dunn, *The Theology of Paul the Apostle*, 344.

his exposition of predestination to an end in 8:28, then we could accept Dort's doctrine of double predestination that promises God's preservation of the elect for salvation while passing by or reprobating the rest. But Paul could not stop there because that would mean that God is "unrighteous," no longer faithful to the promises made to Abraham and Israel through Moses.

Romans 8:18–11:36 reveals to us that God works his election and rejection out according to God's own timetable. God's decree of election and rejection of Israel is worked out in the changing contexts of history. In 9:25-29, it is revealed that Israel, the elect ("my people") are longer "my people" and those who were not "my people" are told that they shall be called "children of the living God." Only by the grace of God are a remnant saved. Israel can no longer trust in its striving "for the righteousness that in based on the law." Its righteousness is fulfilled in its faith relationship to the Messiah Christ (9:31–10:4). Romans 10:5-21 reveals that according to God's timetable the old separation between "Jew and Greek" has come to an end as both confess that "Jesus is Lord and believe in [their hearts] that God raised him from the dead" (10:9). The old division between Israel and the other nations has been abolished. Everyone who calls on the name of the Lord will be saved.

Romans 10:14-21 reveals that God's timetable does not contradict the nature of God's eternal election from the foundation of the world; God's plan of salvation includes time for the proclamation of the good news. According to Romans 9-10, Paul's anguish for the Gentiles was that they were not yet able to confess that Jesus Christ is Lord because no one had yet proclaimed the gospel message to them (10:14) and that the Jews were refusing to confess Jesus as Lord because their hearts were hard and sought to fulfill their own righteousness on the basis of the law (9:27-30). Both need the "righteousness that comes from faith" (10:3). Faith comes from the message that is heard through the word of Christ (10:17). The old division between Jew and Greek is overcome in confession of the fact: Jesus is Lord, raised from the dead by God the Father.

Nevertheless, in God's timetable, the gospel is not proclaimed to all people at the same time. According to Romans 10:18-21, the gospel was being preached to the Jews as well as the Gentiles, but the Jews refused to listen. In 10:19-21, Scripture is quoted to say that Moses already foresaw that the Jews would not listen. Therefore, God turned to give the gospel message to others in order to make Israel "jealous of those who are not a nation." God says, "I have shown myself to those who did not ask for me." But God has not yet finally rejected Israel: "All day long I have held out my hands to a disobedient and contrary people."

God's righteousness is demonstrated by the course of God's timetable. In the eleventh chapter, we read that Israel is at one time rejected and then restored again to God's favor. There are many twists and turns in God's election of God's people. In Romans 11:1-19, we read that God has not wholly rejected his people in spite of the fact that they killed God's prophets and demolished altars to the true God. By God's grace, a small remnant of the people have been chosen on the basis of God's grace, "no longer on the basis of works" (11:6). But of those who have been "hardened" in opposition to God, it is said that through their "stumbling," the riches of the gospel, and their inclusion into the people of God, other peoples enjoy their riches (11:12). Paul writes that he ministers among the Gentiles "in order to make my own people jealous and thus save some of them." Paul sees those converted by his ministry to be "first fruits" looking toward to those who will be brought to faith later. They are the yeast that leavens the whole loaf. "If root is holy, then the branches also are holy" (11:16). In Paul's mind, those Gentiles who respond to his preaching are the first fruits of the full number of the nations who were once rejected by God. Paul's words here go beyond what he fully knows. The remnant in Israel is the yeast that purifies the lump of dough. That is why he calls it a "mystery" that will become fully known at the end of time.

After the twists and turns in God's election of Israel, Paul finally comes to understand the mystery of God's relation with Israel, God's elect people. God hardened the part of Israel "until the full number of the Gentiles has come in. And so all Israel will be saved" (Romans 11:25). Paul is writing with a universal hope for all those in the course of history who have been disobedient. At this point we must be careful not to go beyond what Paul is saying when he addresses his "brothers and sisters" (11:25),

> As regards the gospel they are enemies of God for your sake; but as regards election they are beloved, for the sake of their ancestors, for the gifts and calling of God are irrevocable. Just as you were once disobedient to God but have now received mercy because of their disobedience, so they have now been disobedient in order that by the mercy shown to you, they too may now receive mercy. For God has imprisoned all in disobedience so that he may be merciful to all. (Romans 11:28-32)

James Dunn suggests that here Paul is writing in his role as a missionary to the Gentile nations more than as Paul the theologian. The scattering of the nations following the debacle of the Tower of Babel was in God's calling being replaced by the ingathering of nations at the end of history. Paul "probably saw it as the final outreach to the sons of Japheth in accordance with the table of nations and its correlated geography, as originally envisioned in Genesis 10."[36] In God's plan of salvation, those nations who were removed from their land in order to make space for a time for Abraham and the Israelites—the Amorites, the Canaanites, the Hittites, the Perizzites, the Hivites, and the Jebusites (Exodus 34:10)—would in the end participate in the mercy of God, along with Israel, whose dead bones would rise again (Ezekiel 37:1-13).

In spite of the fact that Dort's doctrine of election and reprobation has often been interpreted to be a deterrent to evangelism and world mission, we must here note that the Canons of Dort view the proclamation of the gospel to all people more urgently than other confessional statements of the Reformation era. Article I,3 urges, "In order that people may be brought to faith, God mercifully sends messengers of this joyful message to the people and at the time he wills. By this ministry people are called to repentance and faith in Christ crucified." In Article I,14, we read that "By God's wise plan, this teaching concerning divine election was proclaimed through the prophets, Christ himself, and the apostles, in Old and New Testament times. It was subsequently committed to writing in the Holy Scriptures. So also today in Christ's church, for which it was specifically intended, this teaching must be set forth with a spirit of discretion ...." The Canons urge that

> It is the promise of the gospel that whoever believes in Christ crucified shall not perish but have eternal life. This promise, together with the command to repent and believe, ought to be announced and declared without differentiation or discrimination to all nations and people, to whom God in his good pleasure sends the gospel.[37]

In Article III/IV, 7, the Canons recognize that in God's divine forbearance (Romans 3:25-27), God does not reveal the secret of divine election to all people all at once. In the New Testament it was revealed

---

[36]    Dunn, 531.
[37]    Canons, II,5.

to only a small number without distinction, but now it is being revealed to a large number, not because one nation is better than another, but because it is in the good pleasure of God to do so. Article III/IV,15 says that in regard to those "who have not yet been called, we are called to pray to the God who calls things that do not exist as though they did. In no way, however, are we to pride ourselves as better than they, as though we had distinguished ourselves from them."

The Synod of Dort made a serious error when it admonished us in Article I,18 to reverently adore God's wisdom revealing his "secret decree" of double election and reprobation. Article I,18 reflects Paul's universal hope for Jews and Gentiles, not an eternal decree that eternally separates the elect from the reprobates. Romans 11:33-36 calls upon us to adore God's wisdom in revealing his plan of salvation for the Jews first, but also the Gentiles:

> Oh the depths of the riches both of the wisdom of and knowledge of God! How unsearchable are his judgments, and his ways beyond tracing out! For who has known the mind of the Lord? Or who has been his counselor? Or who has first given to God, that God should repay him? For from him and through him and to him are all things. To him be the glory forever! Amen.[38]

### The Place and Function of the Canons of Dort Today[39]

Our review of the verses quoted in Articles I,6 and I,7 leads to the conclusion that Acts 15:18, Ephesians 1:11, Ephesians 1:4-6, and Romans 8:30 do not support the doctrine of election and reprobation as taught in the Canons of Dort in those articles. We can agree with Allan Janssen when he writes that "there have been versions of the doctrine that are very difficult to accept, let alone defend."[40] Because Articles I,6 and I,7 stand at the heart of the Canons of Dort, we cannot avoid considering the place and function of the Canons today as a historic and faithful witness to the Word of God. We can say that the Canons of Dort still function today as a historic and faithful witness that we are saved by grace alone, not by our own obedience of faith. It rejects all Pelagianism and semi-Pelagianism. It testifies that we are elected *to* faith and holiness, not *because of* our faith or holy living. In spite of its blindness about God's election of Israel and the Jews, the Canons bear

---

[38]    As quoted in Canons I,18.
[39]    Janssen asks this question in *Confessing the Faith*, 5-7.
[40]    Janssen, 66.

historic witness that God is all in all and that, in his just judgment, God is free to show mercy to whom he wills to show mercy.

The serious exegetical blindness to what Paul wrote in Romans 8:28–11:36 must no longer be covered over in the Reformed confessional tradition. The Canons of Dort can no longer function as a legal document that requires strict adherence of every sentence and proposition on its five main points of doctrine. We need no longer to defend Dort's doctrine of the double decree,[41] but we recognize that the synod was on right track when it pointed to Acts 15:18, Ephesians 1:11, Ephesians 1:4-6, and Romans 8:30 as focal points of comfort and assurance of election in Christ. With a renewed understanding of the doctrine of predestination in mind, the Canons of Dort serve to overcome temptations to pride and anxieties about our perseverance in the faith[42] as we read in III/IV,11:

> By the effective operation of the same regenerating Spirit, God also penetrates into the inmost being, opens the closed heart, softens the hard heart, and circumcises the heart that is uncircumcised. God infuses new qualities into the will, making the dead will alive, the evil one good, the unwilling one willing, and the stubborn one compliant. God activates and strengthens the will so that, like a good tree, it may be enabled to produce the fruits of good deeds.

The Canons of Dort do not belong sealed in a glass case in the back corner of the church's museum. As the product of a seventeenth-century controversy, they should be kept in an accessible spot in the archives of the church where they can be used to teach God's predestination "at the appropriate time and place" ... "for the glory of God's most holy name, and for the lively comfort of God's people."[43]

---

[41]    Canons, I,6.
[42]    Canons, V,10,11.
[43]    Canons, I,14.

CHAPTER 7

# Dutch Twentieth Century Protestant Theology at its Best: The Voice of Oepke Noordmans

Karel Blei

Allan Janssen has been interested in Dutch Reformed theology for many years. He reads Dutch, even difficult theological Dutch texts, and understands them, which is quite admirable. Especially, his interest is in the work of Arnold A. van Ruler, who, in the twentieth century after the Second World War, tried to revitalize theocratic thinking and in that post-war period played an important role in the renewal of the Netherlands Reformed Church. Van Ruler died early and unexpectedly in 1970 at the age of 62. At present, he seems largely outdated and forgotten. Yet since 2007, a republication and partly new publication of Van Ruler's *Verzameld werk* (*Collected Works*) has been under way in an impressive series, eight volumes of which have already appeared, with several more in preparation. It was on Van Ruler that Al Janssen in 2005 did his Ph.D. dissertation, *Kingdom, Office, and Church*. He has been able to get acquainted with Van Ruler's specific thinking and to reflect on it. That as such deserves a warm tribute!

Another important Dutch Reformed twentieth-century theologian with whom he became acquainted is Oepke Noordmans. Noordmans also contributed largely to the renewal of the Netherlands

Reformed Church, already in the years before the Second World War. Many ideas about church life and about the function and authority of dogma and confession, as they became well known later, were first worded by him. He died in 1956 at the age of 84. His *Verzamelde werken* (*Collected Works*) were published in 11 volumes between 1978 and 2004.[1] On his life and work, I myself published a book in 2010 in which I incorporated many Noordmans quotes. Noordmans had a special style that, even for Dutch readers, can sometimes be difficult to understand. Al Janssen translated that volume, including the translation of those quotes. That must have been a hard (but beautiful!) job for him. The English version of the book appeared in 2013 in the Historical Series of the Reformed Church in America under the title *Oepke Noordmans: Theologian of the Holy Spirit.*

Al Janssen also did a lot to involve other American theologians in his own interest in Dutch church and theology. Over many years, he organized study weeks during which New Brunswick students stayed in the Netherlands and met with Dutch church representatives and theologians. So they were introduced into Dutch society and church life, and discussions on present-day church, society, and theological issues were possible. I was happy to contribute to many of these meetings and keep them in good memory.

## A Contemplative Turn in Theology?

The theological and church landscape in the Netherlands developed and changed significantly over the last decades. In today's Dutch society, the churches have been, to a great extent, marginalized. In the Netherlands, we are now living in what is often called a secularized country. That does not mean that that people are not interested in matters of religion anymore. On the contrary, people are looking for new insights into what may help in discovering the meaning of life anew. But they usually do that apart from the established churches, each in his or her own way. Religion has become, to a large extent, individual business. In that context, religious experiments are flourishing. The churches try to respond to that tendency as best as they can. New and experimental ways of being church and of representing the gospel have been and are being developed.

Dutch theology, as it is produced today, is also different from what it was in the past. Nowadays more than in former times, one

[1]    Oepke Noordmans, *Verzamelde werken* (hereafter referred to as *VW*) (Kampen: Kok, 1978–2004).

focuses on how to present the Christian message so that it may join in today's emphasis on religious feelings and emotions. The issue of how faith in God and in Jesus Christ can be made plausible to a modern audience is on the forefront, more so than discussions of Christian, or Reformed, doctrine. Can Christian faith be presented so that it responds to today's religious feelings and desires? It is said that in recent years a contemplative and ritual turn seems to have been taking place in the theological scene. Theological speech and thought are no longer dominated by questions of intellectual truth and cognitive representation. In theological projects, one is now emphasizing the crucial roles of contemplation, prayer, and ritual, according to the ancient adage *lex orandi lex credendi.*

Yet despite the great changes in Dutch society and churches over the last decades, one should not overemphasize the difference between doing theology then and now. One should not do theology now as if it was previously just a matter of intellectual truth and cognitive representation. The theology of Noordmans, for instance, was different.

Well-known are Noordmans's many biblical meditations. Here, he liked to describe the church as more than an institute, as "mother church," like he had experienced it already as a child at home in the family. When he received an honorary doctorate of theology (Groningen, 1935), in his word of thanks[2] he referred to these youth experiences. In that "mother church," he said, "my theology is also embedded"; in other words, it is there that it had its origin. Therefore, theology, as Noordmans understood it, can only be (in that sense) "church theology." To him, the church, not just as institute, but rather as a lived reality, was the breeding ground and supposition of his theology as such. If one speaks today of "a contemplative turn in theology," it can rightly be said that such a "contemplative turn" has already become manifest in the theology of Noordmans.

## Noordmans, in Discussion with Karl Barth

Protestant theology of the twentieth century—in its first half, anyway—was colored to a large extent by the influence of Karl Barth, and this includes theology in the Netherlands. It is true that in the first decades of the twentieth century, there was among the Reformed in the Netherlands a lot of criticism of Barth. That was especially the case among the "neo-Calvinists," the followers of Abraham Kuyper,

---

[2]   Noordmans, *VW,* 4:13ff.

who had separated from the Netherlands Reformed Church and had formed their own Church denomination toward the end of the nineteenth century, the Reformed Churches in the Netherlands. In their view, Barth was much too critical about human efforts to create a better, "Christian" culture (and so to prepare for the coming kingdom of God). But Barth's theology was already in the twenties welcomed and introduced by a couple of important theologians. Among them, Noordmans was prominent. He was, however, not just a follower of Barth's, but, in taking up Barth's theological approach, he developed a couple of specific objections.

Noordmans and Barth met in 1926. In that year, Barth paid a visit to the Netherlands for the first time. In the context of that visit, a meeting was organized in Amsterdam for a small group of Dutch theologians so they could speak to Barth in person. Noordmans was one of them. On that occasion, he used the opportunity to put his reservations about Barth on the table. In 1926, Barth had not yet begun his *Church Dogmatics* (*CD*).[3] He had entered the theological discussion with his *Letter to the Romans*, a commentary on Paul's Epistle to the Romans in the New Testament.[4] Barth had commented on that apostolic epistle in an unusual way for biblical scholars at that time, not discussing matters of text criticism, but rather, carefully listening to what is really said in the epistle, thus listening to the *message* of the text. That approach made Barth's book more like a sermon *on* the texts of the epistle.

Noordmans had read Barth's *Letter to the Romans* with great appreciation. He completely agreed with Barth's main thesis: we do not know God, but God knows us. Barth rightly put that God's gracious and judging word comes first. God knows us, but, Noordmans said, Barth does not pay sufficient attention to the renewing effect of that word on our lives. In other words, in Barth's approach, Noordmans saw a lack of sufficient attention to the issue of sanctification.[5]

Later, in the thirties (by that time the first volume of Barth's *Church Dogmatics* had been published), Noordmans elaborated on his reservations. Barth, he said, knows about God's Word as a flashing, intervening event, but he does not know about it as being "a lamp to our feet and a light to our path,"[6] a lamp and light in which we can proceed,

---

[3]    Karl Barth, *Church Dogmatics*, 4 vols. (Edinburgh: T&T Clark, [1932-1967] 1956-1975).

[4]    In particular, the second edition of 1921.

[5]    Noordmans, *VW*, 3:561-572.

[6]    Psalm 119:105.

so that indeed, in one way or another, some continuity becomes visible. Barth does not pay attention to the Spirit who guides and accompanies us, creating continuity in our lives. According to Noordmans, Barth's theology was too much a "theology of moments"—Barth knows the Spirit "who, in the sermon, says the *final* word," but he does not know the Spirit sufficiently as "the speaker of the *next* word, i.e., as the Advocate who abides with us" (cf. John 14:17).[7]

In these critical remarks, we already see signs of Noordmans's own theological thinking. Later, his criticism of Barth's theology deepened. In 1945, Barth had published the first part of his doctrine of creation.[8] It was that view of creation that raised Noordmans's most serious objections. It is worthwhile to look a bit more carefully into what was, according to Noordmans, at stake in this discussion. In doing so, we cannot leave Noordmans's own "doctrine of creation" outside of consideration. And in dealing with that, we have to get to the heart of Noordmans's theology. That is what I would like to discuss in the rest of this essay.

## Barth's Doctrine of Creation

Firstly, let us take a short glance at Barth's doctrine of creation. Barth's starting point is his conviction that we know God only in Jesus Christ, and, according to him, the belief in God the creator is possible just as a specific way of believing in Jesus Christ. In Jesus Christ, God is Immanuel, God with us. That is what tells us that God is not alone. There is also a world, a reality, a humankind, a congregation as God's people with him—namely, that world in which the Word became flesh. And so we also know that humankind and God's world are not alone: they are created, living from and dependent on God in his grace; and that God, in Christ, powerfully comes to those who are his. Therefore, it is only in Christ that we get to know the reality of creation. That means that this reality has Christ, first of all, as its ontological foundation.

That is why, according to Barth, believing in God the creator is totally different from some kind of philosophy. It is taking seriously that the reality in which we live and of which we are part belongs to God as workshop and material. It is living in the presence of the Creator who makes everything new, an acknowledgement of his power (as saving power!) over everything and of his right (as right of grace!) to his creature. It is an acknowledgement of the *goodness* of the Creator.

---

[7]    Noordmans, *VW*, 2:188-193
[8]    Barth, *CD* III/1.

This is, in short, the opening paragraph of *CD* III/1. As a sequel to that, Barth deals with the relationship between creation and covenant. His thesis is that the creation, as God's first work, is to be seen as immediately connected to all God's further works in redemption and completion; in the same way as these, the creation is to be seen as a work of the triune God. Therefore, it is clear that the creation is just destined to make possible the covenant history of God with humankind in Jesus Christ. Creation is the arrangement and design of the space in which this covenant history is now going to take place.

Being the "first" of God's acts, creation is also to be considered a "historical" reality. It is important to see that the Bible proclaims creation in the form not of philosophical consideration but of a story of what happened: the prehistory of Israel (and so of Jesus Christ). But this "historical" character of creation is, of course, itself history-without-prehistory. As such, it stands in "direct relation to God" (what cannot be said of the history that comes after creation). To ordinary "historical" investigation, it is unaccessible; it is what Barth calls "*unhistorical* history." That is why the biblical creation stories are not to be considered historical information but rather "legends," or sagas," which are, according to Barth, again different from "myths" (stories about what in reality is timeless, happening "anywhere and nowhere"). On creation, one can only speak in "sagas"—poetic images.

In what follows, Barth unfolds his doctrine of creation in the form of a careful exegesis of Genesis 1 and 2. So he makes clear that creation is "the outward ground of the covenant" directed toward the covenant, that is, the tendency of the first creation story. And the covenant is "the inner ground of creation" that has covenant-like features in itself already, that is, the tendency of the second creation story. Already, creation itself appears to be an act of benevolence, a manifestation of God's goodness. It is already in his creating activity that God speaks his "yes": what is created is allowed to be. God favors it; in his eyes it is good! The Creator is identical with the God and Father of Jesus Christ.

## Noordmans on Creation: "Creating is Dividing"

But our main concern here is Noordmans. How does he comment on Barth's doctrine of creation? That is to be seen in a short text that he prepared for a small discussion group in 1947 and now is published in Noordmans's *Collected Works*.[9] He is very critical here. His main

---

[9]    Noordmans, *VW,* 3:685ff.

objection is "that Barth, when he, starting from Jesus Christ, noetically ... goes to creation, swerves too much from the center of faith to the periphery." In the center of faith, the issue is not the coordination, nature-grace, but rather the contrast, sin-grace. Whoever in their theological thinking really wants to start from Jesus Christ has to depart from the cross; in other words, depart from Christ's work, the work of "grace as reconciliation." "Doing so, one ends up in Genesis 3, rather than in Genesis 1 and 2." Barth instead starts from Christ's two natures; "not from the cross, but from the incarnation"; not from the center but from the periphery of the gospel. Thus, in Noordmans's view, Barth has chosen a wrong point of departure.

This criticism, dating from 1947, is just a continuation of the line of thought Noordmans had already drawn in the thirties, particularly in his book *Herschepping* (*Re-creation*) from 1934.[10] There he had already argued that whoever emphasizes that creation is an article of faith has to realize that, by consequence, it is a critical concept. The God whom we get to know in the Bible is a God who judges, who separates. That is what God does in Christ, on Golgotha, in reconciliation. It is also what God does through the Spirit, in sanctification: old human is separated from new human. Well then, at creation it cannot be different. So God's creating is also separating. Only then "the work of the Father fits with the work of the Son."

It is true, Noordmans says here, the Bible begins with Genesis 1 and 2. But in reality, it starts with Genesis 3, the fall. That, in the preceding chapters, we hear "that everything was good" in the preceding chapters just gives us a criterion to see that everything has fallen. The reality of the fall is the creation with which we have to make do; there is no other creation. The misery, as it comes together around Jesus—that is the real creation the Bible shows us. So that God is creator means that God (as the God of Joseph) does flow the good from the bad, that God "creates the light out of the dark of sin."[11] And reading Genesis 1 and 2, there we see something other than the origin of beautiful forms, of unbroken, still harmony. "In the beginning God created the heavens and the earth. That is the first great division. It is the act of a spirit, a judgment. That repeats itself with the days of creation. Light and darkness, day and night are divided. The waters above from the waters beneath. The sea from the dry land."[12] Division: already there!

---

[10]   Noordmans, *VW*, 2:214ff.
[11]   Noordmans, *VW*, 2:246.
[12]   Noordmans, *VW*, 2:251.

We have to unlearn, says Noordmans, to speak of creation "as a complete, finished work of God,"[13] work made that, despite the disturbance that came in between, would give us a bearing ground under the feet. When we speak of creation like this, the work of the Son and of the Spirit—redemption and sanctification—is considered just a work of restoration, an incident, an episode. In that case, it is misunderstood that creation itself has been touched by sin, that "sin goes as far as creation." No, "we cannot just leave creation behind" as if it were a finished stage. "Creation accompanies us until we have arrived on Golgotha."[14] There, at the cross, God's creating judging, God's dividing creating, comes to its climax: God himself takes his stand in the judgment; God goes along in the fall.

So, whoever wants to give a "doctrine of creation" cannot do that other than by telling a story, the story of the "procession towards the cross." Between "creation" and "history," there is only a "floating" borderline. In the Twelve Articles, after the opening words "I believe in God the Father," "Creator of heaven and earth" is added.[15] This addition certainly does not mean to fix our thoughts on Genesis 1 and 2. These words, "Creator of heaven and earth," tell us that the Father "is also the God of the Old Testament." The word "creation," well understood, comprises the Old Testament history as a whole as "procession towards the cross."

## Noordmans in Opposition to Neo-Calvinist Theology of Culture

As I said, Noordmans's book *Re-creation* appeared in 1934. In 1935, he had another reason to speak on the belief in God the creator. In that year, he presented a paper to theological students of the Free University in Amsterdam on the theme "Critical Tensions in Reformed Theology."[16] Here, Noordmans is in discussion with Abraham Kuyper's doctrine of "common grace" and with Klaas Schilder's theology of culture, both theological concepts in which creation as a positive datum in itself plays an important role. It is in that discussion that Noordmans feels encouraged to present his own view in a sharpened way, like this:

Of key importance is the *direction* ... whether the Bible, that is: the knowledge of salvation history and the prophecy that

---

13   Noordmans, *VW*, 2:253.
14   Noordmans, 2:257
15   Apostles' Creed.
16   Noordmans, *VW*, 4:107ff.

explains it is there just in order to let us know the creation, to have it function in the right way again, to take off the brake of sin that lies on it and so to make itself superfluous. Or that we have to consider what in the Bible is said on creation like putting the pieces on the chess board in order to see only then start at the fall the beginning of the awe-inspiring cosmic game of sin and grace; so that not only all attention has to be focussed on that, but we also feel our past, to-day and future existentially taken up into that attention of faith. In the last case, we feel that creation is not a quiet datum, waiting for the opportunity to take up its function again, rather: an exciting life-and-death history, a concept of faith.[17]

Of course, Noordmans's position is the last one. The Bible is about "the awe-inspiring cosmic game of sin and grace," in which "Abraham, Moses, the prophets, Christ, the apostles" play their roles.

Only here, the wood of creation has been cut up to a sharp expression, so that I discover the face of the gracious Trinity, the knowledge of Whom is what the Church is about and what the Bible wants to teach us. I refuse to consider that main content, no: the only content, of the Bible just a means to restore what would lie waiting under the threshold of sin, until the biblical game has finished, in order to take up again the pure ministry of early createdness .... So, to me, everything is going in the direction of the cross.[18]

Noordmans concludes by saying here what he says at other occasions too: "To me, creation is not a kind of utter darkness, waiting around the Bible, but a spot of light around the cross itself."

As I said, Noordmans developed these thoughts over against Kuyper's and Schilder's neo-Calvinism. In that neo-Calvinist creation theology, he saw a dangerous parallel of that thinking in terms of creation that was practiced in Germany—by the "German Christians" with their appeal to "blood and soil." Of this confrontation, *Re-creation* also bears the marks. That book appeared in the same year (1934) in which Barth published his brochure *Nein!* (*No!*), which was addressed to Emil Brunner's doctrine that humans have already out of themselves

---

[17]   Noordmans, 4:114f.
[18]   Noordmans, 4:114f.

a "point of contact" for the gospel. In his 1935 paper presented at the Free University, Noordmans mentions this brochure, underlining his approval. He fully agrees with Barth's rejection of all natural theology.

As we saw, 12 years later, the relation between Noordmans and Barth had drastically changed. Noordmans had become Barth's opponent. In 1947, Noordmans was developing the same line of thought but now over against Barth's doctrine of creation. His problem with that doctrine was not that Barth took his starting point in Christ; Noordmans himself wants to do the same. His objection was, on the contrary, that Barth was not sufficiently consequent in taking this position. His "thinking from Christ" means: beginning from the incarnation, not from the cross. To Noordmans, that means that he does not *really* start from Christ.

The difference of view between Barth and Noordmans can become clear to us when we look at the metaphors used on both sides. Both Barth and Noordmans see the creation as the signal for salvation history. But while Barth clarifies his ideas by using the metaphor of the *space* in which—or rather, the *stage* on which— this salvation history is now going to happen, Noordmans uses a different metaphor: that of putting the pieces on the chess board so that the game (of sin and grace) can begin—i.e., at the fall, not earlier.

## Creation as Aiming at Continuity

Noordmans's position, as we just analysed it, may easily give the impression of unworldliness. Noordmans's strict focus on the cross, his abjuring anything that bears only a slight likeness to a positive evaluation of createdness, seems to push us to the conclusion that Noordmans is just obsessed by negativity. That however is a misunderstanding.

Well known is Noordmans's contrast between "shape" (or "form") and "Spirit." He elaborates on that contrast in the biblical meditations he published under that title toward the end of his life.[19] In this series of meditations, he promotes the idea that the Spirit is breaking every shape or form. It is this idea that fits with his conviction about "creating" as "separating," "dividing." So "shape," or "form," appears in a negative light, as sinful reality. But in other contexts, Noordmans uses the terms "shape" or "form" in a positive way, as raised by the Word. In another lecture given by him at the University of Groningen in 1935 (again that year!), on "The Problem of the Continuity within the Dialectical

---

[19]    Now brought together in Noordmans, *VW*, 8.

Theology," we see that Noordmans can understand creating also as shaping, forming.[20]

It is true; in that context, he immediately warns against misunderstanding: "We should not forget that the power of the divine creative Word is necessary to keep the *tohu wabohu* [i.e., "formless void" Genesis 1 and 2] of the paradoxical existence in control. We should not forget that it is God's creative Word, that divides light and darkness and keeps them apart." We should always realize "how dearly such a piece of continuity, that we call: a day, has been bought."[21]

This is about the distinction between "harmony" and "creation," in other words, between "pagan" and "Christian" understanding. "We should not enter into the form as 'harmony' and get in love with it in such a way that God's Word is put in the shadow; that Word that throws its judgment over 'the substance of the things.'" "The form is that fragile, and the tension behind it is that big. The act, the Word, creation is more important the its result."[22]

We see that Noordmans does not abjure his slogan, "creating is dividing." But we see now even more clearly what he has in mind in saying that. What is that "dividing," that in the Word goes over "the substance of the things"? It is "the division that has to be carried out *in order to make the form possible*"! Sure, "dividing" is opposite of "forming." But seen from another point of view, "dividing" and "forming" are exactly *not* in opposition to each other. Seen in that perspective, "dividing" appears to be directed to "forming," or even, the two seem to be almost synonymous. "God speaks and it is; He commands and it stands. God divided light from darkness: the first day. And *with that* form and shape; so: continuity."[23]

## Creation and eschatology

In conclusion, Noordmans's critical "doctrine of creation" is full of positivity. Does this mean that he is closer to Barth's doctrine of creation (as he would later develop it) than he himself must have realized? No, that is not the case. Let us again look carefully. Barth sees, from Christ, the creation as reality, as "form," directed to the salvation history; its "outward ground" preceding that. According to Noordmans, it is exactly the other way around: God's first act is not "forming" but "dividing." To put it in Noordmans's terms, according to Barth, the

---

20  Noordmans, *VW*, 3:646ff.
21  Noordmans, *VW*, 3:655-657.
22  Noordmans, 3:655–657.
23  Noordmans, 3:655–657, italics added.

"form" is there to make possible the work of division (i.e., the covenant history of judgment and grace as such); according to Noordmans, the "division" happens in order to make the form possible. In Noordmans's view, the "form" is not the beginning but the end.

And this, to him, is a matter of life and death. Fully entering into the "form" and the "harmony," already now has, he says (in 1935!), "terrible consequences." It is dangerous, a playing with gunpowder. If we stick to our way of life, dominated by philosophy and science, just on our own, that is, if we don't live from grace, if we are not looking forward to re-creation, then together we get lost.[24]

I just said: here, Noordmans uses the term "form" in a positive way. But that needs to be specified. To Noordmans, more than the "form," or "shape," the "substance," the quality is important. Our faith, he says, is not—not yet—allowed to stay with the "form." That still has a quality of sin. Behind it, there still is chaos, the tohu wabohu of Genesis 1. It stands under the judgment of the Word of God. In other words, the "creation" still has to get through the re-creation. In the re-creation, all things get a different quality. And only then, says Noordmans, the creation will be completed. Only the, there will really be creation as "form."

In fact, Noordmans's "doctrine of creation" is eschatology. One of his famous statements is: "Believing in the Creator is believing in the kingdom of God."[25] What he, in his criticism of Barth's doctrine of creation, actually has in mind is that Barth's theology (as doctrine of creation) misses the right eschatological accent.

It is not by accident that Noordmans published his later Heidelberg Catechism commentary in 1949, in which he especially discussed the Catechism commentary on the Twelve Articles of the Apostles' Creed under the title "The Kingdom of Heavens."[26] That makes all the more clear how much his theology is future, eschaton oriented. A key chapter in that book is Noordmans's commentary on the Catechism—"Lord's Days 9 and 10." These paragraphs deal with creation and providence. Sharp is his criticism especially of Lord's Day 10 on providence. Here, Noordmans says, the Catechism speaks religious, not according to the gospels. It should have dealt here, not with "creation and providence" but with "God's kingdom and election." "Then, the Kingdom would have replaced Creation. The future would have replaced the past. The justice (Matthew 6:33) would have put the providence and care backward

---

[24]    Noordmans, *VW*, 3:657.
[25]    Noordmans, 2:250.
[26]    Noordmans, 2:433ff.

(Matthew 6:31). Both these Sundays would have shown a less pious and a more believing character." They would have spoken in a more evangelical and also modern and real way. As we know, the "troubles of our time" do not so much refer to natural theology. "They do not have to do with creation as such, but with the kingdom of God, because that doesn't come." In summary, God (the Father, of the Twelve Articles) "is much more the God of the future than the God of the past."[27]

## The Spirit as Re-creator

We spoke already of Noordmans's famous biblical meditations, published under the title *Gestalte en Geest* (*Form and Spirit*). In his view, it is the Spirit that breaks every shape or form and that—through this breaking and crushing and judging activity—realizes in the end the true form: the re-creation. I just said that Noordmans's "doctrine of creation" in fact is eschatology. I now have to add that that "doctrine of creation" is essentially Pneumatology. To him more than Christology, Pneumatology is the main point of Christian faith. We can see that in a profound statement he gave in *Re-creation*: "Again and again, God has other possibilities ... If speaking is not sufficient, He comes; if coming is not sufficient, He comforts."[28] This is the way Noordmans discusses the dogma of the Trinity. In doing so, he makes clear that the coming of the Comforter, the Spirit, is the summit of God's coming to us.

With preference, Noordmans calls the Spirit the re-creator. It is true, he says, even in the work of the Spirit, that "creating is dividing." However, now we are no longer like sinners, driven toward Golgotha. "Now, life comes in from the other side. It begins at the resurrection of Jesus ... The Spirit separates old man from new man." That, however, "does now not mean fall anymore, but resurrection" for us also! "In the re-creation the critical character of creation receives its completion." So now, creation as "form," or "shape," finally is established. It has rightly been said that in Noordmans's view, it is only in the Pneumatology that Genesis 1 is fully realized.[29]

Indeed, in Noordmans's theology, the Pneumatological and the eschatological accents are closely connected. As he says, the (re-)creating work of the Spirit "comes to us from the end" and "has eschatological character."[30]

Noordmans is a theologian who still gives us a lot to think about!

---

27    Noordmans, *VW*, 2:453–470.
28    Noordmans, 2:223.
29    Noordmans, 2:299f.
30    Noordmans, 2:299f.

CHAPTER 8

# Van Ruler on the Sacraments

Abraham van de Beek

According to the Dutch theologian Arnold van Ruler, three factors are constitutive for the church: the proclamation of the Word, the sacraments, and office.[1] Allan Janssen wrote a study on Van Ruler's doctrine of office.[2] This article will be directed to the sacraments in Van Ruler's theology.

## Introduction

Van Ruler did not write a study explicitly devoted to the sacraments. Though he conceives of the sacraments as a constitutive element of the church, he does not systematically and extensively deal with it. There are only a few longer texts, especially a chapter on the Lord's Supper in his book *Reformatorische opmerkingen in de ontmoeting met Rome (Reformed Observations in the Encounter with Rome)*[3] and a few

[1]   A.A. van Ruler, *Religie en politiek*, (Nijkerk: Callenback, 1945), 24f, 90f.

[2]   Allan J. Janssen, *Kingdom, Office, and Church: A Study of A.A. van Ruler's Doctrine of Ecclesiastical Office*, The Historical Series of the Reformed Church in America, 53 (Grand Rapids: Eerdmans, 2006).

[3]   Van Ruler, *Reformatorische opmerkingen in de ontmoeting met Rome* (Hilversum: Paul Brandt, 1965).

short sections in other works. For the rest, we have to collect his ideas from short remarks in texts about other issues. By consequence, the context must always be taken into consideration for understanding what these remarks on the sacraments mean there.

This is even more important because Van Ruler can develop very different positions on a subject depending on the conversation partner or opponent he has in view. There is a famous anecdote about two meetings of the General Synod of the Netherlands Reformed Church, which Van Ruler attended as an advisor. In the first meeting, he pleaded for an opinion about a subject and elucidated this with 12 arguments; the synod was fully convinced. During the next meeting, a similar issue was on the table, and Van Ruler argued for the opposite than in the previous meeting. One of the members of the synod asked, "Professor, how can you say this, as you argued for the opposite with even 12 arguments in the previous meeting?" "Well," replied Van Ruler, "what I say now is also valid, and I will explain this with also 12 arguments." And he did so. This does not mean Van Ruler was inconsistent in his thought. It was far more the conviction that theological truth, as any truth, is too complicated for a linear discourse. There are always other aspects, even opposing arguments, which must be taken into account. A brilliant spirit like Van Ruler always saw many aspects to any issue, as one can easily observe in his work. It was the abundance of variation in aspects that he discerned that hindered him to write a systematic theology. When, during a conversation about the doctoral study that I intended to do under his supervision, I asked him if he would not write such a dogmatic, he told me, "I am not able to do so. I cannot arrange my thought so systematically. I always see immediately arguments which refute my position. Theology is too kaleidoscopic for a systematization. I always see new rays of the diamond."[4] So Van Ruler's argumentation depends on the focus that he had in view at the moment he wrote his texts. Sometimes this focus is clear; sometimes one can only guess. This is even more important since most of his writings are the result of lectures or spoken papers he delivered for students or other groups. Consequently, one must pay specific attention to returning argumentations and consistencies in his work and be careful with a single remark, how very striking this may be.

Another important consideration is the development of Van Ruler's thought in time. In studies about Van Ruler, there is often

---

[4]    Cf. D. van Keulen, "Een korte introductie. De theologie van Van Ruler." *Kontekstueel* 26, no. 2, (2011).

insufficient attention paid to this fact.[5] However, as will be explained below, it is of great impact on his thought on the sacraments. Therefore, we begin our investigations with a periodization of Van Ruler's doctrine of the sacraments, which is related to the contexts in which it was developed.

## Periods

### The Forties

Van Ruler's first substantial publication immediately showed his position as an independent theologian. After his study in Groningen, he took his time to get acquainted with his ministerial work. As he once said, in his parsonage in Kubaard, he did not hasten himself, living quietly like the farmers of his congregation and taking time to read the newspaper. This totally changed when he became a minister in Hilversum, the city where the national broadcasting institutes were and where he was challenged how to deal with war and occupation. It was there that he came to his own theological position resulting in his book *Religie en politiek* (*Religion and Politics*). What is the relation of religion and politics, of church and state? And this relation implies the question: How does the state relate to God? Van Ruler's answer is clear; he pleads for theocracy. The state is servant of God, and she must arrange society according to God's commandments. So Van Ruler can call for a Christian society—for the Christianization of life in all its aspects. Van Ruler speaks about this, first of all, as a calling for the Netherlands, but this is only because this is his direct context. His view goes wider. Christianization is a calling for all nations, as all nations should be baptized in the name of the triune God. Therefore, he pleads for colonization: in the colony, especially the Netherlands India (the present Indonesia), the Netherlands have a calling to introduce theocracy in such a way that it can be the national identity of a future independent nation on the Indonesian archipelago.[6]

Van Ruler published several books on his theocratic thought in the years after World War II. This was his most productive period,

---

[5]   An exception is van Hoof, *Intermezzo. Kontinuïteit en diskontinuïteit in de theologie van A.A. van Ruler. Eschatologie en cultuur* (Amsterdam: Ton Bolland, 1974). My own findings are not identical with Van Hoof's, but this is not the place to elaborate this.

[6]   Van Ruler, *Visie en vaart*, (Amsterdam: Holland Uitgeversmaatschappij, 1947), 128–199.

when he had a clear focus. It was also the time that he got his doctoral degree: *De vervulling van de wet* (*The Fulfillment of the Law*), which actually also deals with theocratic thought.[7] He was appointed as professor in Utrecht in the same year. Theocracy was his ideal in this time so that he even became the motivating power for a theocratic political party, the *Protestantse Unie*. However, in the 1946 elections of the parliament, this party did not gain any seat and did not participate in later elections.

It will not be overdue to consider this period as the most powerful and motivated time of Van Ruler's career. Certainly there are aspects that continue and characterize his work in the following decades, but these have never motivated him to such an extent as theocracy in the forties as a prolific writer on that theme.

### The Fifties

In contrast to the later forties, Van Ruler did not publish any substantial book in the following decade. He had noticed that there was not any interest in theocracy, neither in politics nor in the church. It remained a dream for him until the end of his life, but he knew it was over and nothing was left other than politicians who had only limited human interests of their own group, to whom nothing was left other than dividing the jobs among their political friends, as he once bitterly uttered during an examination (this was the time that an examination was still a conversation of a professor with a student in the professor's study room in his home!).

So Van Ruler missed his focus. He took his motivation from his students and from his morning meditations for a national broadcasting corporation. Theologically, his interest in concrete material life continued, not so much as theocracy but as created reality and restoration by the Holy Spirit. One cannot see this interest isolated from the theological context of that time. Barthian theology was dominant in leading circles in the Netherlands Reformed Church of the time. Van Ruler's emphasis on creation and Pneumatology must be understood in contrast with Barth's focus on Christology. So it was not Christology as such that Van Ruler opposed but *Barthian* Christology. Actually, Christology was very important for Van Ruler, however not as an ideological power but as the concrete suffering, death, and resurrection of Christ on behalf of the salvation of sinners. One can hardly find

---

[7]    Van Ruler, *De vervulling van de wet. Een dogmatische studie over de verhouding van openbaring en existentie*, (Nijkerk: Callenbach, 1947).

deeper thought about Christ than in Van Ruler's meditations on Mark 14–16.[8] Van Ruler actually opposed idealistic theological thoughts that did no justice to the real human condition as sinners who are in need of salvation for their concrete lives, which God will restore to lives in God's kingdom, which, in this world, always has the shape of the kingdom of Christ. A mere calling on Christ as vision for the future of the world as God's kingdom is superficial. Human beings cannot erect signs of the kingdom unless these are the work of the Holy Spirit, who does not dwell in an ideal world but inhabits human beings in the church with much tension. So Van Ruler's stress on creation and the Spirit is not because of an optimistic view on good life and empowerment but is related to a deep sense for human reality. The failure of his theocratic project has only deepened this conviction. Nevertheless, Van Ruler can speak about joy. This is not a superficial joy in human successes but in the knowledge of God's work in Christ, who in the image of the cross saves concrete human lives by the Spirit who indwells them. It is not exuberant joy with visible expressions. Van Ruler prefers to speak about chuckles—when human beings in the celebration of God's salvation in Christ see what they really are as God's creatures.

Because of his aversion of idealistic designs, Van Ruler distances himself increasingly from dominant theology in the Netherlands Reformed Church. If there is focus in his theology of the fifties, this focus is the *church*, the church that is just as concrete as the state was in his theocratic project. The church and its theology are the first problem now, and this problem continues for Van Ruler as long as he lives. Though he was enthusiastically involved in the design of the new church order of the Netherlands Reformed Church of 1951 and his hand can be traced back in the final draft, he became increasingly disappointed about its concrete application. The apostolic task of the church for the world was not filled in with the salutary work of Christ and conversion of society and nation to the commandments of God but as an human ideology in the name of Christ. It was understood not that, for Van Ruler, everything was directed to creation as the kingdom of God, but that, for him, everything turned on the hinge of the atoning work of Christ on the cross. Instead of his infralapsarian approach, the church opted for Berkhof's *Christus, de zin der geschiedenis (Christ, The Meaning of History)*[9] and the worldwide projects of the World Council of Churches

---

8   A. A. van Ruler, *Marcus 14. Vs. 1–41* (Kampen: Kok, 1971); *Marcus 14 (vervolg), 15 en 16* (Kampen: Kok, 1972).

9   H. Berkhof, *Christus, de zin der geschiedenis* (Nijkerk: Callenbach, 1958).

on the way to the assembly in New Delhi with the theme *Jesus Christ: The Light of the World* (1961). Van Ruler did not disagree about the goal of the World Council but about the optimism of theologians and church leaders who did not pay real attention to the human condition. He is not against Christology but against this easy Christology that does not see real life and the depth of the suffering of Christ— a Christology without Christ crucified on behalf of us because of our sins. As a result, such a Christology is not salutary for real human beings who only will be renewed by the Holy Spirit. Consequently, Van Ruler was in a position as a young theologian recently characterized my own theology: "He is far from the church but close to the people."[10]

Van Ruler, who was so interested in politics, finished his life co-operating in a probing message to the church against political preaching without attention to conversion and salvation by the death of Christ as atonement of sin.[11] This is not a U-turn from his early work. It is, rather, a confirmation that the church did not see how deep the need for salvation is. If there is distance from his early work, it is that he had noticed that not only the nation but also the church lacked interest in God's government over the world and that he was much too optimistic when he was younger. Sin is more deeply rooted in humanity than he thought before, and even the church does not discern this. She does not stand for what she should stand for in the proclamation of God's salvation.

### Vaticanum II

The second Vatican Council dominated theology in the beginning of the sixties. Leading Protestant theologians in the Netherlands such as Berkouwer and Bronkhorst attended it and wrote about it, and Van Ruler also contributed to the reflection. He did so not by analyzing what happened in Rome but by writing down what, in his opinion, were the specifics of the Reformation in relation to the Roman Catholic Church. So his first substantial book since 1949 appeared: *Reformatorische opmerkingen in de ontmoeting met Rome* (*Reformed Observations in the*

---

[10]   W.M. Dekker, 'Is het verdriet al in je leven gekomen?' in *Nederlands Dagblad*, November 22, 2018.

[11]   G.van Itterzon e.a., *Getuigenis*, 1971, https://www.digibron.nl/search/detail/9d5c5d a12312c934ca2d49bd0bba1f7b/getuigenis [December 12, 2018].
       The *Getuigenis* was finished after Van Ruler's death. His wife, J.A. van Ruler-Hamelink, continued his participation.

*Encounter with Rome*). It is in this book that his most extensive reflections on the Lord's Supper are found.[12]

The book must not be considered as a profound comparison of Roman Catholic tradition and Reformed theology. It is, rather, a set of remarks, as the title indicates, from a Reformed perspective related to Van Ruler's own ideas on the Romana, which is actually not so much in his focus compared to his Protestant colleagues who enthusiastically wrote about Rome. It is also directed to tendencies in the Reformed churches in the Netherlands in general. So actually, his discussion partners were not the Roman Catholics but Reformed theologians and church leaders. It was the debate of the fifties that is continued, now, at the background of Vaticanum II.

### His Last Years

Van Ruler's last half-decade displays a different character than before. He struggled with his health these years. One could expect that his theological power would also fade out. However, the opposite is the case. In 1969, he published a book that shows almost the spiritual power of his early work: *Waarom zou ik naar de kerk gaan? (Why Should I Go to Church?)*[13] In this book, it is not the state and politics that attract his attention now. He is biologized about the church, not the church as a theological idea, not even the church in its organization and church law, but the concrete gathering of the congregation, coming to the proclaimed Word and celebrating the sacraments. It looks if this concrete church restores Van Ruler's theological enthusiasm. Certainly, he had always been an interesting man, a celebrated professor, and a devoted teacher. However, it is clear in this book that something has grasped him. The church has grasped him. The kingdom of God did not disappear, and creation and the Holy Spirit are always present in his thought, but now this is all concentrated in the church, which celebrates eternal life in the encounter with God.

It is amazing that Van Ruler did not learn this by intensive theological research. He discovered it in the worship of his parish church, the Janskerk in Utrecht. Due to his weak health, Van Ruler was not able to preach during these years. So he attended the services as a common member of the congregation. It was the high liturgy of this church that opened his eyes for another reality: the reality of liturgy.[14]

---

[12]  Van Ruler, *Reformatorische opmerkingen*, 201–237.
[13]  Van Ruler, *Waarom zou ik naar de kerk gaan?* (Nijkerk: Callenbach, 1970).
[14]  Van Ruler, 7, 170–175.

Of course, this had impact on his ideas about the sacraments. This new discovery does not mean that he accepted everything uncritically. His critique is that the worship is not concrete enough: bringing the Word closer to human lives and hearts and speaking about personal conversion and the joy of new life.[15] However, worship gave Van Ruler a new focus, a new enthusiasm as he had got in the years after the war. In spite of his fragile health, he wrote a book of 175 pages with dense lines of small letters. It is this book that shows the mature theologian, the church professor, who has grown by frustration, disappointment, and ecclesiastic superficiality to the reception of the gift of joy: celebrating worship and so coming home.

The different perspectives wherein Van Ruler operated had impact on his thought on the sacraments. They are present throughout his whole career but with changing meaning and increasing value.

**Sacrament as Beginning of the Kingdom**

Van Ruler's first period as a theologian of his own standing was marked by his work *Religie en politiek* (*Religion and Politics*). The tone was set for the following books here and these can be seen as spin off, explanation, and elaboration of his first masterwork. The sacraments are remarkably present in this book. One would not expect so in a book on religion and politics, and this shows that the sacrament was not a minor topic for Van Ruler.

For explaining the meaning of the sacrament, Van Ruler uses the couple "visible – invisible."[16] God's salvation in Christ is invisible in the world. He left the world at his ascension, and his salutary work on the cross cannot be demonstrated in the world. The world is horrible. God's salvation in Christ is proclaimed in this world by preaching. Human beings are called to conversion, from being under God's condemnation to eternal life in God's love. However, though ministers preach and preach again, we do not see any change in the world. God's kingdom is invisible. It can only be believed.

Then Van Ruler makes a next, decisive step. The church does not only preach as a critical message to the world, where it does not have impact. The church also has the sacraments. One can conceive these as visible preaching. Because the verbal preaching is so elusive we have visible signs[17]: it is about bread and wine, food and drink, which both

---

[15]    Van Ruler, 173.
[16]    Van Ruler, *Religie en politiek*, 23.
[17]    Van Ruler, *Sta op tot de vreugde*, (Nijkerk: Callenbach, 1947), 32.

remember us to the body and blood of Christ but also refer to eternal life. But also these signs do not produce realization in the visible world if they were mere preaching, a message about something else.[18] They do not only refer to Christ in heaven; they are *themselves* visible reality, precisely in their blunt visible presence. We see a piece of white bread and the red wine,[19] but in faith we raise our hearts to heaven where Christ is with all his grace and benefits. The visible elements refer to the invisible grace, which is Christ himself as the King of kings in his kingdom on God's throne. This kingdom is hidden to the world. But in the elements, we see it with our eyes and taste it with our mouths. This is the sacramental reality. This cannot be explained by reference to other realities. The sacrament has its own characteristics of reality, the *praesentia sacramentalis,* and its language is only relevant for this reality. It is a *phraseologia sacramentalis.*[20] This reality is the reality of the communion of Christ with the celebrating congregation and of the celebrating congregation with Christ. In this communion with Christ, the members are bound together as the members of his body as a real presence through the Spirit. The church is not merely a group of people who come for listening to a message of how the world should be. They are a real community, and in them the Word of God becomes reality, because in the elements of the sacrament, Christ himself shares their lives.[21] They are the visible presence of the kingdom of Christ in the world wherein all equally participate, irrespective of their position in church and society.[22]

The sacramental reality also has impact on the understanding of the preaching. The proclamation of the Word in the Sunday morning worship is not directed to a coincidental group of people. It is for the congregation who gathered for worship. The Word is not only a message; it is proclamation of what these people really are. It is proclamation of God's sentence: judgement and condemnation of the human being under sin and salvation because of the crucified Christ. So the sermon, too, gets a sacramental character.[23]

This sacramental character also affects the day of worship, Sunday. It is a day whereon the church celebrates saved reality as eternal

---

[18]   Van Ruler, *Religie en politiek,* 48f.
[19]   Van Ruler, 35.
[20]   Van Ruler, 94.
[21]   Van Ruler, 196.
[22]   Van Ruler, *Sta op tot de vreugde,* 85.
[23]   Van Ruler, *Religie en politiek,* 85. See also 94f.

life. This is not an interruption of daily life. It is rather concentration and sign of what life really is.[24] Consequently, the sacrament effects the whole life. Its reality is the real presence of God's salvation and prolepsis of the kingdom, and from this reality, Christians live in their families, they go to their work, they participate in political responsibility, they enjoy art and sports. "So the totality of life is lived in circles around the cross of Christ. The first circle is the Lord's Supper, the second circle is political order, the third circle is marriage, the fourth circle is work, the fifth circle is amusement."[25] Wherever Christians live and come, they bear the reality of being Christians, members of the body of Christ. And so the whole life becomes a visible reality of the kingdom. The whole life gets a sacramental character. Therefore, the church practices the *censura morum*: Are her members really involved in the communion with Christ? Does the practice of their lives not deny their very being? And also, the censura morum for the Lord's Supper is not an isolated event. It is embedded in the supervision of the elders over the congregation, which is regularly executed by the house visit. The house visit is also sacramental,[26] as it deals with visible life of the church in her members.

It must be clear: the sacrament is not the fullness of the kingdom.[27] It is a sign[28] as are the healings of Jesus, which are recorded in the Gospels. It is always in the perspective of visible – invisible. Visible is only the sober reality of bread and wine, of a normal family with conflicts and reconciliation, of human beings who do hard work and train for sports. But all this refers to the invisible reality of Christ in heaven who healed human life, and when the church celebrates the Lord's Supper, this reality becomes visible in the sacramental presence of the Lord,and it spreads over the lives of all the participants. Certainly the presence of the kingdom in the sacramental life of the church and her members is fragmentary.[29] The bread is broken in fragments. But these poor fragments of bread are real, precisely as fragments that refer

---

[24]    Van Ruler, *Verhuld bestaan,* (Nijkerk: Callenbach, 1949), 168. The Sunday is celebration of Easter fifty two times a year. In a world where people live with ideals to be realized, the Sunday turns our minds to what was realized in creation and salvation. The Sunday is not empowerment for the realization of our ideal, but living in the reality of the rest that God has provided by his work ('De zin van ons leven' [1945], in D. van Keulen [ed.], *Dr. A.A. van Ruler. Verzameld werk 3.*

[25]    Van Ruler, *Religie en politiek*, 33.

[26]    Van Ruler, 104.

[27]    Van Ruler, 47.

[28]    Van Ruler, *Religie en politiek*, 53.

[29]    Van Ruler, 35.

to the salvation of the world in the death of Christ.[30] The kingdom is the salvation in Christ. Van Ruler relates both with a simple "=" symbol.[31]

The community of the church is not a corporation of individual persons. It is a real community and a social entity. It is so not only for a moment but also in time, from generation to generation. "We stand with our children, with our ancestry and our progeny on the ground of salvation."[32] The sacramental Communion is communicated to the children.[33] Therefore, they are baptized. The sacrament of infant baptism is essential for the understanding of the reality character of the sacrament. Human beings are really, with all they have and are, sacramentally participants of the kingdom.[34] Exclusion of infants from the sacrament would spoil the whole sacrament because it denies real communion and real presence. It turns the sacrament to a mere choice of individual persons who accept the Word of God as a task for human beings. They want to join the project, and they express this by getting themselves baptized as their free answer to the calling, like the response to participate in a useful organisation. For Van Ruler, the sacrament is not the answer and a promise of *human beings* to participate in the realization of their good intentions but the reality of *God's* promises in the fulfillment of his law. It may be fragmentary, and it must remain fragmentary, as it is about expression of God's kingdom in the sign of the cross where Christ bore the sin of the world, but nevertheless it is reality. There is a baptized family in communion with other families but firstly with the kingdom of God wherein also other families participate.

Christians do not live in isolation. They are participants in humanity; they belong to their town, to the city, to the nation. It is there that they participate in work and amusement. So the reality of the kingdom flows over to the whole society, most of all in its structures by the organization of government. That is not only because Christians participate. It is far more because the kingdom of God, which is sacramentally present in the church, is aimed for the whole world.[35] The world must be God's kingdom, and the church is only

---

30  Van Ruler, 68.
31  Van Ruler, 61, see also 59.
32  Van Ruler, *Sta op tot de vreugde*, 73.
33  Van Ruler, *Religie en politiek*, 177, 196.
34  "He sets us on the ground of his forgiveness and mercy" (A.A. van Ruler, *Sta op tot de vreugde*, 25).
35  In *De vervulling van de wet* (207), Van Ruler expresses the fragmentary character of the sacramental reality somewhat differently. No element of created reality is excluded from the work of the Holy Spirit, but his work in creation is not only sacramental

instrumental to this. Therefore, the structures of the government reflect the structures of the kingdom. In the execution and enforcement of laws, the government is a sign of the fulfillment of God's law for the world. So the government is sacramental too. By her system of justice, she participates in the censura morum.[36] She is extension of church discipline in the discipline of society.[37] She is called to promote justice and obedience to God's will. She operates in God's name and by consequence she is representation of God's kingdom. Certainly, this representation is fragmentary as all sacramental reality is. Nevertheless, it is *praesentia realis* as any sacramental reality, and the sacramental phraseology is applicable to the work of the government as it is to the celebration in the church. The concept of the *communio sanctorum* is not limited to the communion with fellow Christians or to the elements of the sacrament; ultimately, it refers to the whole reality.[38]

This turn to normal daily reality is, according to Van Ruler, basic for Reformed identity, in contrast with the Roman Catholic Church, where the ecclesiastical sacrament is the full presence of the divine Christ. Van Ruler affirms this Reformed conviction strongly. However, as early as 1947, he already wondered if it was not too one-sided. Should the church in a secularizing culture not reconsider Rome's position?[39] One cannot live in the world without having been in the church. "First celebrating the Lord's Supper ... and *then* into life, and

---

but also mystical and ethical. Van Ruler is always averse of viewing any topic under one label. Reality is not univocal but complex. Systematic theology is inclined to strive for harmony of all elements. "But this harmony appears to be in its essence God's mystery. We must walk and act in it but both the reflection on and life from this harmony are and remain broken and fragmentary" (*De vervulling van de wet*, 528). Therefore Van Ruler judges Van der Leeuw's sacramentalism as uncritical (G. van der Leeuw, *Het beeld Gods* [Amsterdam: Holland Uitgeversmaatschappij, 1939], 34f). Van Ruler refers to the duality of state and church (*De vervulling van de wet*, 219f). Though the state is expression (*uitbeelding*) of the kingdom, she cannot do without the church, where salvation is proclaimed and celebrated. And the church is not the kingdom; it is the place where salvation is proclaimed and where the sacrament is celebrated as a *sign* (*De vervulling van de wet*, 456f). Van Ruler does not intend here to minimalize the sacrament as a mere symbol. His aim is rather to stress both the importance of created reality and the necessity of the church. This is basic for his theology. The sacraments of the church belong to the intermezzo (*Religie en politiek*, 44), and Christian existence is a shadow (*De vervulling van de wet*, 529) of the fulfilled kingdom of God.

[36]    Van Ruler, *Religie en politiek*, 178: "The task of the state can only be considered as extension of the *censura morum* task of the presbytery." Cf. *Religie en politiek*, 49f, 177.

[37]    Van Ruler, 33, 49.

[38]    Van Ruler, 84f.

[39]    Van Ruler, *De vervulling van de wet*, 531.

*then* into suffering, and *then* into death. First Christ and the abundant mercy in him and then reality, also with all its horrors."[40] For "the cross is the centre of world history."[41] From this centre, which is proclaimed and commemorated in the sacraments of the church, the sacramental presence of God's kingdom spreads over the world.[42] The law of God, in the form of the decalogue, must be read in the church, and by doing so, the minister reads the law for the government in order to proclaim to the worldly powers what justice is.[43]

The sacrament has a wide scope in this early work of Van Ruler. Infants and states are involved in it. It has no limits. It is the vision of the kingdom of God. It may not be forgotten that it is in the shape of the cross now,[44] which means that it is fragmentary, and therefore nobody can claim the fullness of the kingdom at any place. The state cannot do so, and consequently, she is never fully right. Theocracy is the best guarantee of tolerance,[45] for the fragmentary sacrament can never be totalitarian. Also, the church cannot make such claims. An infallible pope denies the sacramental character of the church and makes claims that only belong to the fulfilled kingdom of God. On the other hand, it may never be forgotten that sacramental presence is real. There exists a church where Christ is present, and there is a government that is representative of God's coming kingdom.

---

[40]   Van Ruler, *Sta op tot de vreugde*, 90.

[41]   Van Ruler, *Sta op de vreugde*, 104; *Verhuld bestaan*, 105. See also *Verhuld bestaan*, 42: God is only found in the sacrifice of the expiation of sin.

[42]   This does not only refer to the world as human political society but to the whole of nature (*Religie en politiek*, 45), with all its horrors. It would be interesting to compare Van Ruler's position with M.E Brinkman (*Schepping en sacrament. Een oecumenische studie naar de reikwijdte van het sacrament als heilzaam symbool in een weerbarstige werkelijkheid* (Zoetermeer: Meinema, 1991) and *Het leven als teken. Over de verschrikkelijke en verrukkelijke natuur* (Baarn: Ten Have, 1986) who also relates nature to sacramentality. See also A.A. van Ruler, "De bevinding in kerk en theologie" (1946), in D. van Keulen, ed., *Dr. A.A. van Ruler. Verzameld werk 4B. Christus, de Geest en het heil* (Zoetermeer: Boekencentrum, 2011), 504.
This aspect of Van Ruler's theology may be an eye-opener in Christian theology of environment. See also *De meeste van deze is de liefde*, J.N. Voorhoeve, Den Haag s.a., 67. Cf. Dirk J. van Keulen, "Leads for Ecotheology in Arnold A. van Ruler's Work," in Ernst M. Conradie, ed., *Creation and salvation. Dialogue on Kuyper's legacy for contemporary Ecotheology*, Brill, Leiden, 2011, 197–211.

[43]   Van Ruler, *Religie en politiek*, 260.

[44]   "Life and world must be as they are, as gruesome; otherwise the light of the cross would disappear" (A.A. van Ruler, *Religie en politiek*, 50).

[45]   See also his later article "Theocratie en tolerantie" (1956), in A.A. van Ruler, *Theologisch werk 1* (Nijkerk: Callenbach, 1969), 191–215.

## The Fifties

Van Ruler's productivity in the fifties shows a contrast with it in the forties. He produced only short publications in this period. Also, he did not write very much about the sacraments. There are only some short remarks in texts on other topics. So we cannot draw too far reaching conclusions from these.

Van Ruler continues his attention for the whole creation. Infants and states are comprehended in the work of the Spirit.[46] When speaking about the sacrament, we must think that "we are in the church but we are also in the world."[47] However, a shift also can be noticed. While Van Ruler's perspective was to the horizons of reality in the forties, he now focuses on the church. His attention is to the *Christians* who are in the church and the world. And even this is not sufficient: we must go back to the historical revelation of salvation in the coming of Christ and the descent of the Holy Spirit, to substitution and inhabitation.[48]

So Van Ruler concentrates his thought more to salvation. His focus is not to the horizon but to the center, where the salutary work of Christ comes to us. This is also reflected in his thought on the relation of preaching and sacrament. He explicitly elaborates the classic distinction that the Word works faith and the sacraments empower it.[49] The sacrament cannot be without the Word and always follows it. Consequently, he now rejects the idea that preaching itself can be called sacramental.[50] There is a clear distinction between Word and sacrament. Both are necessary, but both have also their own standing.

He also speaks differently about the sacrament itself. His attention is not to the sacrament as beginning realization of salvation, spreading to ethics and politics, but to the celebration of reconciliation with God in Christ. The risen Christ is in heaven. "It is there that He bears the sacrifice. It is there that He is the transformer, through which all reigning of God goes, so that it is reigning of Christ. ... In the sacrament of the Lord's Supper we have communion with this Christ through the Holy Spirit, are we set into heaven, and do we share eternal life in

[46]    "Hoofdlijnen van een pneumatologie" (1957), in A.A. van Ruler, *Theologisch werk* 6 (Nijkerk: Callenbach, 1973), 31.

[47]    "De categorie 'realisering' als theologisch begrip" (1953), in A.A.van Ruler, *Theologisch werk* 4, (Nijkerk: Callenbach, 1972), 79.

[48]    Van Ruler, *Theologisch werk* 4, 79.

[49]    "Grenzen van de prediking" (1952), in A.A. van Ruler, *Theologisch werk* 3 (Nijkerk: Callenbach, 1971), 36.

[50]    Van Ruler, *Theologisch werk* 3, 37f.

an unspeakable way. What could we actually want more?"[51] The joy of salvation is the core of his speaking about the sacrament. Salvation is mediated by the sacrament.[52]

When Van Ruler relativizes the sacrament of the church now, it is not because it is only part of a wide sacramental presence of the kingdom but because it refers to Jesus who is more than the sacrament. "We cannot be content with the things which God Himself or Christ gave us. Not even with the sacrament. The sacrament of the Lord's Supper is without doubt a most important form, wherein we participate in this [eternal] life, in this bread, in Jesus Christ. But it is not the one and only form. And: it is just *only* a form! It is not *the* bread of life. The bread of life is Jesus Christ Himself, or also: God in Christ."[53]

It can be wondered what is the cause of this shift. It is not due to a fundamental turn in Van Ruler's theology. He still has the whole creation in mind, and he continues to do so until the end of his life. The kingdom of God as the fulfillment of the whole creation was still his focus in his classes at the end of the sixties. Salvation is only an instrument on behalf of creation, though a necessary element which cannot be missed in human lives and society. We can only enjoy soccer on Sunday afternoon after having been to the church on Sunday morning. However, in his writings of this period he does not elaborate the wide impact of salvation but rather its centre. "To say it in one word: only if one goes to the church ... full human dignity is preserved. The apex of humanity is attained in the liturgy, where to culture according to her essence never can come, at least not in this expressivity."[54]

I suppose this has to do with his disappointing experiences in the late forties and early fifties. Society and politics were not interested in his theocratic ideals. This does not mean that Van Ruler gave them up, but he realized he had to do much homework first. Without understanding

---

[51] "Vijf bepalingen over de hemel" (1956), in A.A. van Ruler, *Blij zijn als kinderen. Een boek voor volwassenen* (Kampen: Kok, 972), 99f. See also 152: The ascension of Christ is the concentration of all mysteries of Christian faith. "We cannot keep out of its way or embezzle it." See further "God is mens geworden" (1955), in Gijsbert van den Brink and Dirk van Keulen (ed.), *Van schepping tot Koninkrijk. Teksten (1947–1970) uit het theologische oeuvre van A.A. van Ruler* (Barneveld: Klassiek licht, Nederlands Dagblad, 2008), 161f.

[52] Van Ruler, *Theologisch werk* 6, 30. It should be well distinguished that the sacrament does not create *faith* (this does the Word only) but that it mediates *salvation,* and we participate in salvation by the sacrament indeed (*Van schepping tot Koninkrijk*, 162),

[53] Van Ruler, *Vertrouw en geniet. Zestien toespraken over Jezus Christus en de wereld* (Den Haag: J.N. Voorhoeve, n.d.), 13.

[54] "De apartheid van de kerk" (1959), in *Blij zijn als kinderen*, 205.

salvation, people will not understand theocracy. This became even more clear when he noticed that not only did society and politics not take up his paradigm but also the church took different tracks. Though Van Ruler enthusiastically participated in drafting a new church order for the Netherlands Reformed Church, he soon noticed that both church leadership and his fellow professors understood the task of the church for renewal of the world very differently from his own conviction. This became explicit when the synod of the church published a pastoral letter on *Being Christian in Dutch Society*.[55] Van Ruler reacted with sharp critique.[56] He blames the church, criticizing that she focuses on human activities.[57] In the letter, the synod does not deal with the church in her catholicity but "with the modern issue of the free organization, the association and the party."[58]

The pastoral letter states that the members of the church are called to erect signs of the kingdom.[59] At first sight, this might sound very Van Rulerian. However, Van Ruler is of a different opinion. The synod makes a shortcut. She walks from the proclamation of the Word immediately to societal and political ethics. Because of unclear formulations in the pastoral letter, one can easily forget the specific character of the form of God's presence in Christ for the Christian.[60] "The aim is the Kingdom of God and true humanity. But the eschaton is never given to us in pure culture. For us, the Kingdom of God is only present in the shape of the Kingdom of Christ and consequently true humanity only in the shape of being Christian, true culture only in the shape of Christianization."[61] By that shortcut, the synod makes the preaching of the Word a propaganda speech for a social and political program. Van Ruler objects that the proclamation of the Word must be pronouncing what God has done in Christ and is doing in his Spirit to human beings. They must be converted to God and saved from their sins. This must be celebrated in the sacrament. And the sacrament is not only a community of human beings who are gathered as individuals

---

[55] Herderlijk schrijven vanwege de Synode der Nederlandse Hervormde Kerk, *Christen-zijn in de Nederlandse samenleving*, 1955.

[56] Van Ruler, *Achtergronden van het herderlijk schrijven*, Geschriften betreffende de orde der Ned. Herv. Kerk 5, Veenman en zonen, Wageningen 1955.

[57] He already objected to this fallacy in *Religie en politiek*. "Theocracy is not an ideal that we can strife for. It is purely a gift and wonder of God which He sets into the world sometimes" (50f).

[58] Van Ruler, *Achtergronden van het herderlijk schrijven*, 11.

[59] Van Ruler, 25.

[60] Van Ruler, 26.

[61] Van Ruler, *Theologie van het apostolaat* (Nijkerk: Callenbach, n.d.), 36f.

for their task in the world. The sacrament is also related to the "things": bread and wine as the body of Christ, and the body of Christ is not only a gathering of people but also an institution.[62] The church is taken into communion with God in Christ through the Spirit. The Spirit erects signs of God's kingdom in the world. The church is not the subject of building the kingdom; she is only instrumental. In short: Van Ruler blames the synod, that she replaces Pneumatology with anthropology and God's work with human activities. By consequence, the signs of the kingdom in society are not the sacramental presence of God but mere signs of human successes which will not last long.

So Van Ruler turns to the center, not because the horizon is not important but because the horizon is out of sight in the church since she does not understand the center and therefore skipped it. So much work must be done in teaching the church, its leadership, and the fellow professors. They have to start with basic catechesis about the fundamentals of Christian faith.[63]

> Rediscovering the catholicity of the church is the law of the moment for Protestantism in the twentieth century. That means ... that the church is again experienced as body of Christ, wherein Christ, or even better: God in Christ, is present. This *praesentia realis*, this real presence of God in Christ, not *only* in the sacrament, but *also* in the sacrament and subsequently in the whole being of the church as God's mystery in history, is the irrevocable essence of the church.[64]

## Encounter with Rome

The most extensive text on the sacraments by Van Ruler is the last chapter of his book on the encounter with Rome.[65] Similar ideas are found in a few other publications of this period. The chapter consists of three parts. In the first section, Van Ruler continues the track that we found in his publications of the fifties. He stresses even more the distinction between preaching and sacrament. Both deal with God's

---

[62]  Van Ruler, *Achtergronden van het herderlijk schrijven*, 27.
[63]  The Netherlands Reformed Church published a confessional document *Fundamenten en perspectieven* in 1949, in line with Barth's *Christengemeinde und Bürgergemeinde*. It is remarkable that Berkhof prescribed it to his students until his retirement in 1981, while I cannot remember Van Ruler ever speaking about it.
[64]  "Taak en toekomst van het protestantisme in Nederland" (1955), in *Blij zijn als kinderen*, 211.
[65]  Van Ruler, *Reformatorische opmerkingen*, 201–237.

salvation in Christ. This salvation must be communicated to us. The gap in time between the historical Jesus and us must be bridged. There is also the distance of the risen Lord in heaven and us on earth. And, finally, the Mediator is someone other than us. Also these distances must be bridged.[66] This is done by tradition, and the preaching of the Word is the way tradition is applied to us. God in Christ comes to us in the Word.[67]

However, this is not sufficient for an encounter of God and us. It is not only Christ who must come to us, but we also must go to him, or at least accept his coming. There is not only tradition but also *reception*.[68] This is not an independent human activity. It is the work of the Holy Spirit, but he convinces us without destroying our identity. It is really *we* who accept Christ's coming. The preaching of the Word is complemented by faith from our side. The acceptance of the work of Christ from our side is a mystery, which is just as high and deep as the mystery of incarnation and atonement.[69] The Holy Spirit of God *in* us is an equal mystery with God *with* us in the incarnation. So far, the sacrament is not yet involved. It is only an elaboration of the thesis that the Word creates faith. This is the way we become Christians, by being reconciled with God through the atonement and expiation of sins by Christ.[70]

Only *after* this reconciliation does the sacrament come into view.[71] The Eucharist is the celebration of the reconciliation.[72] It is the embracement of God and a human being with the kiss of love. This is the subject of the second section.[73] It is the most personal and existential text on the sacrament in Van Ruler's oeuvre. It is about the communion with God in Christ. It is the real presence of God in Christ in a real unity with human beings, as the bread and wine are really the body and blood of Christ. Van Ruler does not make objections to the idea of transubstantiation.[74] The unity of sign and reality is the unity of Christ with us. It is the unity of bride and bridegroom and even deeper. It is

66    Van Ruler, 204f.
67    Van Ruler, 212.
68    Van Ruler, *Reformatorische opmerkingen*, 206.
69    Van Ruler, 206.
70    Van Ruler, 212f.
71    Van Ruler, 161, 213.
72    Van Ruler, 221.
73    Van Ruler, 215–228.
74    Van Ruler, 222.

the present eschaton, united with Christ in heaven and his eternal life.[75] This unity cannot be explained; it can only be celebrated. Any discourse about it can only produce tautologies. Like the celebration of the unity of God and human beings is one, so is sacramental phraseology. It cannot be substituted or replaced by something else.[76]

This perfect unity does not mean that human identity would be absorbed by God. That is not even the case in the unity of divine and human in Christ, though there is a *unio personalis*. In the sacrament, the human person is fully intact. The inhabitation of the Holy Spirit is of a different character than the incarnation. That does not mean it would be of a lower character. It is the amazing reality that God in the Spirit celebrates love with a human person. And precisely because it is an encounter, an embracement, both must keep their own identity. "The Lord's Supper is a twofold act: God in Christ gives Himself in his grace to man and man gives himself to God. This way they jointly constitute the sacrament. ... God who gives Himself is not the only constitutive factor. Man who gives himself is so just as much. They give themselves to each other. They celebrate their communion."[77]

In this perspective, Van Ruler in the third section brings in the question of whether the Lord's Supper is a sacrifice.[78] It is so, indeed, as Christ's giving himself for us. He gives himself to us as we give ourselves to him, accepting his love. This is the sacrifice of reconciliation.[79] One can even think about atonement and expiation. Certainly, this was done by Christ once and forever for us.[80] But when we accept his substitutional sacrifice and confess that we cannot save ourselves, we are drawn in his sacrifice and sacrificed with him.[81] However, this is not a new atonement. Expiation was done, once and forever. When the atoning sacrifice is applied to human beings, they sacrifice themselves to God in Christ, not as expiation but in sanctification. So the atoning sacrifice gets the shape of sanctification in us.[82] This is expressed by

---

[75]  Van Ruler, 220, 225.
[76]  Van Ruler, 221f.
[77]  Van Ruler, *Reformatorische opmerkingen*, 216.
[78]  Van Ruler, 229–237.
[79]  Van Ruler, 233.
[80]  Van Ruler, 231, 234f.
[81]  Van Ruler, 231.
[82]  Van Ruler, 235f. See also: A.A. van Ruler, "Structuurverschillen tussen het Christologische en Pneumatologische gezichtspunt" in J. de Graaf (ed.), *De Spiritu Sancto. Bijdragen tot de leer van de Heilige Geest bij gelegenheid van het 2e eeuwfeest van het Stipendium Bernardinum* (Utrecht: Kemink, 1964), 216.

the service of offerings in the liturgy.[83] This offering is not a separate offering next to Christ's sacrifice. It is the same sacrifice wherein we are involved.[84]

Consequently, Van Ruler turns his attention to human daily life, and here notions of his early work come into view: work, society, politics.[85] The celebration of the Eucharist is directed to this life. The Eucharist is not an aim in itself; it is a way, or even an instrument, for the kingdom that must become manifest in the world since sin was taken away.

After the overwhelming intensity of the second section, the third section contrasts as somewhat dim. It seems as if Van Ruler wants to bring in his ideas about the kingdom as the goal of all God's works, but he does not succeed to connect this with his ideas on the eucharist. Maybe the word "consequently" at the beginning of the previous paragraph should rather be "subsequently"; it is done, but it has no intrinsic connection with what precedes. It seems that the distinctions that Van Ruler rightly observes in the theological discourse become separating lines between aspects of Christian life. We celebrate the eucharist, and this is so intense that nothing can exceed this. How, then, can life and work in creation be the goal of this eschatological intensity? Certainly, Van Ruler would produce 12 arguments when asked, but the contrast has rather to do with the intensity wherein he pushes subjects to the ultimate. Because he in this chapter deals with the Lord's Supper, it is pushed to eschatological height and depth with the most profound metaphors. Consequently, daily life in sanctification becomes pale. This in contrast with his focus on politics in 1945 when the idea of sacrament was only an instrument for the notion that God is relevant for the whole world, and so the sacrament lost its own identity. Everything was brought under the paradigm of the kingdom in 1945, whereas distinct topics are not really connected in 1965. How far this reaches can be illustrated by the relation of preaching and sacrament. Van Ruler argues that the whole salvation is applied to human beings by the Word. The sacrament comes only after the reconciliation as its celebration. This goes so far that Van Ruler considers to celebrate the Lord's Supper in separate services.[86] He focuses so exclusively on the Word first and subsequently on the sacrament that he—even in a

---

[83]    Van Ruler, 232.
[84]    Van Ruler, 232.
[85]    Van Ruler, 236.
[86]    Van Ruler, *Reformatorische opmerkingen*, 220.

discourse on Reformed remarks to Rome—does not keep to the intrinsic connection of Word and sacrament.

Van Ruler first deals with preaching with such a focus that all other aspects are excluded. It is the preached Word that must be received by the hearers. This gives the impression as if they hear the Word for the first time and must answer by their assent. However, there is an existing congregation, a church, a community wherein, where to, and where about the Word is spoken. This should establish the sacramental character of the sermon that Van Ruler initially opted for and that he succeeded to substantiate in the church order of 1951. After his explicit rejection of this idea in 1957,[87] it now no longer even comes to the horizon.

A similar observation can be made about infant baptism. While Van Ruler focuses fully on the sacrament of the Lord's Supper, he does not take baptism into account. In his discourse of 1965, it should actually be concluded that baptism has to be inserted between the preaching of the Word and the eucharist—that would imply baptism of adults. This would be in full contrast with Van Ruler's ideas about salvation that extends to ancestry and progeny, which he did not abandon after the forties. Still, in his classes in the late sixties, he could stress that we are baptized—lock, stock, and barrel—including our children.

It seems that Van Ruler, in his opposition to Rome (or his own construction of what Rome would be), forgets the church as a real entity with continuity, connecting and intertwining all aspects of faith. Consequently, the Lord's Supper is interpreted as a mystical union to such an extent that daily life can only be experienced as a rainy Monday morning after a wonderful Sunday with your partner. Work and life is something what comes after the celebration of love. Nevertheless (or maybe, unfortunately?), work is the most important—the beginning of the kingdom.

Is this the only way the metaphor of partners can be elaborated for the relation of God and human beings? Can the only consequence be none other than a bad conscience? Was not my work at the expense of giving enough attention to my partner, the world at the expense of the celebration of the eucharist?[88] Could the metaphor of partners not better be filled-in as living together with the joy of the sacrament of love

---

87   Van Ruler, *Theologisch werk* 3, 37f.

88   "De verhouding van de mens en de wetenschap in het licht van de theologie" (1968), in *Theologisch werk* 1, 14. Cf. the review of the volume by K.R. Popma, 'Van Rulers medicijn tegen theologisch amateurisme,' *Leidsch Dagblad,* October 3, 1970, 13.

as an apex, which spreads throughout all days of life? By claiming that the goal of creation is the kingdom of God, after having dealt with the sacrament in such a deep relational way, Van Ruler is at risk to end with a kingdom without the triune God with his whole history with human beings, because Christ is only the *autobasileia* for the time being until the incarnation will be undone in the consummation.[89] Living with Christ is, for him, only a matter of an intermezzo, but what will living in the kingdom be without living with this God who saved me?

## The Finale

During the last years of his life, Van Ruler struggled with his health. Consequently, he was not able to preach on Sundays and went to church as other members of the congregation. He attended the worship in the medieval Janskerk in Utrecht where the service had the character of high liturgy. This liturgical setting opened news perspectives for Van Ruler.[90] Liturgy came into the centre of his thought with the Lord's Supper as its culmination point. This impact on Van Ruler's theology can be found in two publications that he wrote in his last years, the book *Waarom zou ik naar de kerk gaan? (Why Should I Go to Church?)* and the long article "Ultragereformeerd en vrijzinnig" ("Ultra-Reformed and Liberal").[91] He finished that article six days before his death.[92]

Van Ruler's thought on the sacraments in these articles follows the lines of the second section in his expositions in *Reformatorisch opmerkingen*. The Eucharist is the celebration of the unity of God and human beings. However, it is not placed in opposition to other theologies or to other aspects of theology and Christian worship and life. The distinctions are not dominant, but the positive meaning of the Eucharist is decisive.

Van Ruler speaks about the sacraments in the most elevated language. It is the celebration of love and the fulfillment of God's

---

[89] Van Ruler is aware of this tension. He speaks about contradictions in theology between the topics and even about a cleft between church and Christianized life. "This duality of the ecclesiastical and the extra-ecclesiastical, of the *corpus Christi* and the *corpus Christianum* causes an enormous cleft in the realization of salvation. This never will be overcome" ("Verscheidenheden en tegenstrijdigheden in de realisering van het heil" [1964], in *Theologisch werk* 4, 90).

[90] Van Ruler, *Waarom zou ik naar de kerk gaan?*, 7, 174f.

[91] Van Ruler, "Ultragereformeerd en vrijzinnig," *Wapenveld* 21(2/3), 1971.

[92] K. van der Zwaag. "Van Ruler worstelde met bevinding" in *Reformatorisch Dagblad*, June 10, 2011, accessed December 14, 2018, https://www.digibron.nl/search/detail/0134b4a33691c0eca2ab4392/van-ruler-worstelde-met-bevinding/2.

coming to humankind and humans"believing in God's promises. It is the fulfillment of salvation, "the truth and reality of communion."[93] God and humans are united in the embracement of reconciliation. The sacrament is the eschatological fulfillment. It is the concealed eschaton.[94] It is not only a sign; it is the celebration of salvation, and celebration is realization.[95] "We have left behind any mediation. We stay in full reality."[96] "The sacrament is the feast of complete salvation, of salvation as of God and men. It is *the* shape of eternal life!"[97] Human beings with their whole being, body and mind, and God as the triune God are united in the sacrament of the Eucharist[98]—as one great liturgy of thanks for creation and salvation. It is the celebration of love as the unity of man and wife in the mystery of sexuality.[99] This does not mean that humanity is absorbed by God. For the celebration of reconciliation, two persons are needed.[100] It is the intimate unity of the two, the human body of the church and the triune God, that constitutes the wonderful event of eschatology, and both enjoy themselves and each other.

For expressing the realization of the eschaton, any form and any language of earthly life is insufficient. "But then there is the sacrament! It is so unique both in form (it is an extremely erratic block in our daily lives) and in capacity (the *unio sacramentalis* of sign and the signified), that it appears to be a vessel wherein we can bear safely eternal life with us on our travel through time."[101] The sacrament must remain such an erratic block, for it is the *concealed* eschaton. "A handful of water, a bite of bread, a nip of wine ... Life is nowhere poorer and harder than in the sacrament ... The more sacramental ... we think and live, the more we stay in the awe-inspiring reservation, wherein the gospel sets human existence."[102] However, "concealed" does not mean "not real." It is the reality of what the eschaton is, but in the concealment of time, and therefore only seen by the believing community, which is the church.[103]

---

93   Van Ruler, *Marcus 14*, 67.
94   Van Ruler, "Ultragereformeerd," 27.
95   Van Ruler, 27.
96   Van Ruler, 27f.
97   Van Ruler, 27.
98   Van Ruler, *Waarom zou ik naar de kerk gaan?*, 86.
99   Van Ruler, *Waarom zou ik naar de kerk gaan?*, 84.
100  Van Ruler, 86f; see also A.A. van Ruler, *Ik geloof. De twaalf artikelen van het geloof in morgenwijdingen* (Nijkerk: Callenbach, 1968), 127; the unity of the two also implies tension and conflicts, precisely because it is inhabitation, the two in one body.
101  Van Ruler, "Ultragereformeerd," 27. See also *Blij zijn als kinderen*, 197.
102  Van Ruler, 28.
103  Van Ruler, 28.

This does not mean that the unity with Christ is less real. It is precisely in the concealment that he is present, for we celebrate his death.

> The Kingdom of glory has appeared in Him. The Savior gives part in Himself for this, in the shape of the bread with which He unites Himself. We stay in the sacrament of the Lord's Supper first of all—though in veiled shape—in the final state and destination of the whole created reality and of the whole process of world history. However, who Himself exposes this way must go through death ... The Lord's Supper is not only the feast of eternal glory, it is also a sacrificial meal.[104]

However, concealment is not decisive. This is rather the reality of being with God, the fulfillment of our lives. In the liturgy we encounter God, the ground of all being, not veiled but clear and distinct, in his full glory.[105]

Though the distinction is still present between the preaching by which faith is worked and reconciliation is attained on the one hand and the sacrament as celebration on the other hand,[106] the distinction is not so strong. The proclamation of the Word itself also receives somewhat of the glory of the sacrament. Everything is set in the right light by the proclamation of the Word, and so everything is set right according to the order of the kingdom.[107] Word and sacrament are bound together in the one liturgy of the worshiping congregation as expression of the one church, the body of Christ into which human beings are incorporated by baptism.[108] The perspective is more from the church as celebrating community than from the way human beings are reconciled and live with God, as it was in 1965. This can also be remarked from the close connection between infant baptism and the Lord's Supper. Both intrinsically belong together.[109] The sacraments are one, and it is impossible to baptize your children and to not participate

---

[104]  Van Ruler, *Marcus 14*, 68f.
[105]  Van Ruler, *Over de Psalmen gesproken. Meditaties over de Psalmen* (Nijkerk: Callenbach, 1973), 104. See also A.A. van Ruler, *De menselijkheid in de theologie*, (Kampen: Kamper Cahiers 3, Kok, 1967), 10.
[106]  Van Ruler, *Waarom zou ik naar de kerk gaan?*, 72; "Ultragereformeerd," 26.
[107]  Van Ruler, *Waarom zou ik naar de kerk gaan?*, 12f. This recalls the sacramental character of politics in *Religie en politiek*. However, the structure is different. The ultimate fulfillment of the relation of God and creation is not in the world, wherefor the church would be only instrumental, but the fulfillment is in the liturgy of the church. "Liturgy cannot be limited to the street" (*Waarom zou ik naar de kerk gaan?*, 174).
[108]  Van Ruler, *Waarom zou ik naar de kerk gaan?*, 83; *Ik geloof*, 127.
[109]  Van Ruler, "Ultragereformeerd," 28.

in the Lord's Supper. Sacraments also cannot be separated from ecclesiastical office.[110] The whole liturgy is one, and this is reflected in the unity of Christian life and also in daily work and social and political participation. However, it is now a spin-off of rather than the beginning of the kingdom that must be fulfilled in the world after the task of the church in the service of reconciliation will have been fulfilled. We go to church for the communion with each other, with God, with Christ.

> This threefold communion is such a high reality, such a great mystery, that we, all in all, cannot keep it in any other external or internal form of life. We need the church for it. That is just the way it is. The church is the form of this communion par excellence. She *is* the communion with the Mediator, with the triune God and with each-other-in-Christ. We must enter into it again and again. So every new going to the church is not only embodiment and demonstration, but also realization and celebration of the communion, and so it can also be called real incorporation.[111]

The world is brought into the church. This is most clear in the service of the offering. What are human beings more devoted to than to money? Maximally, sex and alcohol can compete.[112] It is this worldly life that we bring into the church, as bringing our whole being.[113] Therefore, the church wants to make converts.[114] "The church is turned inwardly ... The church is the bride of Christ. And does the bride not frequently stay before the mirror?"[115]

The Eucharist is the center, and everything is directed to its celebration, even the preaching of the Word. The Word never can fully express what the fullness of salvation is. Words are insufficient. It is only attained in the sacrament.[116] "I think about this curious event of the lecture and the address at the table of the Lord's Supper. Scripture is just barely read there. But sacramentally, we stay full well in the abundance of salvation. Therefore, we lay Scripture quickly away."[117]

---

[110]   Van Ruler, 28.
[111]   Van Ruler, *Waarom zou ik naar de kerk gaan?*, 87f.
[112]   Van Ruler, *Waarom zou ik naar de kerk gaan?*, 100.
[113]   Van Ruler, 100.
[114]   Van Ruler, "Apostolisch en apostolair" (1969), in *Blij zijn als kinderen*, 195.
[115]   Van Ruler, *Blij zijn als kinderen*, 194.
[116]   Cf. Hilarius of Poitiers: Real Christian life is celebrating and living the communion with Christ. Theology is only needed for refuting heretics. And its words are always insufficient (*On the Trinity* 2,2).
[117]   Van Ruler, *Vormen van omgang met de Bijbel. Zeven radiovoordrachten* (Amsterdam: Nederlands Bijbelgenootschap/Driebergen: Bijbel Kiosk Vereniging, 1970), 30.

Van Ruler's thought in these publications, and even more his own feedback about what happened in the liturgical worship, give the impression of coming home. He himself uses even the phrase "a kind of conversion."[118] He found a new perspective for theology, and it can even be supposed that he would have found a paradigm for a systematic theology now. In the perspective of the sacrament, salvation and creation are united. It is not a mere word and an internal belief. It is material, bodily, and it fills mind and feelings. The whole human being is involved, and the fullness of the triune God is involved.[119] This is eschatology, indeed. In this testament of Van Ruler, the splendor of eternity and the glory of God's works is expressed.

The consequence can be none other than leaving behind the idea of the intermezzo. How can such a celebration of the eschaton ever be an intermezzo only? This is fulfilled creation—a creation with its whole history: with sin and grace, with atoning love, with dying of the old and resurrection in eternal new life. The last consequence would also be to leave the infralapsarian structure of theology that dominated so much the earlier work of Van Ruler. Not merely creation but also the celebration of salvation—the unity of God and human beings in the embracement and kiss of reconciliation—is the end of all God's works. The transition from the old creation to the new is a transfer. "Baptism is being buried with Christ and being resurrected with Him. We are cut off from the old trunk of Adam and inserted into the new trunk of Christ. We become a member of his body by baptism."[120] The celebration of the Eucharist is anticipation of the eschatological fulfillment. Creation is anticipation of the same.[121] When the Eucharist is concealed eschaton in the remembrance of the death of the Lord, then creation cannot be other than anticipation of the eucharist, directed to the reconciliation in the death of Christ.

In the reception of Van Ruler, the focus is most on his earlier work, especially on his thought on theocracy and his stress on creation. His last publications did not influence the image of Van Ruler's theology

---

[118] Van Ruler, *Waarom zou ik naar de kerk gaan?*, 7.

[119] Certainly such a theology in sacramental perspective by Van Ruler would have a different character from Anglican sacramental theology and the incarnational theology of sacrament of G. van der Leeuw (*Sacramentstheologie* [Nijkerk: Callenbach, 1949]). Sin, judgment, atonement, the cross, and the death of Jesus would have a substantial place. Actually, the absolute necessity of the work of Christ is the most constant element of Van Ruler's theology from its beginning to its end.

[120] Van Ruler, *Waarom zou ik naar de kerk gaan?*, 84.

[121] Van Ruler, 161.

very much. However, if it would be done, a different Van Ruler might arise. Unfortunately, his theological way was broken off suddenly, as was his life. It remains a mystery what the development of his theology would have produced if he would have lived longer, but maybe this is fully in line with Van Ruler: theology is always a torso, and one can and must start always anew.

CHAPTER 9

# Van Ruler's Quest: A Theology of Joy For the Human Being Living in This World

Christo Lombard

During the early days of a two-year research period at the Centre of Theological Inquiry (CTI) in Princeton, 2003-2005, I received a visit from the Rev. Allan Janssen, who had heard about my Van Ruler agenda: that I am working on a project to make the theology of the Dutch theologian, Arnold A. van Ruler (1908-1970) more accessible in the English-speaking world. He himself, it turned out, was busy writing a doctoral dissertation on Van Ruler's theology of the "church offices."[1] I then made available to him whatever I had on Van Ruler, including the extensive bibliography on which I have cooperated with the *Oude Handschriften* (archival) section at Utrecht University.[2] We had several

---

[1] His early contributions on the organization and church order of the Reformed Church in America (*Gathered at Albany*, 1995, and *Constitutional Theology*, 2000, both published in the Historical Series of the Reformed Church in America, by Eerdmans), would now consolidate their theological foundations in his doctoral dissertation, *A Study of A.A. van Ruler's Doctrine of Ecclesiastical Office with Implications for the North American Ecumenical Discussion* (received at the Free University, Amsterdam, in June 2005).

[2] *Inventaris van het archief van Prof. Dr. Arnold Albert van Ruler (1908-1970)*, 1997, ed. E.M. Kempers, Utrecht University Library (with introductory articles by A. De Groot, F.C. Immink and C. Lombard).

animated discussions and started doing some theological things together. I was, for instance, invited to speak on the Belhar Confession in his congregation and even later at the Reformed Church in America's General Synod meeting in June 2004, having been one of the few white members of the Dutch Reformed Mission Church (DRMK) in Southern Africa (which became part of the Uniting Reformed Church in Southern Africa [URCSA] on the basis of the Belhar Confession).[3]

Some time during this period of research in Princeton, I was also invited by Allan to participate in a conference at New Brunswick Theological Seminary in a session focusing on Van Ruler's theology. The text of that presentation in 2004, in which I tried to give an introduction into the main themes in Van Ruler's theology, and of which I handed out a brief summary, was never published. In this contribution to the festschrift for Allan Janssen, who over the years became a good friend, I shall present a more elaborate version of the part dealing with "theology for this world."[4]

Having inspired one another through all these discussions and activities, we then also started a "working group" on Dutch theology at the American Academy of Religion (AAR) in 2004, which resulted in quite a number of exciting and successful sessions. All of these bits and pieces of kingdom work, playfully provoked by God's Spirit, can herewith be celebrated together with Dr. Janssen's many other fine contributions to Reformed theology and church practice. May he joyfully carry on being fruitful in God's vineyard!

This contribution on Van Ruler's theology concentrates on one his one main passions and hopefully explains or illustrates, to some extent, the keen interest Dr. Janssen and I share in Van Ruler's general approach to doing "theology for this world."[5] The focus here is thus

---

[3]    It was with great joy that we could receive the news some time later that the serious study project on the Belhar Confession by the RCA, to which I and Dr. Mitri Raheb from Palestine could contribute at the Synod of 2004, led to acceptance of Belhar as its own Confession by the RCA.

[4]    For the bigger horizon of this work, see my dissertation on Van Ruler, C. Lombard, *Adama, Thora en Dogma: Aardse lewe, Skrif en Dogma in die denke van A.A. van Ruler* (Cape Town: University of the Western Cape, 1996). See also C. Lombard, "The Relevance and Challenge of Van Ruler's Theology," in J. Mouton and B.C. Lategan, eds., *The Relevance of Theology for the 1990s* (Pretoria: HSRC, 1994), 97–124.

[5]    For a concise and very useful summary of Van Ruler's eschatological and Trinitarian, kingdom-oriented theology, see chapter two (40–79) in Janssen's dissertation. In my contribution here, I affirm his analysis, pointing out specifically Van Ruler's accent on the human being, living in this concrete earthly world as the terrain of God's rule.

primarily on theology for "this world," this earthly world (*"adama"*) from which and for which *"adam"* was created. Since Van Ruler's untimely death in 1970, "Van Ruler" has become a code name for a belief shared in many contexts worldwide, and also by leading theologians such as Jürgen Moltmann, that a consistent (non-dualist) reading of Calvin, as provided by Van Ruler, has positive contributions to make in the ongoing ecumenical "theology of the ages."[6]

Like few theologians before (and after) him, Van Ruler brought together, in one comprehensive theological vision, God, humanity, and "this world."[7] Allergic to all dualisms that would try to think of God and humanity, or humanity and world, or God and world, as separated from one another, Van Ruler drew the lines of the so-called Calvinistic horizontalism further through than even Calvin.[8] According to this view, there is but *one* reality, namely, this earthly reality as created, saved, and sanctified by God as God's "kingdom." Van Ruler posited this thesis as a conscious contribution to the ecumenical theology of the worldwide church.

In this essay, we shall briefly indicate how Van Ruler, without blinking or flinching, made adama (a *chiffre* for "humanity and this

[6]    J. Moltmann, "First Round," in Jürgen Moltmann, ed., *How I Have Changed. Reflections on Thirty Years of Theology* (Harrisburg, PA: Trinity Press International, 1998), 15: "After Karl Barth's monumental *Dogmatics*, I thought, there could be no more theology (just as there could be no more philosophy after Hegel), because he had said it all and said it so well. Then in 1957 I got to know the Dutch theologian Arnold van Ruler. He cured me of this apprehension. I discovered the Reformed kingdom of God theology and the Dutch apostolate theology." In his contribution at the centenary celebrations of Van Ruler's life and theology in Amsterdam in 2009, Moltmann said similar things. See "Gestaltwerdung Christi in der Welt. Zur aktuellen Bedeuting der Theologie Arnold van Rulers," in Dirk van Keulen, George Harinck, and Gijsbert van den Brink, eds., *Men moet telkens opnieuw de reuzenzwaai aan de rekstok maken* (Zoetermeer: Boekencentrum, 2009), 113–125.

[7]    On this, researchers with different evaluations of Van Ruler's theology agree. Cf. P.W.J. van Hoof, *Intermezzo. Kontinuïteit en diskontinuïteit in de theologie van A.A. van Ruler: Eschatologie en Kultuur* (Amsterdam: Ton Bolland, published dissertation, 1974), 5, 7, 25 and J.J. Rebel, *Pastoraat in pneumatologisch perspektief: een theologische verantwoording vanuit het denken van A.A. van Ruler* (Kampen: Kok, published dissertation, 1981), 49, quoting Van Hoof in a section called "new attention to the world": "The true Anliegen of Van Ruler can be summarized with the words: God, humanity, and world."

[8]    In the Foreword to his book, *Reformatorishe opmerkingen in de ontmoeting met Rome* (Hilversum/Antwerpen: Paul Brand, 1965), Van Ruler says that in the ecumenical conversation he has tried to free himself from modern Protestant ideas and "to go back to the pristine positions of the Reformation," but also that he was aware of the fact that he had drawn some lines of the original Reformation's position through quite far and could seem somewhat "headstrong" in this respect.

world") the clear focus of his entire theology. It is a well-known fact that Van Ruler shared this contextual, "worldly" focus for theology with, for instance, Dietrich Bonhoeffer and JB Metz.[9] Although we cannot deal with the methodological side of Van Ruler's theology here, it should become evident *where* he, as self-avowed arch-Reformed theologian, has fetched the playfulness—the philosophical, speculative, almost scholastic, qualities—that characterize his theological approach.[10] Frequently, Van Ruler indicated that he, as a child of the Reformation, would like to think through, much further, along the lines of Calvin, in search of the optimal reformed contribution to be made theologically to the "catholica". In one of his last contributions, on "New questions after 15 years", in 1970, he explicitly stated that as a theologian one should never give up on the dream of a "comprehensive, catholic synthesis".[11] He was concerned about the deepest intentions of the Reformation and how we as theologians could extrapolate them meaningfully for today's world.[12] The purpose of this contribution is simply to suggest that his very concrete, Old Testament or Torah-based thinking about the human being and this earth provides the "horizon" for his dogmatic thinking in which adama, Torah, and dogma are intricately intertwined.

Van Ruler sadly died at the age of 62, and for researchers (including ones from other contexts than the Dutch one) who discovered various

---

[9]     See Van Ruler's appreciative and critical reflection of 1966 on Bonhoeffer's theology, "Vragen, door Bonhoeffer aan de orde gesteld," in G.C. Berkouwer and A.S. van der Woude, eds., *Revolte in de theologie* (Nijkerk: G.C. Callenbach, 1968), 116–131. See also *Theologisch werk V* (Nijkerk: G.C. Callenbach, 1972), 171–187. For Metz, see J.B. Metz, *Theology of the World* (London: Burns and Oates, 1969).

[10]    Cf. G.Th. Rothuizen's introduction to G.C. Berkouwer and A.S. van der Woude, eds., *In gesprek met Van Ruler* (Nijkerk: G.F. Callenbach, 1969), 7–13, "If this is called scholastics ..." In the same publication (17) Van Ruler is quoted as saying: "I wish to say—with emphasis—that all thinking that has not reached the level of sophistication of scholastic thinking, is still immature and unfinished."

[11]    Van Ruler, "Nieuwe vragen na vijftien Jaren", in *Theologisch Werk V* (Nijkerk: Callenbach, 1973), 175.

[12]    Various anecdotes from Van Ruler's colleagues about the intentions of his theology convey in a playful way the serious goals he set for the Reformed theology of the future: J.M. Hasselaar, for instance, was convinced that Van Ruler wanted to integrate the Aufklärung into "Calvin." Stating in various ways that theology's task is a Christian philosophy of history (or of revelation), Van Ruler wished to integrate "Kierkegaard" into "Hegel" in order to answer "Sartre." He wanted to promote "theocracy" but in such a way that the Schleiermacher question could receive a proper answer: to understand revelation as "in service" of human progress. Bronkhorst gave another version of the answer owed to Sartre: Van Ruler wanted to combine Hoedemaker's theocracy with Kraemer's apostolate to reverse the existentialism of Sartre! See Lombard, *Adama, Thora, Dogma*, 55–57.

rich perspectives of his thought only after his death, many prominent ecumenical "tasks" for future theological gymnastics stand out. One can think of the *anti-dualist motivation* of his theology: against a "nova creatio" eschatology of Anabaptism (signals of which Van Ruler even suspected Moltmann!); a "deification" of humanity, in Roman Catholic and Neo-Protestant theology; or a "Christologized" humanity, in Barthian theology. One can also think his peculiar choice of *beacons for a theological framework,* such as eschatological, trinitarian, and pre-destinarian; or his *soteriology,* based on the vicarious-incarnational Christological and inclusive-adoptional Pneumatological work of God; or, finally, the *application of his "theocratic" understanding of God's reign.*[13] However, in this contribution, we shall merely investigate his overall theological approach to the root theme of adama. I deliberately include a few longer quotations (my own translations) from the master himself to whet the appetite for those who understand and enjoy theology more as art, as poetry, as wisdom, than as science or dogma per se.[14]

## "Adama" (This World as God's Terrain or "Kingdom")

"Adama" is here used in a playful way to designate the total living world of the human being, Adam, who was created out of the "adama," with the purpose of living a full life on this concrete earth.[15] "Adama" thus includes the human being in its "dustiness" and materiality, its biological and sexual determinedness, but also in its cultural and spiritual dimensions; in all its relations of life on this earth. Researchers are unanimous that this richly "earthy" character of Van Ruler's theological work is the most striking feature thereof, and whether one can fully agree with it or not, this gives a fascinating concreteness and true-to-reality quality to the whole construct of his thinking.[16] Bearing in mind Van Ruler's deepest quest, namely, how his way of doing theology leads to a meaningful, dynamic, and adaptable "theological existence" that can also be relevant in this new century, we now turn our attention to the first of three aspects of his adama-theology.

---

[13] These aspects are dealt with in detail in chapters 4-6 of my dissertation on Van Ruler (Lombard, 1996).

[14] This is also done to remind Allan and other interested theologians that we still have a dream of translating the "full Van Ruler" into English (and hopefully other languages as well).

[15] Cf. Lombard, 89–103.

[16] H.W. de Knijff, "Arnold Albert van Ruler: zijn leven, zijn actualiteit: een interview met J.M. Hasselaar en H.W. de Knijff," in *Areopagus.* 14/2 (1981), 60–72.

"This world as God's kingdom" would be an apt typification of Van Ruler's entire *Anliegen*. What Van Hoof, as Catholic scholar, called Van Ruler's "reformational horizontalism" (i.e., the horizontalizing, secularizing accents, or the attention which "this world as the only human world" receives in Van Ruler's theology) can probably be seen as the most typical characteristic of his thinking.[17] For Van Ruler, the Reformation has been—and remains to be—a unique event in the historical and politico-religious annals of "Christian Europe," and from there into the *oecumene*, a political event that led to the birth of a new type of human being with a new experience of reality: the type of human that experiences that his or her life is lived in total dependence of God, but horizontally, secularly, in front of God's countenance (*coram Deo*), in full responsibility for this one, visible, and tangible reality, with an earthly instead of a heavenly expectation.[18]

According to Van Ruler, the statement that there is but *one* reality must be maintained absolutely when we wish to think strictly and consistently eschatologically.[19] There is only one terrain for God's kingdom: this visible, material, and relative world in which we live.[20]

---

[17] See Van Hoof, *Intermezzo*, 1974, 27–35, and Rebel, *Pastoraat*, 1981, 49–64. Cf also A.N. Hendriks, *Kerk en ambt in de theologie van A.A. van Ruler* (Amsterdam: Buijten en Schipperheijn, dissertation, 1977), 48–56; B.J. Engelbrecht, *Ter wille van hierdie wêreld. Politiek en Christelike heilsbelewing in Suid-Afrika* (Cape Town: Tafelberg, 1982), with the title meaning: "For the Sake of This World."

[18] Cf. e.g. Van Ruler, *Religie en politiek* (Nijkerk: G.F. Callenbach, 1945), 213; Van Ruler, *De vervulling van de wet* (Nijkerk: G.F. Callenbach, dissertation, 1947), 58; Van Ruler, *Visie en vaart* (Amsterdam: Holland Uitgeversmaatschappij, 1947), 9, 12–15; Van Ruler, *Na 100 jaar kromstaf. Onze houding tegenover Rome* (The Hague: Voorhoeve, 1953), 15–18. Van Ruler was convinced that this "idealized" version was the only antidote to the threat of "modernism" and "secularism," but then it had to be taken seriously and not watered down. To really think anthropocentrically we have to look at humanity through the eyes of God and not at God through the eyes of humanity.

[19] Van Ruler, *Vervulling van de wet*, 27; Van Ruler, *Heb moed voor de wereld* (Nijkerk: G.F. Callenbach, 1953), 34; Van Ruler, *Religie en politiek*, 166, 295; Van Ruler, "De kern van de zaak is: vreugde!", *AVRO-bulletin* (December 20, 1964); also in *Blij zijn als kinderen*, (Kampen: Kok, 1972), 131–132.

[20] On "this life" or "natural life," cf. Van Ruler 1960, "De waardering van het aardse leven" in *Wending*, 15/2 (1960), 94–109; also in Van Ruler, *Theologisch Werk V* (Nijkerk: G.F. Callenbach, 1972), 19–31; Van Ruler, 1968, "De kern van de zaak: hoe waardeert men de stof?" *Wapenveld*, 18/1 (1968), 2–7; also in *Theologisch Werk* V, 9–18. On the "relativity" of life, cf. Van Ruler, *Religie en politiek*, 399: "The a.b.c. and the x.y.z. of all theocratic wisdom is that we should take the relative aspects of life seriously. Theocracy moves in relativity and knows that it will never overcome this relativity, or be able to overcome it, or be allowed to overcome it, and also should not be wishing to overcome it."

The real secret that theology has to contemplate is the mystery that this earth truly is God's kingdom.[21] This world is God's real work of art.[22] All dogmatic loci serve one purpose: to prevent a flight from this one good creation, God's world, and God's kingdom:

> Thus we in the Christian faith are prevented from all sides— through the Trinity, the creation, the predestination, the apostolate, the incarnation and the eschaton—from walking out of this earthly life. We are surrounded. We are being pushed back in the present. Here and here alone is our place. And, when we think through all points in a Christian way, this has nothing suffocating about it. Even the being together with the other is in no way to be seen as a hell, at least not when lived through in the *agape*. Christianity teaches us to live with a limitless positivity: only *Weltbejahung* and—there lies the *Pudel's Kern!*—only self-affirmation, without reserve and without qualification. [23]

Systematic theology, as it were, stands watch at the portals of reality to exorcise any lot-affirming resignation and to urge the full affirmation of common, profane, secular life: of the world as "pure world."[24] Theology should take seriously this principled earthiness of our self-understanding.[25] For Van Ruler, there is simply no other, higher world next to our empirical world, in which our problems can be solved or in which the kingdom of God can be erected.[26] He is totally averse to any dualism between "world" and "kingdom."[27] The problem he sees with all dualistic approaches is that they simply cannot accept that "dust" (adama)—the material basis—of "this world" has been posited

[21]  Cf. Van Ruler, *Reformatorische opmerkingen in de ontmoeting met Rome* (Hilversum/Antwerpen: Paul Brand, 1965), 145-6: "The real mystery is this world as kingdom of God. In fact, this is the *pleróma* of the *mysterion*." See also Van Ruler, *Vervulling van de wet*, 42; Van Ruler, *Waarom zou ik naar de kerk gaan?* (Nijkerk: G.F. Callenbach, 1970), 160.

[22]  Van Ruler, *Vervulling van de wet*, 27; Van Ruler, 1953, *Heb moed voor de wereld*, 151.

[23]  Van Ruler, *Waardering van het aardse leven*, 27.

[24]  Van Ruler, *Religie en politiek*, 28; Van Ruler *Vervulling van de wet*, 78; Van Ruler, *Sta op tot de* vreugde (Nijkerk: G.F. Callenbach, 1947), 143; Van Ruler, *Waardering van het aardse leven*, 24-27.

[25]  Van Ruler, *Droom en gestalte* (Amsterdam: Holland Uitgeversmaatschappij, 1947), 197; Van Ruler, "Grenzen van de eschatologisering," *Vox Theologica*, 37/4 (July 1967), 167-185. This seminal piece is also in *Theologisch Werk IV* (Nijkerk: G.F. Callenbach, 1972), 102-118; cf. also G.C. Berkouwer, "Over de theologie van A.A. van Ruler," *Gereformeerd Weekblad*, 26/43 (1971), 298.

[26]  Van Ruler, *Vervulling van de wet*, 35; Van Ruler, *Visie en vaart*, 243, 360.

[27]  Van Ruler, *Vervulling van de wet*, 36-38.

by God, the creator, with a *valde bonum*, and that this is to be the crucial question for all theology (talk about God): "How do we evaluate the 'stuff'?"[28]

In a very original essay on "Appreciation of the Earthly Life," Van Ruler probes deeper into this question and analyses the most important components of our earthly existence: *materiality* that has to be appreciated equally to spirituality; *corporality* which is protected by the article on the resurrection of the body from any degradation; *individuality*, which also means: limitation, uniqueness, and even loneliness; *sexuality* ("Adult persons do not play around with a top ["*priktol*"] any more, but when they do not fool around in the sexual aspects of married life, they are almost dead."); *temporality*, which means that existence has a beginning and an end, with the passion and strivings of a limited life in between; *communality*, which also means the depersonalized being of "*das man,*" in economics, politics, social life; the *historical* or *genealogical* realities that relativize the individual to a moment in the chain of the generations.[29]

Over against all the other possible answers on the question how one should evaluate this concrete, earthly existence (e.g., that it is [1] the antipode of real being, namely, "non-being"; [2] an appearance, an imagination, an infatuation; [3] a veil over the real being; [4] an image, shadow, or gleam of the true and eternal being; [5] a punishment for pre-existent but fallen spirits; [6] a purification toward the true and essential life; [7] an exercise or preparation in view of eternal life—all seemingly viable philosophies of which people from east and west avail themselves to make sense out of "this life"), Van Ruler explores this option:

> The eighth possibility is this: earthly life as the *true and only life*. This is truly what God is about. This is also what has been given and designated to us. From time to time this penetrates to our mind. Then we say: This is it! We live but this once! Life can be hard. We can also waste our chances. It can also be surprising. Unfathomable it will remain anyway. However, whichever way we experience it, this earthly life—this is what it is about; I simply cannot think a way around this. I also cannot live a way through it. I can simply accept and live this life.[30]

---

28    For a detailed analysis of what this question entails, cf. Van Ruler, *Hoe waardeert men de stof?*, 1968, 9–18.
29    Van Ruler, *Waardering van het aardse leven*, 19–22.
30    Van Ruler, 22–23.

This life is not necessary, but it is good. This world is not divine, also not demonic; it is no emanation out of God's being, but it has been willed and posited by God; it is thus fully real and is no shadow performance; it is part of a small, relative history in a corner of the universe, but it is fully historical; this is where the true human history takes place; it is underlined by the fact that God incarnated Godself in this history, to save the world so that this world—our one and only world—should be carried through to the eschaton.[31]

In his exposition of what he calls Van Ruler's "cultural theology," Van Hoof emphasizes that Van Ruler's accent on this world, right through into the eschaton, is aimed at the elimination of all false dualisms, i.e., dualisms that start off from two opposed intra-mundane realities. Any dualism that could possibly jeopardize the mystery of this world as terrain of God's reign must be avoided and fought theologically: a spatial or ontological dualism of another world next to or above this world; a dualism of time where the eschaton represents another time—a pure futurism—over against our time; or an existential dualism in which human existence is dissected between time and eternity.[32]

Van Ruler's accent on the acceptance of this *one reality* is very deliberate in order to explain that humanity's destination (*telos*) is not in salvation as such, or in the covenant, or even in God, but solely in humanity's (i.e., the human being's) own saved existence in front of God, over against God.[33] The kingdom of God—this world that is being saved and will be fully saved—is bigger and more comprehensive than the grace of God in Christ, the covenant, the church, special revelation, or the *summum bonum* of human thinking.[34]

---

[31]  Van Ruler, 24–27.

[32]  According to Van Hoof, *Intermezzo*, 60–61, Van Ruler placed himself outside of the tradition within Calvinism where a distinction is made between heavenly and earthly, or spiritual and secular realities. He shares Metz' war against dualism (109–111). He allows the "competition" between God and humanity to spend itself in Christology, so that in Pneumatology a synthesis, incorporation and cooperation becomes possible again (99, 128–129, 228, 268, 286). It is important, however, to note that Van Ruler does indeed distinguish *legitimate and necessary dualities* such as Creator-creature, revelation-existence, salvation-world, mediator-humanity, Spirit-matter, and church-state, and *false dualisms* such as interior-exterior, material-spiritual, body-soul, cosmos-ethos, heavenly-earthly (see Van Ruler, *Religie en politiek*, 308–309).

[33]  Van Ruler, *Heb moed voor de wereld*, 33: "All future expectation in the Bible is focused on this: not that we 'see' God, but that we—blessed by God's glory —'inhabit' this earth." Cf. also Van Ruler, *Reformatorische opmerkingen*, 26.

[34]  Cf. Van Ruler, 1968, "Bijbelse toekomstverwachting en aards perspektief," 1968, as published in *Theologisch Werk II* (Nijkerk: G.F. Callenbach, 1971), 220–240, for

Hendriks is correct in arguing that, from Van Ruler's eschatological kingdom-perspective, the relationship between God and the
world forms the central theme and question around which the biblical
knowledge of God turns.[35] Thinking and speaking as Christians, we
do not get rid of this world, not even in eternity.[36] The eschaton is
the created reality in its saved state.[37] The eschaton is, per definition,
nothing else than the salvation, sanctification, and glorification of the
whole earthly, historical, and communal human reality.[38]

Such an eschatological approach has certain consequences
for Van Ruler's entire dogmatic work. The idea of God's kingdom or
rule has its roots in the concept of God itself, so that these two, God
and kingdom, cannot be separated or abstracted from one another.[39]
The handling of the God concept as a separate *locus de Deo* is an
impossibility in Van Ruler's theology. Such an approach to God falls

---

a detailed development of this theme. In Van Ruler's theology, humanity finds its
goal and destiny in that this humanity is restored in God's kingdom, where the
"social ideal" of *shalom* is realized. God's purpose with humanity thus is more
comprehensive than the covenant [see Van Ruler, *Bijbelse toekomstverwachting*,
227, and Van Ruler, "Gerechtigheid en rechtvaardigheid," 1969, as published in
*Theologisch Werk IV*, 43]. It is also more than salvation or particular revelation or
grace [Van Ruler, "Methode en mogelijkheden van de dogmatiek," in *Theologisch
Werk I*, (Nijkerk: G.F. Callenbach, 1969), 60–61; Van Ruler, *Theologie van het apostolaat*
(Nijkwerk: G.F. Callenbach, 1953), 36]; it is more than the church [Van Ruler,
*Theologie van het* apostolaat, 24; Van Ruler, *Het apostolaat der kerk en het ontwerp-
kerkorde* (Nijkerk: G.F. Callenbach, 1948), 55,74]; it is more than ethics (Van Ruler,
*Vervulling van de* wet, 84); more than theology [Van Ruler, *Dwaasheden in het leven II*
(Nijkerk: G.F. Callenbach, 1966), 122]; yes, even more than Christ and the Spirit
(Van Ruler, "De betekenis van de mozaïsche wet," 1947, *Theologisch Werk* I, 137).
God's overall goal and purpose is God's kingdom, coming on this earth (Van Ruler,
1969, Gerechtigheid en rechtvaardigheid, 44).

35    Hendriks, *Kerk en ambt in de theologie van Van Ruler*, 48. Cf. Van Ruler, *Vervulling van
de* wet, 27: "To really think from the perspective of God's kingdom, means that we
absolutely persist with this assertion that there is only one reality, viz. this visible,
tangible reality in which we stand, and that everything God does is completely and
exclusively focused on this reality."

36    Van Ruler, "De mens, de zin van de geschiedenis," 1963, published in *Theologisch
Werk* VI (Nijkerk: G.F. Callenbach, 1973), 79.

37    Van Ruler, *Reformatorische opmerkingen*, 225.

38    Van Ruler, *Hoe waardeert men de stof?*, 17.

39    Van Ruler, *Vervulling van de wet* (my translation), 38: "We cannot even distinguish this
world from its origin; since she does not have an 'origin'; she is out of 'nothing.' And
in and onto this world God performs his work, omnipotently. He is her Lord. That
is why we can also not distinguish the world and God ontologically-dualistically.
We can simply let the world in fact be posited by God and allow God to act in and
with her. On the 'relationship' of God and world we can get no overview. Thus the
idea of the kingdom has its deepest roots in the idea of God.

prey either to platonic idealism or to ontological speculation, both of which in essence, in his perspective, are heathen options. Over against the idealistic or the ontological concept of God and the accompanying *Seinsverständnis* (total construct of reality), Van Ruler posits his own eschatological-theocratic view of reality, which operates on at least three levels: as structure of theological thinking about any matter; as political structuring of reality, by both the church and the state; and as a comprehensive Christian view of life—a biblical antidote for all sorts of philosophical-heathen Seinsverständnis.[40] Thus, Van Ruler chooses to speak about God only in God's relations to humanity as God's partner and about the world as God's world, and this he does in terms of the dynamic terms of God's eschatological reign over his creation.[41] Over against "autonomous man" who approaches reality, through his rigid ontological mindset, principally in a static way, we have the living God who constantly does brand new things (*"gloednieuwe dinge"*),[42] who is unthinkable, unimaginable, and incomprehensible, in principle.[43] This God can possibly be approached through the mythical images of dogmatic faith symbols[44] but without penetrating to an understanding that rests on the foundation of "evidence."[45]

All dogmatic loci, in Van Ruler's thinking at least, connive and work together to keep God, humanity, and world together for time and eternity. Right through his vast oeuvre, and especially in his preaching, this characteristic *Weltoffenheit* plays through—this intense affirmation and acceptance of life, as created and carried by God's grace and faithfulness.[46]

---

[40] Note the central place Van Ruler himself gives to the notion of a "theocratic concept of reality," in his *Religie en politiek*, 153–170.

[41] Van Ruler, *Vertrouw en geniet! Zestien toespraken over Jesus Christus en de wereld* (The Hague: J.N. Voorhoeve, 1955), 85; Van Ruler, 1945, *Religie en politiek*, 390–392.

[42] Van Ruler, *Vervulling van de wet*, 189; Van Ruler, *Visie en vaart*, 34.

[43] Van Ruler, *Visie en vaart*, 206; Van Ruler, *Religie en* politiek, 29; Van Ruler, "De aard van onze kennis van God," 1958, published in *Theologisch Werk* VI, 63; Van Ruler, *Ik geloof* (Nijkerk: G.F. Callenbach, 1968), 17.

[44] Van Ruler, "Het visoen van de Reformatie" (lecture delivered at Hilversum and other places, 1949–1955); Van Ruler, "Grenzen van de eschatologisering," in *Vox Theologica*, 37/4, (1967), 177 (also as an article in *Theologisch Werk* IV, 102–118).

[45] Van Ruler, *De aard van onze kennis van God*; cf. Van Ruler, *Het visioen van de Reformatie*.

[46] Van Ruler, "Die Weltoffenheit des Christlichen Glaubens," (Hamburg and Göttingen, 1956), a remarkable lecture, and never published. Cf. further Van Ruler, "De waardering van het aardse leven," a lecture delivered in various places and

### God's Purpose: Human Partners (in Creation and History)

In his study on the concept of "religion" in both Schleiermacher and Van Ruler, Paul Fries has clearly indicated, as also suggested by Hasselaar, that in Van Ruler's thinking, the Schleiermacher-*Frage*, as to the value and worth of religion for our humanity, has been central.[47] Fries concludes:

> Consciousness, conscience, reason, ethos, ethic, culture, freedom, autonomy, tolerance, etc., all find their human content and meaning in Christian theocracy. Thus Van Ruler is indeed concerned with the issues of our time, including that one with which this study is concerned, i.e., the true humanity. Rejecting the solution to this problem offered by many thinkers in our time, that religion inhibits the true humanity, Van Ruler, with Friedrich Schleiermacher, contends that (true) religion is the *conditio sine qua non* for the truly human existence. In the eschaton the song of praise to God will be sung without the accompaniment of religion; until that time the chorus glorifying God will be led by its great and many-voiced orchestra.[48]

It is easy to demonstrate that Van Ruler's theological work is fraught with reflection on aspects of true humanity, such as quoted above, "consciousness, conscience, reason, ethos, ethic, culture, freedom, autonomy, tolerance, etc." This focus on the essentials of what it means to be "human" is clearly illustrated in captions he had given to talks or theological reflections throughout his career: *The Idea of Freedom* (1945)[49]; *Social Justice and Its Biblical Backgrounds* (1946)[50]; *Politics, a Holy Matter* (1946)[51]; *For What Are We Living?* (sermon from 1949)[52];

---

published in *Wending*, 15/2, April 1960, 94–109 [also in *Theologisch Werk V*(Nijkerk: G.F. Callenbach, 1972), 19–31].

[47]   For his analysis of Van Ruler, cf. his chapter: "Van Ruler on the Christian religion and the true humanity," Paul Fries, *Religion and the Hope for a Truly Human Existence: An Inquiry into the Theology of F.D.E. Schlieremacher and A.A. van Ruler with Questions for America* (Utrecht: Rijksuniversieit, dissertation, 1979), 123–179.

[48]   Fries, *Religion and the Hope for a Truly Human Existence*, 165–166.

[49]   Van Ruler, "De vrijheidsgedachte", radio talk, December 3, 1945, in *Visie en Vaart* (Amsterdam: Holland Uitgeversmaatschappij, 1947), 12-15.

[50]   Van Ruler, "Het sociale recht en zijn Bijbelse achtergrond", radio talk on VARA, February 27, 1947, in *Visie en Vaart* (Amsterdam: Holland Uitgeversmaatschappij, 1947), 16-19.

[51]   Van Ruler, "Politiek is een heilige zaak", paper at a meeting of the Protestant Union (PU), April 25, 1946, published as a brochure by PU.

[52]   Van Ruler, "Waarvoor leven wij?", sermon on Mark 2:27, January 19, 1949, in *Verhuld*

*Religion as Opium for the People?* (sermon from 1953)[53]; *Dogmatic and Critical: An Antithesis?* (1955)[54]; *Biblical and Modern Existentialism* (sermon from 1955)[55]; *The Conscience, The Ethical as Fraction, Not as Firmament*, and *Problems in the Idea of Tolerance* (all from 1956)[56]; *Knowledge of God as the Destiny of Humanity* (sermon from 1957)[57]; *Appreciation for Reason* (1958)[58]; *The Worth of Culture in View of Christian Faith* and *Inhuman Elements in the Gospel* (1960)[59]; *What Has Happened to Humanity?* (1961)[60]; *Praise Song for Virtue* (1962)[61]; *Faith Also Comes after Reason* (1963)[62]; *Definitive Realization of Reality* (sermon from 1964)[63]; *Theocracy and Tolerance* (1966)[64]; *Questions Put Forward by Bonhoeffer* (1966)[65], *Carpe Diem!*, *Do Not Exclude Reason*, and *The Ethical Deed in the Absurd Existence* (sermons from 1966)[66]; *Gospel*

---

*Bestaan* (Nijkerk: Callenbach, 1949), 112-114.

53 Van Ruler, "Godsdienst als opium voor de mens?", sermon on Zechariah 13:5, October 20, 1952, in *Heb moed voor de wereld* (Nijkerk: Callenbach, 1953), 128-131.

54 Van Ruler, "Dogmatisch en kritiisch – een tegenstelling?", opening lecture at Utrecht University, October 5,1955, in *Theologisch Werk IV*, (Nijkerk: Callenbach, 1972), 30-39.

55 Van Ruler, "Bijbels en modern existentialisme", talk in Rotterdam Cantine, March 20, 1955.

56 Van Ruler, "Het geweten", talk at Nederlandse Gesprek Centrum, March 1956 (brochure); "Het zedelijke als fractie, niet als gesternte", article in *Elzeviers Weekblad*, July 7, 1956; "Vragen rondom de verdraagzaamheid", talk at Wednesday evening club, October 10, 1956

57 Van Ruler, "De goddelijke kennis is de bestemming van de mens", sermon on I Cor. 13:12b, in *De meeste van deze is de liefde* (Den Haag: J.N. Voorhoeve, 1957), 163-169. (also in English: *The greatest of these is love* (Grand Rapids MI: Eerdmans, 1958), 103-107).

58 Van Ruler, "De waardering van de rede", four radio talks (February 3, 10, 17 and 24, 1958), in *Theologisch Werk IV* (Nijkerk: Callenbach, 1972), 9-29.

59 Van Ruler, "Het inhumane in het evangelie", article in *Utrechts Nieuwsblad*, November 12, 1960; also in *Blij zijn als kinderen* (Kampen: Kok, 1972), 63-65.

60 Van Ruler, "Wat is er met de mens gebeurd?", lecture in the Aula, Utrecht University, October 4, 1961 (published in *Bezinning*, 17/2, February 1962).

61 Van Ruler, "Loflied op de deugd", article in *Utrechts Nieuwsblad*, August 11, 1962 (also in *Blij zijn als kinderen* (Kampen: Kok, 1972), 44-46.).

62 Van Ruler, "Her geloof komt ook ná de rede", article in *Utrechts Nieuwsblad*, 15 June 1963 (also in *Blij zijn als kinderen* (Kampen: Kok, 1972), 104-106).

63 Van Ruler, "Het definitiewe bezef van realiteit", meditation on I Cor. 15, in *De dood wordt overwonnen* (Nijkerk: Callenbach, 1964), 43-46.

64 Van Ruler, "Theocratie en tolerantie", in *Vrijheid, horizon der geschiedenis*, eds. W. Nauta and J Sperna Weiland (Nijkerk: Callenbach, 1966), 121-135 (also in *Theologisch Werk III*, (Nijkerk: Callenbach, 1971), 164-177).

65 Van Ruler, "Vragen, door Bonhoeffer aan de orde gesteld", radio talks on NCRV, December 5, 12 and 19, 1966 (in *Theologisch Werk V* (Nijkerk: Callenbach, 1972), 171-187).

66 Van Ruler, "Pluk de dag!" (meditation on Ecclesiastes 5:17); Schakel de rede niet uit!" (meditation on Ecclesiastes 10:10), and "De ethische daad in het absurd

*and Ideology* (1968)[67]; *Democratizing the Factor of the Will* (1969).[68] The list can continue.

It is also remarkable to note how many articles and talks through which Van Ruler engaged in conversation with the Humanist tradition in Holland, especially with the *"Humanistisch Verbond."*[69] In all the articles in which Van Ruler reflects on the accents needed for a realistic Christian anthropology, the central question always remains regarding the purpose and destiny of true humanity.[70]

So, what is the true destiny of the human being, according to Van Ruler? The answer to this question had been wrestled from serious grapplings with various theological answers, given in the course of the Christian tradition by Rome, Neo-Protestantism, Anabaptism, and Barthian theology.[71]

Over against the vision of Rome and, ironically enough, Neo-Protestantism, who teach that that our humanity is determined through incarnation, through the unification of the "godly" and the "human," through which it becomes possible for the human to be "elevated" out of the earthly existence to participate in the Trinitarian life of God; over

---

bestaan" (meditation on Ecclesiastes 11:1), all taken up in *Dwaasheden in het leven* (Nijkerk: Callenbach, 1966) (radio talks on AVRO radio from 1966), Vol. 1:88-91; Vol. 2:39-42 and Vol. 2:75-79.

[67] Van Ruler, "Is het evangelie een ideologie?", lecture at the Faculty of Theology, Leiden, December 18, 1968; published as "Evangelie en ideologie", in *Theologisch Werk II* (Nijkerk: Callenbach, 1971), 56-77.

[68] Van Ruler, "De democratisering en de wilsfactor", arrticle in *Leeuwarder Courant*, August 2, 1969, p. 2.

[69] Cf. e.g. Van Ruler, "De idee der humaniteit in de opvoeding," (lecture in Esplanade, Utrecht, 1947); Van Ruler, "Christendom en Humanisme," (lecture in Hoogeveen, 1948); Van Ruler, *De overheid in Nederland en het* humanisme (The Hague: Keulen, 1954), also in *Theologisch werk III* (Nijkerk: G.F. Callenbach, 1971), 191-207; Van Ruler, "Christendom en humanisme," (lecture in Utrecht and surroundings, 1959–1961).

[70] Van Ruler, "Calvijns betekenis voor West-Europa" (lecture, 1959), also published in *Blij zijn als kinderen*, 1972, 223-226; Van Ruler, "Das Leben und das Werk Calvins" in *Calvin-Studien 1959*, edd J. Moltmann, Neukirchener: Verlag, 1960), 84-94.

[71] The anti-dualistic motives that play along in Van Ruler's opposition to these answers and profoundly determining the tone and focus of his theology have been developed with some consistency as illustrated by numerous altercations with these other options, cf. Van Ruler, *Gestaltwerdung Christi in der welt* (Neukirchen: Verlag der Erziehungsvereins, 1956), 32-34 [this piece, which deeply influenced Moltmann, is taken up in *Calvinist Trinitarianism and Theocentric Politics* (editor and translator John Bolt, Lewiston: The Edwin Mellen Press, 1989), 105-148]; Van Ruler, "De mens, de zin van de geschiedenis," 1963 (published in *Theologisch werk* VI, 67-84. See also "Ultra-Gereformeerd en vrijzinnig" in *Theologish werk III* (Nijkerk: G.F. Callenbach, 1971), 141-144.

against the Anabaptist doctrine of a totally new creation, according to
which the "old human being" (i.e., the old creation) can be tossed away
like an old pair of shoes; and over against Barth and his school, who
teach that the purpose and meaning of human history lies in Christ
alone and has indeed already been realized through Christ's life—thus
in contrast to these strong traditions that somehow live alongside one
another (and also within the Protestant tradition), Van Ruler offers his
own answer:

> The purpose of creation is that the creature finds joy in itself
> before God and as such exists as liturgical service of God. Through
> salvation the Lord God had to make an enormous detour. This is
> because of sin. For that the Mediator had to come. The sinner
> must learn to live from grace. That will never happen without
> the work of the Holy Spirit. To do this work, the Spirit had to be
> poured out and had to dwell in. All of that is an enormous process.
> It is more than anything else a process of shattering; shattering of
> God in death and in the offer (sacrifice), and shattering of the
> human in the acknowledgement and confession, and even more,
> in the letting go, of the guilt.
>
> For all of this the whole apparatus of Israel, its Messiah,
> and the church, was necessary. But the purpose of it all does
> not lie in the fact that the sinner must be brought to his or her
> knees, and that God grants him or her God's grace. That, indeed,
> is necessary. There is no other way. This also belongs essentially
> to the true spiritual life. It is even the deepest point thereof. But
> it is not the purpose. The purpose is that creation is again taken
> from the abyss of lostness, is saved in order to again be creation,
> to again exist before God's Countenance, as what it had been
> intended, which is God's creature. Salvation of the creature is
> more important than the Savior. That which is being saved, to
> truly *be* itself again, is more important than salvation. That it can
> exist again, as creature before God, is more important than that
> it is being saved.
>
> The original destiny is also the eventual destiny. It exists
> therein that existence rejoices in itself before God's Countenance,
> serving God with its praises. The experience of the totality of
> the reality of the world, in nature and history, as kingdom of
> God, belongs even more essentially to true spirituality than the
> experience of sin and grace. True spiritual life exists in the natural
> life, experienced in the correct way, that is: through sin and grace,

through death and eternal life, it experiences itself as (saved) creatureliness.[72]

In a concise German summary of the main traits of his theology of means and ends, *Gestaltwerdung Christi in der welt* (*The Configuration of Christ in the World*), Van Ruler uses the same argument of proto-eschatological *purpose* and trinitarian *means*, to emphasize that God is truly interested in the "naked existence" of all "things" created and especially in the true humanity of the human being:

> Protologically and eschatologically, everything is then oriented to the naked existence of things as such before God, without the wrapping of sin, and without the wrapping of Christ. The creation is what it is all about. Or, alternatively, the kingdom of glory is what it is all about. One could also say that it is humanity that is the focus. Then it is also true that the whole of Christianizing is oriented to this goal. The origin of Christianizing is in the middle, in the particular form of God in Christ. Its ultimate goal, however, is to be found in the protological and eschatological purpose of God; not in Immanuel, in God with us, but in humanity, in human beings before God.[73]

Van Ruler's argument about God's purpose with the world and humanity, which remains the same in spite of the additional—and severe—problem of sin, is summarized succinctly in his polemical essay on "Humanity, the Meaning of History."[74] He begins by emphasizing why the meaning of history is so important to Christians, endeavoring *inter alia* to do the following: to prevent the absurd situation that, in the end, it may only be the communists who cling to the idea of "salvation" in history; to ensure that the so-called Christian West, which could always accompany the material benefits it sent out into the world with some spiritual value as well, does not run dry on the spiritual side of its "colonialism"; to remain true to the real content

---

[72]  Van Ruler, "Ultra-Gereformeerd en vrijzinnig," *Theologisch werk* III, 142–143.
[73]  In the text above, I use the dynamic translation in Van Ruler 1989: 131–132, a book in which John Bolt presents eight core articles from Van Ruler's ouevre in English: J. Bolt, ed. and trans., *Calvinist Trinitarianism and Theocentric Politics: Essays Toward a Public Theology by Arnold A. van Ruler* (Lewiston: Edwin Mellen Press, 1989).
[74]  Van Ruler, "De mens, de zin van de geschiedenis," 1963 in *Theologisch werk* VI, 67–84, directed against the Roman Catholic *elevatio* idea, the Anabaptist concept of *nova creatio*, and specifically the Barthian *Christomonistic* anthropology, as represented in Berkhof's book, *Christus, de zin der geschiedenis*.

and message of the Bible, which is that human history is carried by God toward a meaningful end; and, lastly, to preserve the pure humanity, as intended by God—disentangled from the ideological connections with the universe, nature, reason, and the state—as an anthropological "given."[75]

After dealing with other, alternative approaches to a Christian anthropology, Van Ruler returns to what he sees as the core question: "What did God have in mind with creation?" or, "What is the unique meaning of creation, next to salvation?"[76]Fundamentally, one should answer this question, according to my insight, as follows: the meaning of the fact, that we are here, lies in this: to be here! We should think anthropocentrically. The human being stands in the centre, namely of the attention of God. That is more important than that God is there, in the sight of human beings, and that God is in the center of human attention. That the human being is there, before God, is therefore also more fundamental than that God is the God of human beings. The covenant of works is in this sense more fundamental than the covenant of grace.

> What is the meaning of creation? The answer is: that we are there! That we are there in the proper way! That we are there as a community of people, together with the whole created reality! That we are there consciously, articulated, the inside turned out. Speaking and answering! That we are there, transforming, thus eccentric, in distantiation, applying, forming! That we are there singing praises! In other words: the meaning of creatureliness lies in the ethical, the social, the reflexive, the verbal, the cultural and the liturgical.[77]

Van Ruler closes this article on the human being as the meaning of history with eschatological and predestinarian accents. What needs more attention here, in the context of his adama-analysis, is his view on God as the God of history.[78] Amidst his immensely positive assessment

---

[75]  Van Ruler, "De mens, de zin der geschiedenis," 68–70.
[76]  Van Ruler, "De mens, de zin der geschiedenis", from *Theologisch Werk VI,* 1973, 76. Van Ruler put these questions as follows in Dutch: "En de grote vraag blijft om antwoord reopen: wat had God voor met de schepping? Welke is de eigen zin van de schlepping naast de verlossing?"
[77]  Van Ruler, 76–77.
[78]  For this cf. Van Ruler, "Historische kultuurvorming," 1944 (an analysis of the philosophy of history of Ernst Troeltsch), in *Geschiedenis* (Assen: Van Gorcum and

of the humanity of the human being, as the meaning and purpose of history, also and foremostly in God's own view, Van Ruler never hides or minimizes the chaotic seriousness of evil as the most important spoilsport in the historical process.[79] He even asks whether it is possible to think consistently about evil without thinking of the possibility that God, as the main character in history, sometimes participates in making things chaotic; that God creates chaos and plays with it, as with the Leviathan—leaving aside humanity's role in the workings of evil for a moment![80]

As far as human guilt is concerned[81]: this historical problem can only be dealt with historically through God's concrete act of love, through the divinity and historicity of Jesus Christ. Through the cross— in itself the biggest chaos—the order of God's reconciliation is being created in the world. And in this order of love, God keeps us alive in the chaos of the world:

> In Gethsemane and on Golgotha Jesus positively affirms God's judgement, and thus God's world, against which the judgements are directed, thus also the chaos. He accepts, tolerates, works through the chaos, and so overcomes it. The resurrection is bodily. The body shows the signs of the cross. Thus it is taken up in eternity ... Thus, even in love, from the perspective of the gospel of the cross and through the Spirit, we do not really rise above the chaotic. We also do not get rid of it. As long as we still want to do that: to rise above it and get rid of it – we still commit treason against the world. A person of God can really only love the world. The world as it is. This world he or she can simply only love. And love means: saying yes, accept, affirm, working with it, reconciling, sanctifying, keeping the expectation, feeding a silent but immeasurable joy. Through all of this we simply move deeper

---

Comp), 200–221; Van Ruler, "Het koninkrijk Gods en de geschiedenis" (inaugural lecture, Nijkerk: G.F. Callenbach, 1947); this seminal piece is also republished in Van Ruler, *Verwachting en voltooiing* (Nijkerk: G.F. Callenbach, 1978), 29–42; see further Van Ruler, "Bijbelse toekomstverwachting en aards perspectief" (lecture, 1968), published in *Theolgisch werk* II, 1971, 220–240.

[79]  See in this regard his provocative article on "God en de chaos," delivered at various occasions in 1958 and 1959, eventually also published in *Theologisch werk* V, 32–45.

[80]  Van Ruler, 33–34.

[81]  It is important to note that Van Ruler pictures the "Fall" much the same as Westermann (in *Creation*, Minneapolis: Fortress Press, 1974), 108–112: i.e., that the Fall is not to be seen only as the "background" of the biblical story of redemption but is inherently part of it, taken up in the inner plot of the unfolding of the drama.

into the chaotic. ...

Perhaps we shall never really understand this fully, neither with our reason, nor with our heart. But this is what we *are*. We are the chaos. We are the being. We are the play of God. Everything depends on this: not merely the courage to be, but even more so the willingness to play along. May I have a dance with you? God asks from us, and the essence of our being depends on whether we are willing to accept this proposal. But being as this divine play, as play of divine love, is a trans-illumination of being, also of the chaos in being, which may even satisfy and gladden our reason and our heart.[82]

## True Humanity: Use *and* Enjoyment of God's Dynamic Creation

Behind Van Ruler's positive anthropology and his theology of joy, we thus find a playing God, a God who his creation there not only to be used but also to be enjoyed.[83] The play of God's children in and with the world is the only legitimate way of dealing with the "stuff" of creation.[84] God left the play of history to us; God does the actual work of history himself.[85] The whole of reality is in a profound sense to be experienced as a play: "The last reality is not the seriousness. That is deadly. The ultimate is: laugh, jest, dance and song, art and joy, contentment and freedom. The ultimate, ultimate reality is God's absolute freedom."[86]

Life is not only a burden and a task; it is especially also a joy. Life can legitimately be experienced as a burden when so little is seen of the glow of God's glory in the world.[87] Life is also a task: we are servants and

---

[82]  Van Ruler, "God en de chaos," 42, 44.
[83]  See the following on the element of "delight," "joy," in Van Ruler's theology: D. Penninkhof, "De genieting is de wezenlijke: bevinding en aardse werkelijkheid bij A.A. van Ruler," in *De Civitate*, 25/5 (1976), 33–41; A.v.H. (Albert van Heuvel), "Theologie à la Mozart" in *Groninger Kerkblad*, 249/4 (1973), 2–3; D. van Keulen, "Wij zijn een grap van God." Van Ruler over de vreugde, in Dirk van Keulen, G. Harinck, and G. van den Brink, eds., *Men moet telkens opnieuw de reuzenzwaai aan de rekstok maken* (Zoetermeer: Boekencentrum, 2009), 64–79.
[84]  Van Ruler, *Droom en gestalte* (Amsterdam: Holland Uitgeversmaatschappij, 1947), 39.
[85]  Van Ruler, 135.
[86]  Van Ruler, *Vertrouw en geniet*, 89. Translator's note: "God's absolute freedom" is an impoverished version of the wonderful Dutch word "*vrijmacht*": combining God's freedom and God's power.
[87]  In Van Ruler's thinking this legitimate type of "Messianic grief" is clearly distinguished from what he calls "ontological melancholy," which is nothing less than pure sin! See Van Ruler, *De waardering van het aardse leven*, 30.

co-workers of God. We have work to do. We are instruments in God's
hand. We realize our humanity not so much through observation or
contemplation but through action, through actively engaging with
the world. The most important perspective, however, remains: life as a
pleasure or joy:

> Life as a delight. The real task lies in the holy work of the laudation.
> In the praise of God lies the meaning of life. We are, in our essence,
> theo-logoi, God-speakers. However, the real praise happens not by
> turning away from the creatures and fully focusing on and losing
> ourselves in the Creator, but by "enjoying" the Creator's works.
>
> On this point I would wish to break away from a centuries-
> old Christian-European tradition. Since Augustine, it has been
> brought under the formula that we may only "use" (*uti*) the world,
> created reality, and "enjoy" (*frui*) only God himself. As though
> God represented another world, another *object* than this world. As
> though God could be had without his world! While this is nothing
> but his world! And: is the world not truly *theatrum gloriam dei*, the
> theatre of his glory! Earthly life is the realization of the glory of
> God. ... We live *ad maiorem gloriam dei*, to the greater glory of God.
>
> By being there, actually and consciously, we amplify
> the unimaginable abundance of God's glory. Even this—the
> strangeness of the comparative—is a form of play, luxury, of
> delight. The luxury in fact does not only lie in the comparative,
> but already fully in the notion of glory itself. We are in no way
> necessary. But we have positively been posited by the divine
> pleasure. With the rest of creation we are, so to say, a luxury of
> God. This nobility brings responsibility. Therefore, we also have
> to experience our own being as luxury and thus as delight, and
> thus in the modus of enjoyment.[88]

Van Ruler is of course not unaware of the fact that with this positive
and life-affirming approach he is tampering with the boundaries of
tradition. But he asks whether the tradition, which thought it possible
to enjoy God without his creation, is not itself blasphemous:

> The basic question remains: What is the ultimate perspective?
> How should it be formulated? What is the destination of everyone
> and everything? The answer to this can really only be: the joy, the

[88]    Van Ruler, *De waardering van het aardse leven*, 30.

enjoyment of all that is! This thesis is the most modern form of Christianity imaginable. Therein is brought together all the developments since the seventeenth century. Has Christianity not erred on this point, all these centuries? *Grosso modo*, it has always been saying: we may enjoy (*frui*) only God and the eternal things, and that only with our inner being; the exterior world may only be used (*uti*). To my mind this formula has something blasphemous to it: thus we slander the Creator, by thinking of his creation as sub-standard. Moreover, the true relationship between God and the human being is thus distorted: how can the human "have" (and thus enjoy) God without God's world? Human life is the service and praise of God. But is this service and praise possible in any other way than (at least: also) through the enjoyment of God's world? [89]

Van Ruler's addition to this brief excursion on *uti* and *frui* is also quite significant: "Let us not speak disparagingly of the revolution this thesis can bring about in the Christian faith! To my mind, all so-called 'theology of renewal' pales into child's play, in comparison." [90]

As is evident from Van Ruler's sermons, meditative publications, but also many of his serious academic articles, this basic positive view of humanity and the world—in spite of the deep disturbance of evil, sin and guilt—has become the hallmark and the ground-tone of his oeuvre: "Stand Up to Joy!" ("Sta op tot de vreugde!", 1948), "Have Courage for the World" ("Heb moed voor de wereld," 1953), "Trust and Enjoy" ("Vertrouw en geniet," 1955), "Most of These Is Love" ("De meeste van deze is de liefde," 1957), "Death Is Being Overcome" ("De dood wordt overwonnen," 1964), "I Believe" ("Ik geloof," 1968), "Believe with Gladness" ("Geloven met blijdschap," 1971), "Life a Feast" ("Het leven

---

[89]  Van Ruler, *De kern van de zaak: hoe waardeert men de stof?*, 16–17.

[90]  From Van Ruler's article on "Hoe waardeert men de stof?" ("How do we evaluate the stuff?"), 1968, 15ff., it is evident that he in fact wishes to counter the "current one-sided accent on worldliness" through a Christian view on the acceptance, affirmation, and enjoyment of creation. To his mind, modern thinking about the world misses out on at least three things: the accent of the eschaton (revolution is child's play in comparison with the apocalypse!); the importance of mediating salutary institutions as for instance the church, in which the salvation that has already been acquired is being preserved (there are thus other realities of importance that play a role in human life, not only the future, the state, the culture, and society!); the necessary attention that should be given to the individual and the mystic aspects of life (there are not only the big social realities to be reckoned with but also the realities of the individual person!).

een feest," 1972), "Let the Whole World Be a Praise Song" ("Laat heel de aard een loflied wezen," 1973), and "Round Dance" ("Reidans," 1974). His theology is "theocratic" because it lives from the *vision of the joy of God's real work*: concrete sanctification of "ordinary life" or the "liturgy on the street":

> This is why the state should walk in the light of God's Word, to order the chaos of sin, in such a way that the whole of life is saturated by God's grace and God's justice. Only then the state actually becomes what it should be. It then wakes up from the bad dream, that it, itself, is God on earth, and only then can it become servant, liturgist of God, that lets the liturgy, the praise of God, rise up from the whole of existence. In Twente the industry, in Rotterdam the shipping industry, in Amsterdam the stock-exchange, and in the rural areas the plowshare cutting through the earth—all of it one great liturgy, one great service and praise song for Him who has saved the lost life out of guilt and out of death.[91]

---

[91]   Van Ruler, 1947, *Visie en vaart*, 28-29. See also Van Ruler, 1953, *Heb moed voor de wereld*, 129-130: "Yes, in the Biblical testimony it goes so far, that eventually there will not be a special knowledge of God and a separate service, specially directed towards God, any more. The inhabitation of the earth, the cultivation of the land, will be the only and true service of God. The ordinary—simply and only the ordinary—will be holy. ... The farmer is a truer reflection of God's ultimate purposes than the pastor."

CHAPTER 10

# Power, Abuse of Power, and Law in the Church: Apostolate, the Bodies of Assistance, and Church Polity for the World

Leon van den Broeke

## Introduction

This contribution focuses on the question how the Dutch hervormde theologian A.A. van Ruler[1] viewed the *organen van bijstand*—
bodies of assistance—and what, according to him, the notion of an
apostolate church means from a church polity perspective for not
only the church but also for the world.[2] Such bodies assist the general
assemblies, under their leadership and in responsibility to them, in the
service to the care of the church for a certain aspect of life. They are called
*kerkenraadscommissie* (committee of the consistory), *classicale commissie*

---

[1]   Arnold Albert van Ruler (1908-1970), *hervormde* pastor Kubaard 1933, Hilversum
      1940, Ph.D. 1947, professor University Utrecht 1947; L.J. van den Brom, Ruler,
      Arnold Albert van Ruler, in *Biografisch Lexicon voor de Geschiedenis van het Nederlands
      Protestantisme* (*BLGNP*) vol. 6, Kampen: Kok, 2006, 262-264.
[2]   This article is a translation and an elaboration of the lecture I held in Dutch at
      the presentation of volume 5B of the *Verzameld werk: Kerkorde, kerkrecht, ambt*
      (hereafter referred to as *VW*) of A.A. van Ruler on Friday, December 14, 2018, at the
      Diependaalse kerk in Hilversum.

(classis committee), *provinciale commissie* (provincial committee), or *raad* (council).[3]

To choose this specific topic is not difficult: in 2005 Allan J. Janssen defended his doctoral dissertation on Van Ruler, *Kingdom, Office, and Church*,[4] at the Vrije Universiteit Amsterdam (VU) in the Netherlands, just two weeks after I defended my dissertation. Janssen has a passion for Dutch theology, the Netherlands Reformed Church, Van Ruler, the kingdom, ecclesiastical office, and the universal church. The title of his third chapter not only pictures Van Ruler's vision of the church but also Janssen's: "The Church as a Bearer of the Gospel and as Gestalt of the Kingdom."[5] At the end of this chapter, he comes to ten conclusions. Two of them, conclusions eight and ten, concern this function of being gestalt: "The church is, as the body of Christ, a gestalt of the kingdom of God, as it provisionally and fragmentarily exhibits God's intentions for the world in the communion and institution that is this body"[6] and:

> The church as a community of love, bearing an institutional gestalt in this world, nonetheless continues to exist not for itself but on behalf of the world. Van Ruler did not abandon his original apostolic vision of the church but rather deepened it in as the church took on liturgical shape. The church continues, however, to be used by God for God's kingdom intentions.[7]

With these ecclesiological notions on the church as a gestalt of the kingdom that exhibits God's intentions for the world, along with the research question, we are at the core business of the renewed Netherlands Reformed Church in and after the Second World War. Bodies of assistance helped the general assemblies to fulfill their apostolate task for the benefit of the world.

This might need some clarification. In 1816, King Willem I (1772-1843) imposed his own church order—the *Algemeen Reglement* (General Regulations) of 1816—in the *Nederlandse Hervormde Kerk* (the Netherlands Reformed Church). Due to his experience as a ruler in the small territory of Fulda in Germany, he wanted to be a father

---

3    Ordinance 1-23-1, accessed January 4, 2019, http://www.kerkrecht.nl/content/kerkorde-nhk-1951-ord-1-23-1.

4    Allan J. Janssen, *Kingdom, Office, and Church: A Study of A.A. van Ruler's Doctrine of Ecclesiastical Office* (Grand Rapids/Cambridge: Eerdmans, 2005).

5    Janssen, 81–123.

6    Janssen, Conclusion 8, 123.

7    Janssen, *Kingdom,* Conclusion 10, 123.

for the church. Parallel to the political infrastructure, he wanted a centralized church. That was new for this denomination, as in the previous centuries, it was used to a decentralized political and reformed infrastructure. The Kingdom of the Netherlands had just started in 1813. Before 1795, the Netherlands were a republic of seven relatively autonomous provinces. King Willem I did not want the church to discuss doctrine and have discussions or conflicts about it. For him, the church was an administrative body that had to function in an efficient way. Although many pastors did enjoy that their salaries improved, not everyone agreed with the king. Discontinuity was felt with the old (Dortian) ecclesiastical and confessional reformed church of the sixteenth and seventeenth centuries. In 1834, a group of orthodox believers who longed back for the church of Dort left the church. They formed a seceder's church with such pastors as, among others, Hendrik de Cock (1801–1842), Albertus Christiaan van Raalte (1809–1876), and Hendrik Pieter Scholte (1805–1868). In 1886, a new group of believers left the Netherlands Reformed Church under the leadership of Abraham Kuyper (1837–1920), a pastor, theologian, founder-rector-professor of the Vrije Universiteit Amsterdam, journalist, politician, and prime minister (1901–1905). In 1892, the majority of these two groups joined forces and together formed the *Gereformeerde Kerken in Nederland* (the Reformed Churches in the Netherlands). This denomination applied the Dort Church Order of 1619. In this contribution, I will make use of the word "*hervormde*" to refer to those who belonged to the Netherlands Reformed Church and "*gereformeerde(n)*" to refer to those who belonged to the Reformed Churches in the Netherlands.

The gereformeerden were not the only ones who had difficulties with the *Algemeen Reglement* of 1816 when they were still members of the Netherlands Reformed Church but also some hervormde members, especially by the end of the nineteenth- and in the twentieth-centuries. Several plans and draft church orders were composed, but because of the plurality in the church, no agreement could be reached. Due to the circumstances in and of the Second World War, that which had been impossible in the past decades became possible: a renewal of the church appeared to be realistic. Van Ruler was part of this process of renewal of the church and its church order. He played an important role as might become clear below.

Before I will come to my concluding remarks, I will focus in this contribution on Van Ruler and power: the bodies of assistance and abuse of power.

## Van Ruler and Power

In volume 5B of the *Collected Works* that is currently in process, Van Ruler often makes use of the word "*macht*"— power—and often in connection with another word or in a phrase: *machtskwestie* (the question of power),[8] *machtsvorming* (the forming of power),[9] *ambtsmacht* (the power of the office),[10] *overmacht/overmachtig(e)* (superior power/the one of with superior power),[11] *bevolmachtiging/volmacht/gevolmachtigden* (authorization/authorized persons),[12] *beslissingsmacht* (the authority to decide),[13] *sacrale macht* (sacral power),[14] *machtsoverdracht van de Heer aan bepaalde personen* (the transmission of power of God to certain persons),[15] *God gebruikt in zijn vrijmacht mensen om Hem te representeren* (God uses, in his omnipotence, people to represent him),[16] *macht van het Woord [Gods]* (the power of the Word [of God]),[17] *machten van het ongeloof* (the powers of unbelief),[18] *macht der belijdenis* (the power of the confession),[19] *mensenmacht* (the power of humans),[20] *Gods vrijmachtige genade* (God's omnipotent grace),[21] *overmacht van het rijk* (superior power of the kingdom),[22] et cetera.

Van Ruler seems to regard power in a positive way, or at least he gives it a theological connotation. Indeed, power is usually regarded as negative, but that is not necessarily the case. Power is necessary, for example, to avoid chaos or disorder. Moreover, Van Ruler speaks in a theological way about the power of God. Nonetheless, despite beautiful theological phrases, power in the church is still often viewed as something negative. People experience or think that their freedom is limited by power or by those who exercise power. The rationale is usually that they think that it is due to church order. During a break in an ecclesiastical meeting, I noticed people discussing a beautiful—in

---

[8]    Van Ruler, *VW* 5B, 318.
[9]    Van Ruler, 321, 515, 516,
[10]   Van Ruler, 326, 403, 502, 729, 732, 777, 830.
[11]   Van Ruler, 204, 221, 267, 297, 300, 304, 328, 465, 647.
[12]   Van Ruler, 66, 486, 493, 610, 611, 631, 633, 637, 649, 659, 661, 667, 731, 749, 757, 776, 783, 828.
[13]   Van Ruler, 68, 818, 819, 831
[14]   Van Ruler, 56
[15]   Van Ruler, 55.
[16]   Van Ruler, 59.
[17]   Van Ruler, 87, 135, 234.
[18]   Van Ruler, 220.
[19]   Van Ruler, *VW* 5B, 234.
[20]   Van Ruler, 20, 224, 246, 247, 457, 473.
[21]   Van Ruler, 300.
[22]   Van Ruler, 300.

their eyes—renewal plan. They were enthusiastic about it. Nonetheless, those who had to make a decision about this plan were less enthusiastic and voted against it. When the spokesperson of the group was asked why the plan was rejected, he stated "because the church order rejects it."

From this perspective, the German jurist Hans Dombois (1907–1997) had a point when he, in 1967/1968, spoke about the *Rechtsfremdheit* —alienation or distance from law—of theologians as *"skandalon."*[23] The resistance against hierarchy, although understandable against the backdrop of the sixteenth-century Roman Catholic Church, seems to be, for the Reformed, written in stone. Therefore, the words of Van Ruler are refreshing because they are more an expression of a hymn book than of a law book, of a theological rather than a juridical language:

> One must not say that a church order is only human scaffolding *around the church as building work of God.* A church order has more meaning. It does no less than this, that it arranges the church to a certain extent. The church, which—invisible—only stands before God's eyes, becomes, to a certain extent, visible to the eyes of people. One needs to think especially of the sacraments! In its order and law, the church received a wide interface with the world.[24]

Van Ruler connects church with world, order and law with sacraments, and church order ("human scaffold") with church ("God's construction work").[25] Janssen elaborates on Van Ruler's notion of scaffolding:

> This institutional character is not accidental to the church. It is not, as Van Ruler says using one image, the "scaffolding" on the church building, but it is the "cross beams" or the "rafters" on the building. Scaffolding may assist in the building or repair of the church, but it is taken down when the work is done; it is not

---

[23]  The German jurist Hans Dombois (1907–1997) states: "Erzeugt selbst bei namhaften Gelehrten die lang gehegte Abneigung ein schwer glaubliches Maß von Unkenntnis, und die gleiche Unkenntnis nährt wiederum die Abneigung. Aber noch niemals haben sich Lebensprobleme durch ihre Verschweigung oder Unterdrückung lösen lassen." Hans Dombois, "Zur Lage der Kirchenrechtslehre," in , *Zeitschrift für Evangelisches Kirchenrecht,* 13 (1967/68), 368.

[24]  Van Ruler, *VW* 5B, 421.

[25]  Van Ruler, *VW* 5B, 244, 421, 422; Van Ruler also uses "scaffold" to refer to the church (*steigerwerk*); *VW* 5B, 195, 399. Furthermore, he uses the metaphor of scaffold to refer to the offices; *VW* 5B, 796, 809 n. 119.

essential to the building. Or to use another image, the institution is not a "corset" on the body, but the "skeleton" of the body. A body cannot exist without its skeleton.[26]

It is partially due to Van Ruler that the *Hervormde Kerkorde* of 1951 is rooted in the service of Word and sacraments for the benefit of the world. He calls attention to the theological notion that church polity is liturgical law and that church polity is not only focused on the church but also on the relevance of the church for the world and the witness of the church toward the civil authorities and the people.[27] Janssen states: "The communal, the gestalt of the church, finds its institutional expression in the liturgical and sacramental."[28]

**Bodies of Assistance**

Van Ruler considers that bodies of assistance are necessary.[29] In 1948, he stated that he did not want to "smuggle something episcopalian into our church, but just as attempts to bring the nature of the church to full completion."[30] They need to be understood from the perspective of:

> complete development of the original-gereformeerde, presbyterial notions of church polity. By and since Dort the gereformeerde church polity is atrophied, not only in the sense, that the order of the church was exclusive inward-looking, but also in this sense, that it was locked in the local congregation and in an unreformed closed understanding of the office.[31]

He refers to the gereformeerde pastor Herman C. Rutgers (1880-1964)[32] who, in 1910, defended his doctoral dissertation: *Kerkelijke deputaten.*[33] He does not attack the younger Rutgers—the son of the

---

26   Janssen, *Kingdom*, 107.
27   *Hervormde Kerkorde of 1951*, Article III.1.
28   Janssen, 110.
29   Van Ruler, "Het apostolaat der kerk en de ontwerp-kerkorde," in *VW* 5B, 317.
30   Van Ruler, "Het belijden in de nieuwe kerkorde," in *VW* 5B, 203-204.
31   Van Ruler, *VW* 5B, 203.
32   Leon van den Broeke, "Tussenregenten, uitvoerders of leiders met autoriteit? F.L. Rutgers en H.C. Rutgers over kerkelijke deputaten," in Leon van den Broeke and George Harinck, eds., *Nooit meer eene nieuwe hiërarchie! De kerkrechtelijke nalatenschap van F.L. Rutgers,* (Hilversum: De Vuurbaak, 2018) (*ADChartasreeks* 34), 86-107.
33   H.C. Rutgers, *Hun werkkring en bevoegdheid inzonderheid gelijk deze gekend worden uit de handelingen der Zuid-Hollandsche synoden en deputaten,* Kampen: J.H. Kok [1910]; G. Harinck, "Rutgers, Herman Cornelis," in *BLGNP* vol. 3. (Kampen: Kok, 1988), 313-315.

VU professor in church history and church polity, Frederik Lodewijk Rutgers (1836–1917), who was the right hand of the famous Abraham Kuyper. Rather, Van Ruler explains that apostolate connects with the tradition, but it is also a development of it. The church shows, through its bodies of assistance, that it is enabled in the kingdom of God. It is about the service of the church into the world that emanates from the presbyterial-synodical system of church polity, as Van Ruler stated in 1967: "There is no type of church polity which connects the church and the kingdom so closely together, and therefore operates into the world, than the presbyterial-synodical one. That has to do with the three offices and their uniqueness."[34]

According to Van Ruler, gereformeerde deputies were not in this light of the service of the church into the world. He does not seem to be conscious of the fact that, originally, deputies were only deputies of the particular and not of the General Synod, according to Article 49 of the Dort Church Order of 1619.[35] For that reason, Rutgers's dissertation was about the deputies of a specific particular synod, the General Synod. In 1948, Van Ruler stated that deputies were "in accordance with the whole nature of the Dort Church Order and, moreover, of the Reformation, as it developed itself, mainly or even exclusively (except for the relationship with the civil authorities and the book censorship!) on the internal life and work of the church."[36] That is logical because the gereformeerde assemblies and deputies were considered to limit themselves to the ecclesiastical agenda, and that had an internal focus. To Van Ruler, the hervormde agenda did have an external focus. That is understandable because he lived three centuries after the creation of the Dort Church Order of 1619 in a completely different context. To respond to the ecclesiastical agenda, bodies of assistance are necessary. Van Ruler sums up no less than 15 bodies of assistance:

---

[34]    Van Ruler, "De presbyteriale kerkorde en de ordening van de gemeenschap," in *VW* 5B, 416.

[35]    Article 49 of the Dort Church Order of 1619: "Yeder Synodus sal oock eenighe deputeren / om alles wat de Synodus geordonneert heeft / te verrichten / soo wel byde Hooge Overheyt / als by de respective Classen / onder haer sorterende / mede om t'samen oft in minder ghetal over alle examina der aencomender Predicanten te staê : ende voorts in alle andere voorvallende swarigheden dê Classen de hant te bieden / op dat goede eenigheyt / ordre ende suyverheyt der leere behouden ende gestabilieert worden. Eñ zullen dese van alle hare handelinghen / goede notitie houden / om den Synodo rapport daer van te doen / ende soo't geeyscht werdt / redenen te geven. Oock en zullen sy niet ontslaghen wesen van harê dienst / voor eñ aleer de Synodus selfs haer daer van ontslaet," accessed January 2, 2019, http://kerkrecht.nl/node/488.

[36]    Van Ruler, "Het apostolaat der kerk en het ontwerp-kerkorde," in *VW* 5B, 318.

1. the council for the labor among Israel
2. the council for the mission
3. the council for the affairs of church and state
4. the council for the questions of church and society
5. the council for the labor among non-members of the church
6. the council for youth ministry
7. the council for the affairs of church and school
8. the council for the worship
9. the committee for the theological higher education[37]
10. the council for the affairs of church and theology
11. the council for catechesis
12. the general diaconal council
13. the general financial council
14. the council for the salaries and pensions
15. the council for the relation with other churches[38]

He called these councils "an utmost modest number for a massive church in a modern world!"[39] He was not the only one. The hervormde theologian A.J. Bronkhorst (1914–1994)[40] explained that the number of 15 is an artificial one; it should have been more, but because of pressure, the number had to be limited and a number of councils are combined. For Bronkhorst, this strengthens bureaucratism. He preferred 30 simple councils over 15 complicated ones.[41]

To Van Ruler, the name "bodies of assistance" is more than a change of name in relation to the gereformeerde name "deputies." He was not an exception in this. The hervormde professor in theology Th.L. Haitjema[42] was also of that opinion.[43] He also considered that

---

[37]    The other 14 bodies of assistance are called "raad" (council), but this body is called "committee."

[38]    Van Ruler, *VW* 5B, 318.

[39]    Van Ruler, 318.

[40]    Alexander Johannes Bronkhorst, hervormde assistant pastor Utrecht 1939-1940, pastor Wijk aan Zee en Duin 1940, Willemstad 1943, Den Haag 1947, professor Brussels 1954, professor Utrecht Church History of the twentieth century 1966–1984 and docent church polity 1971–1991; A. de Groot, "Bronkhorst, Alexander Johannes," in *Biografisch lexicon voor de geschiedenis van het Nederlands Protestantisme 5*, Kampen: Kok, 2001, 92–94.

[41]    Van Ruler, VW 5B, 351 note 152.

[42]    Theodoor Lambertus Haitjema (1888-1972), pastor De Meern 1914, Hoogmade en Rijpwetering 1916, Apeldoorn 1918, professor 1923-1959; B.J. Wiegeraad, "Haitjema, Theodorus Lambertus," in *BLGNP* vol. 6, 107–110.

[43]    Balke and Oostenbrink-Evers, *De Commissie voor de Kerkorde (1945–1950)* (Zoetermeer: Boekencentrum, 1993), 284.

"deputies" emphasized too much the individual aspect and ignored the unity of the councils. However, not every theologian or jurist who was involved in the renewal process of the Netherlands Reformed Church favored the bodies of assistance. Johannes Severijn (1883–1966)[44] and Oepke Noordmans (1871–1956)[45] objected to the councils[46]: Severijn because he favored [the freedom of] the local congregation and feared the limitation of this freedom due to the bodies of assistance, and Noordmans because the apostolate and the bodies of assistance were extended too far.

The hervormde professor in the history and phenomenology of religion, Hendrik Kraemer (1888–1965), states that apostolate is not a function of the church, but it is the other way around: the church is an expression of the apostolate, though this is the title of a subparagraph in the book of the hervormde church historian A.J. Rasker (1906–1990).[47] Although he was involved in the renewal of the Netherlands Reformed Church and initiated the councils for the mission, he also warned against the shadow sides of these councils.[48] In May 1942, he wrote a report to the General Synod and predicted secularization in the aftermath of the Second World War and that the post-war world would cry for a radical spiritual re-foundation. In that light, he continued, instituting these councils is a way of anticipating the post-war world. These councils are an expression of the fact that "the church, for the fulfillment of its duty, needs councils who have stimulating, exploring

---

[44] Johannes Severijn, pastor Wilnis 1915, Leerdam 1918, Dordrecht 1921, member Second Chamber Dutch Parliament 1929, professor Utrecht 1931–1953; A. de Groot, "Severijn, Johannes," in *BLGNP* vol. 3, 323–110.

[45] Oepke Noordmans, pastor Idsegahuizen and Piaam 1903, Suameer 1910, Laren (Gelderland) 1923, emeritus 1943; A. van Haarlem, "Noordmans, Oepke," in *BLGNP* vol. 1, 220–223.

[46] See for example: W. Balke and H. Oostenbrink-Evers, *De Commissie voor de Kerkorde*, 535.

[47] A.J. Rasker, *De Nederlandse Hervormde Kerk vanaf 1795: Geschiedenis, theologische ontwikkelingen en de verhouding tot haar zusterkerken in de negentiende en twintigste eeuw*, 6th ed. (Kampen: Kok, 2000), 328. See also: 317–330; K.E. Biezeveld, "Rasker, Albert Jan," in *BLGNP* vol. 5, 416–418.

[48] Hendrik Kraemer, who had a passion for mission, studied Indonesian language and literature and Islamology. He was professor in Leiden 1937–1947, Director of the Ecumenical Institute of the World Council of Churches Chateau de Boissy at Celigny near Geneva in Switzerland 1948–1956, and visiting professor at Union Theological Seminary, New York 1956–1957; E. Jansen Schoonhoven, "Kraemer, Hendrik," in *BLGNP* vol. 1, 104–111.

and controlling tasks; in order to keep the church alive and active."[49] A year earlier, Kraemer already wrote about his concerns about a "centrist authority and bureaucratic atmosphere" of the councils.[50]

The fear was that too much authority of the councils, or abuse, or both would challenge the presbyterial-synodical nature of the Netherlands Reformed Church. However, the councils and the bodies of assistance in general get their church order position because of the notion of apostolate in the church for the benefit of the world.

For Van Ruler, from the perspective of the church, bodies of assistance are less exclusive than the gereformeerde "deputies." The latter ones have the connotation of the power of the church, according to Van Ruler, and the bodies of assistance with the service of the church (to the world). The Netherlands Reformed Church moves more toward the world: "Whenever the care of the ministry of the church for the various terrains of life require it, the General Synod calls bodies of assistance into life, charged with information and with the execution of that which gets drawn up in their field of work."[51] He explains that it is about the providing of *information* and the implementation of "which them on that field is assigned." Their labor is "primarily connected with ... the public prophecy of the church in the full life."[52]

He is lyric about the new hervormde church polity and the apostolic church. In 1948, he stated that the notion of apostolate was in the gereformeerd-church polity bud, but it did not blossom: "This flower of the gereformeerde church polity has, mainly through pressure (besides help!) of the civil authorities and through the pressure of the constitutional organization in the Republic, in the morning of its blossoming partly perished."[53] From a church polity point of view, the bodies of assistance form not a constitutive but a regulative principle, says Van Ruler. They are bodies of *assistance* to assist the general assemblies.[54]

---

[49]    Memorandum van "Kerkelijk Overleg" aan de Algemene Synode, opgesteld door H. Kraemer, midden 1942; J. Bruin, *Kerkvernieuwing: Een praktisch-ecclesiologisch onderzoek naar de betekenis van "Gemeenteopbouw" voor de Nederlandse Hervormde Kerk* (Zoetermeer: Boekencentrum, 1992), 72.

[50]    Nota H. Kraemer, in opdracht van de Raad voor de Inwendige Zending, 1942; Bruin, *Kerkvernieuwing*, 71.

[51]    Van Ruler, *VW* 5B, 319.

[52]    Van Ruler, 320.

[53]    Van Ruler, "De belijdende kerk in de nieuwe kerkorde," in *VW* 5B, 203.

[54]    Van Ruler, 320.

This raises the question whether Van Ruler, while trumpeting the bodies of assistance, had an eye for the empirical church. He seems to give account of being familiar with the criticism:

> The Nunspeet Committee did not leave it to this constitutive regulation. It knows all too well the objections, which one in the church has against this institution of bodies of assistance. It sees clearly that it is surrounded by real dangers. Therefore we need not look only to the history of the church since 1940. The old ecclesiastical deputies mentioned in their time exactly the same objections and dangers as the current bodies of assistance. When it comes to this point the church has still to wrestle with a difficulty, which results from the presbyterial structure of its church order.[55]

The "Nunspeet Committee" refers to the Committee for the Church Order that gathered between December 1945 and November 1947 in Nunspeet, a village in the Province of Gelderland. On November 24, 1947, it handed over the draft church order to the General Synod, which resulted a few years later in the *Hervormde Kerkorde* of 1951.[56]

For Van Ruler, bodies of assistance were required: "About the form of the bodies of assistance one can discuss. Also about their number. However, there will be bodies of assistance."[57] At the same time, he is worried about the one-sided way in which others "try to limit these bodies of assistance as much as possible."[58] They also need "play space and elbow room"[59]: "If literally everything needs to be decided by the general assemblies or approved in advance, then the labor, which the church has to do in the world, is doomed. ... But in practice it shall automatically mean, that one must be very careful for animosity."[60]

---

[55] Van Ruler, *VW* 5B, 320.
[56] W. Balke and H. Oostenbrink-Evers, *De Commissie voor de Kerkorde*, xxvi–xxxiv. Members of this committee were the jurist Paul Scholten (1875–1946), chair of the committee until he died; professor in theology S.F.H.J. Berkelbach van der Sprenkel (1882–1967), chair after Scholten died; professor H. de Vos (1896–1980), vice chair; the jurist H.M.J. Wagenaar (1901–1999), stated clerk of the committee; J. Boonstra (1893–1956), pastor; E. Emmen (1902–1985), stated clerk of General Synod, K.H.E. Gravemeyer (1883–1979), secretary of General Synod; Th.L. Haitjema; O. Noordmans; A.A. van Ruler; J. Severijn; the jurist G. Vixseboxse (1884–1963); and W.A. Zeydner (1890–1965), pastor.
[57] Van Ruler, *VW* 5B, 320.
[58] Van Ruler, 324.
[59] Van Ruler, 324.
[60] Van Ruler, 324.

Together with Bronkhorst, Van Ruler states that the Netherlands Reformed Church tries to "meet the existing objections about and the dangers of the institute of bodies of assistance"[61] and also to meet the desires Rutgers mentioned in his doctoral dissertation: limited authority, no appointment by rotation, appointing deputies outside the circle of pastors, a fixed-term for deputies, and the decline of payment to deputies.

## Abuse of Power

Despite the beautiful words, the question remains whether Van Ruler had an eye for the empirical church, the disorder, the abuse of power, and the authoritarian way in which ecclesiastical staff members and officers act. No less than the kingdom of God is at issue. Van Ruler does warn for the Antichrist in church polity when he states:

> With the church order emphasis of the abstractum "office" one readily connects the bad practice of the notion of highness, dignity, honor, esteem, control, power, et cetera. And indeed: the ways and deeds of God become dangerous, when they get a full human form! If Christ enters church polity, he can become the Antichrist. What else can one do, than over and over again, pointing towards the mystical background of all the juridical [context], towards the essential surrounding of the offices by the whole ecclesia, towards the inclusion of the ecclesia in the basileia, to promote in this way the purity of the ethos of the office?[62]

Even though he has an eye for abuse of power, he remains idolate of the apostolate. As long as an officer is conscious of his position and his Sender, it appears, to Van Ruler, that there is no problem at issue:

> The office bearer needs to be careful with an all too authoritative appearance to become the *fâcheux troisième*[63] between those two, who love each other—God and humans. Office is just an instrument. And that is an instrument in which only God is represented. The love can not come from one side. Humankind needs to be involved, as humans, the process of salvation shall come to the completion.[64]

[61] Van Ruler, 324.
[62] Van Ruler, *VW* 5B, 680.
[63] A third person, which is too much.
[64] Van Ruler, 741.

The problem is not so much grounded in the "authoritative" way of acting of an office-bearer, but, moreover, in the authoritarian way of acting and speaking in, for Van Ruler, the sacrosanct presbyterial-synodical system of church polity. He seems to make little distinction between power and authority. His use of words might be a colorful bouquet, and most likely this use will fall on theological good soil, but from a management science point of view, it is not so much the case. This is especially the case when he states: "Authority is more than legitimacy or competence. It has more to do with the assignment: that one says and does in the Name of the Lord."[65] Authority is certainly legitimated when it comes to formal sources of influence to reach the goals of the organization without being formalistic. "Power is related to the extent wherein and the way(s) in which stakeholders execute influence and pressure to dominate an issue."[66] Ideally, authority and power are one. However, in daily life this is often not the case, and that includes the church.

Is there not, despite or as a result of overemphasizing the apostolic ideal, an overload of bodies of assistance? Council Republic was the less-flattering name for the Netherlands Reformed Church with its councils as bodies of assistance.[67] The problem is bigger. The priority of apostolate over confession in the theological constitution in the *Hervormde Kerkorde* of 1951 had a shadow side. J. van der Graaf, a former stated-clerk of the *Gereformeerde Bond* (the Reformed Association) in the Netherlands Reformed Church stated that the Barthian theology with view to the apostolate dominated at the expense of the theocratic view of Van Ruler.[68] The personal aspect of the apostolate disappeared. It was all about society, the institutional apostolate *Kerk en Were* (Church and World), and the World Council of Churches.

By the end of his life, even Van Ruler became disappointed about the political development of the notion of apostolate in his

---

[65]  D. Keuning, *Organiseren en leiding geven*, 2e herz. dr., (Leiden: Stenfert Kroese, 1986), 120.

[66]  D. Keining, 120.

[67]  A.J. Mensink, "Kerk op weg naar 2025: Groeien naar structuur die dienstbaar is aan de verkondiging," accessed December 13, 2018, https://dewaarheidsvriend.nl/blog/kerk-op-weg-naar-2025-2; Karel Blei, "De kerkorde en de generale synode," in W. Balke, A. van de Beek en J.D.Th. Wassenaar, *De kerk op orde? Vijftig jaar hervormd leven met de kerkorde van 1951* (Zoetermeer: Boekencentrum, 2001), 201-205.

[68]  J. van der Graaf, "De kerkorde en het apostolaat," in W. Balke e.a. (ed.), *De Kerk op orde Vijftig jaar Hervormd leven met de kerkorde van 1951*, (Zoetermeer: Boekencentrum, 2001); J. van der Graaf, *De Nederlandse Hervormde Kerk: Belijdend onderweg 1951-1981-2001*, (Kampen: Kok, 2001).

Netherlands Reformed Church. He was concerned about the political preaching, because, according to him, the message of the gospel is not so much political involvement, but it refers to another world. Because of his disappointment, he sympathized with the *Getuigenis* (Witness), a 1971 document that opposed those who considered that they could have a word for the world outside the hervormde congregation.[69] The Getuigenis opposed the politicization and socialization of salvation. Van Ruler not only sympathized with the history of the Getuigenis, but the Getuigenis was born in a conversation with him and the hervormde professor (in, among others things, the theology of the apostolate) G.C. van Niftrik (1904-1972).[70] When the Getuigenis was released, Van Ruler had already passed away. In his name, his widow, J.A. van Ruler-Hamelink (1910-1995), signed the document, together with Van Niftrik, the hervormde theologian W. Aalders (1909-2005),[71] the hervormde professor in church history G.P. van Itterzon (1900-1992),[72] the hervormde professor (in, among other things, the nature and history of apostolate) H. Jonker,[73] and J. van der Graaf. The Getuigenis received support of 60,000 people but also met sharp criticism and rejection. Some of those who expressed their criticism pointed out in an open letter responding to the letter that the Swiss theologian Karl Barth (1886-1968) sent on March 16, 1966, to the organizers of a manifestation in Dortmund, Germany. The motto was "No other gospel." Barth stated that standing up for a sound confession would only be credible when one would be prepared to oppose the nuclear weapons, the war in Vietnam, the outbursts of antisemitism in West Germany, and much more. It demonstrated the post-Second World War developments and tensions in society, politics, and church. In November 1971, the General Synod discussed Getuigenis, the criticisms against it, and the polarization in the church for the first time. It would be followed by two other discussions in the General Synod, in February and November 1972. On the one hand, the synod stated—in November 1972—that any identification of whatever ideology with the gospel

---

[69]    Rasker, *De Nederlandse Hervormde Kerk 1795*, 358–360.

[70]    Karel Blei, "Niftrik, Gerrit Cornelis van," in *BLGNP* vol. 5, (Kampen: Kok, 2001), 384–387.

[71]    P.J. Stam, *"Het oog omhoog, het hart naar boven": Een levenlang leerling van "dominee" Doctor Willem Aalders* (...), (Katwijk: Het Baken, 2010).

[72]    "Catalogus Professorum" entry for Van Itterzon. Accessed January 4, 2019, https://profs.library.uu.nl/index.php/profrec/getprofdata/991/54/127/0.

[73]    J.H. van de Bank, "Jonker, Hendrik," in *BLGNP* vol. 5, 295–296.

needs to be firmly rejected.[74] On the other hand, the synod emphasized that faith and political responsibility are inextricable.

Apart from best practices in the field of apostolate—for example, in the classes of the Netherlands Reformed Church as pastoral care in hospitals, senior citizens"homes, for refugees from Ambon, for the army, for the agricultural sector, for Jews and for Muslims, for seafarers, and for the industrial sector—a few years after the renewal of the Netherlands Reformed Church, the notion of apostolate and the bodies of assistance to be church for the world became problematic and caused conflicts and tension about the nature of the church in relationship to society and politics.[75] It even affected Van Ruler in a negative way. He did not lose his faith in the apostolate of the church but was disappointed in the way it functioned in his church. It became more concerned with the world, with politics than with—and rooted in—the church.

**Concluding Remarks**

Van Ruler was so enthusiastic about the bodies of assistance (including the councils), the church as a gestalt of the kingdom, and the service of the church to the world in general that he minimized the dangers and that the trap of overemphasizing the apostolate of the church was to be more focused on the world than on the church, let alone on church polity. Van Ruler had too little vision for the empirical church, although at the end of his life he became concerned about the politicalization of the gospel and the preaching in and of the Netherlands Reformed Church. Severijn and Noordmans were more realistic, and Kraemer also expressed his concerns about the shadow sides of the councils. Despite best practices in the field of the apostolate church, the Netherlands Reformed Church became deeply polarized about the relevance of the gospel in a post-Second World War context for the society and politics. Even Van Ruler became dissatisfied, not about the notion of the apostolate of the church but about the way it was used in a wrong way in view to the political attitude of the church. Nonetheless, his earlier notions should not be forgotten. On December 21, 1945, he stated that people should not make the order

---

[74]    Handeling van de vergadering van de generale synode der Nederlandse Hervormde Kerk op 20, 21, 22, 23 November 1972 in centrum Hydepark te Doorn, 14–16, accessed January 4, 2019, http://pkn-acta.digibron.nl/overview.

[75]    See for some best practices: C. (Leon) van den Broeke, *Een geschiedenis van de classis: Classicale typen tussen idee en werkelijkheid 1571–2004* (Kampen: Kok, 2005), 344–346.

entirely a servant to life, because the order is also a service instrument to God. Then he became lyric again by pointing out that the order is a piece of a hymn and that it glorifies.[76] The 912 pages of Van Ruler's *Verzameld werk* volume 5B together form a colourful bouquet, in which he, through the presbyterial-synodical church polity, connects church and world. The "scaffold" (church order) around the "construction work" (church) is a hymn. However, flowers wither, a building needs renovation, and sometimes a hymn sounds more an elegy about the abuse of power. To Van Ruler, church polity is firmly about this: it is a flower, a scaffold, and a hymn. That is Van Ruler's strength and power, and he does seem to say, that is the power of the esteemed presbyterial-synodical church polity. In church polity, it is about no less than "holy affairs." These holy affairs need to be safeguarded, and people need to feel secure in church. For that reason, the church should not only be holy (*heilig*) but also secure (*veilig*) against abuse of power. That hymn still needs to be sung.

---

[76]    Balke and Oostenbrink-Evers, *De Commissie*, 134.

CHAPTER 11

# Ordained Ministry: Reformed and Ecumenical Observations

Leo J. Koffeman

## Introduction

It is not only in the Protestant Church in the Netherlands that recent developments in terms of missional ecclesiology have raised serious questions regarding traditional views in church polity, particularly regarding ordained ministry and sacraments. Similar stories can be told from, for instance, the South African, British, and American contexts. [1]

In this contribution, I intend to give a survey of discussions within the Protestant Church in the Netherlands over the last two decades. My main question after that overview will be: How do these discussions relate to the ecumenical convergence (and, to some extent, consensus) that has been found—since the "Baptism, Eucharist and

---

[1]   This contribution elaborates some experiences and thoughts I presented in a workshop in Stellenbosch, South Africa (November 2018), "Challenges to the Reformed View of Ministry, from the Perspective of Missional theology." See also: Leo J. Koffeman, *In Order to Serve: An Ecumenical Introduction to Church Polity* (Zürich: LIT Verlag, 2014), 111–128.

Ministry" (BEM) reports of 1982—on the issue of ordained ministry? Is the Protestant Church in the Netherlands in fact distancing itself from ecumenical discourse in this respect? Or, from a different perspective: How and to what extent does ecumenical theology challenge the Protestant Church in the Netherlands in this respect? It is my intention to recognize the value of the Reformed tradition in these questions and at the same time to argue within the wider context of ecumenical theology and dialogue. As far as I can see, my considerations may also help to understand and interpret discussion in the American context. That is, at least, my hope.

At the same time, what I bring forward might show my congeniality with Allan Janssen on these issues. In his doctoral dissertation on A.A. van Ruler's doctrine of ecclesiastical office, Janssen characterizes Van Ruler's view of the relation between office and ordination as a "loose end": "[T]he question remains as to the link between ordination and office. Are, for example, ministers to be ordained but not elders and deacons? If that is the case, does that not devalue the "office-character" of elders and deacons and place in jeopardy Van Ruler's entire understanding of office?"[2]

My frame of reference is multilateral ecumenical dialogue as promoted by the Faith and Order Commission of the World Council of Churches. In its most recent ecclesiological report, "The Church: Towards a Common Vision," ordained ministry is characterized like this:

> Ordained ministers assemble and build up the Body of Christ by proclaiming and teaching the Word of God, by celebrating the sacraments and by guiding the life of the community in its worship, its mission and its caring ministry. All members of the body, ordained and lay, are interrelated members of God's priestly people. Ordained ministers remind the community of its dependence on Jesus Christ, who is the source of its unity and mission, even as they understand their own ministry as dependent on Him. At the same time, they can fulfill their calling only in and for the Church; they need its recognition, support and encouragement.[3]

---

[2]    Allan J. Janssen, *Kingdom, Office, and Church: A.A. van Ruler's Doctrine of Ecclesiastical Office* (Grand Rapids: Eerdmans, 2006), 277, cf. 276.

[3]    *The Church, Towards a Common Vision*, Faith and Order Paper No. 214 (Geneva: World Council of Churches, 2013), § 19.

Three fundamental tasks of ordained ministry are distinguished: proclaiming the Word of God, celebrating the sacraments, and guiding the life of the community. Those who are ordained should focus on these responsibilities, and those who are called to take these tasks upon them should be ordained! Therefore, I can largely narrow down my leading question to the issue of the authority to administer the sacraments of baptism and the Holy Supper. Who is able to do this, why, and under which conditions?

First, I will describe how the church order of the Protestant Church in the Netherlands has dealt with this issue. Next, a survey of recent discussions in the General Synod of the Protestant Church in the Netherlands may show the dilemmas at stake. And finally, I will give some theological observations that may help to clarify the theological issue of ordained ministry.

## Church Order Developments in the Netherlands

Slight changes in the view of ordained ministry within the Protestant Church in the Netherlands and the three churches that united into it have occurred in the church order of the Protestant Church in the Netherlands as it was developed in the 1990s and became church law in 2004. After that, and step by step, further changes were introduced. But let me begin with the classical Reformed position.

### Before 2004

The church orders of the three churches that united into the Protestant Church in the Netherlands—the Netherlands Reformed Church, the Reformed Churches in the Netherlands, and the Evangelical Lutheran Church in the Kingdom of the Netherlands—were unanimous in that they left no room for anyone else but an ordained minister to administer sacraments.

The church order of the Reformed Churches in the Netherlands presents a clear example. It starts from the rule that not only ministers (in the church order called "ministers of the Word") and "proponents" (licensed ministerial candidates) can have permission to preach; others are entitled to do so if they have received a license according to the rules as enacted by the General Synod. In practice, however, this meant that, particularly in the Reformed Churches in the Netherlands, many people were licensed to preach, or—in the language of this church order—"to lead and officiate in a worship service." The Netherlands Reformed Church and the Evangelical Lutheran Church were more reticent in this respect.

However, there is a limit in terms of church law, also in the Reformed Churches in the Netherlands: "[I]n exercising this competence they will refrain from all actions that have an official [*ambtelijk*] character."[4] What is meant with such "official actions" (i.e., actions that are part of the office of minister) can be concluded from another article that deals with the tasks of the minister. Apart from preaching, the minister has as his or her tasks "the administration of the sacraments; giving the benediction; leading all further official actions in worship, like in particular the administration of public profession, making announcements regarding admonishment and discipline, confirming office-bearers, confirming marriages and catechesis."[5] The same limitations were in place for licensed ministerial candidates.

Under no circumstances someone could legally administer the sacraments without being ordained as a minister.

*2004: A New Church Order*

As of May 1, 2004, the Protestant Church in the Netherlands is a fact, and a new church order is in place, consisting in a constitution (*Kerkorde*), 14 ordinances (*ordinanties*) as by-laws, and a set of general regulations (*generale regelingen*), which contain technical elaborations. Three churches had come to a common position regarding the authority to lead worship services.

It is regulated in Ordinance 5, on Worship, Article 5. The first paragraph of this article deals with the authority of the ministers of the church and of churches with which the Protestant Church in the Netherlands has an ecumenical relationship. The second paragraph (ord 5-5-2) regulates the authority of others: licensed ministerial candidates, students who get a license as part of their theological training, and a third category, "those to whom—in accordance with the rules of the "General regulation regarding the granting of a license to lead worship services"—a license has been granted to preach in the Protestant Church in the Netherlands, i.e., in worship services of those congregations mentioned in the license." In the next sentence of the same paragraph, the limitations are set: "The authority meant in this paragraph does not include the administration of baptism and the

---

[4]    *Kerkorde van de Gereformeerde Kerken in Nederland* vastgesteld door de generale synode van Assen (1957) met de door volgende synoden daarin aangebrachte wijzigingen, aangevuld met uitvoeringsbepalingen, (Kampen:Kok, 2001)Article 69.3.
[5]    *RCN*, Article 10.

Holy Supper, the administration of public profession, confirming office-bearers, confirming marriages, and giving the benediction."

The "General regulation regarding the granting of a license to lead worship services," usually known as general regulation on preaching licenses, includes further limitations regarding those who can apply for a license. It distinguishes three categories that may qualify for a preaching license: those who attend the theological training for ministry, those who have completed such training without having become ministers, and those who work in a congregation as "church workers." The latter category consists of people with a professional but non-academic theological training; after they have completed this training, they are registered in a special register and can apply for a position as church workers. Many of them had no job and therefore did not qualify for a preaching license in 2004. According to ord 3-12-4, church workers could not be elders or deacons in the congregation in which they worked, because they are employees of the church council in terms of civil labor law (which is not true for ministers).

According to a transitional stipulation, those who had had a preaching license in one of the three churches before the unification and would no longer qualify were given the option to apply for a continuation, the criterium for granting such a license being in "the interest of the church." In practice, most licenses were prolonged.

So in fact, not much changed. However, one new rule in the ordinances opened another door. During the long process of working on a church order (1991–2004), the longing for more focus on the missionary task of the church instead of that on church order regulations had increased year by year, and, from its very first session after the unification, the General Synod of the Protestant Church in the Netherlands focused on mission. In one issue, this was reflected in the new church order. In ord 2-18, the classical assembly was given the authority to make special arrangements for a congregation in an urban area and in "special missionary, diaconal and pastoral circumstances."[6] Among these possible arrangements, one was specified: "granting to one or more elders or deacons the authority to perform—in case of the absence of a minister—official acts of a minister, like leading worship

---

[6] Ordinance 2-18-1. Congregations in rural areas needed permission from the General Synod. See for the original 2004 version, as well as the outdated 2016 and the now operative 2018 version of the church order: https://www.protestantsekerk. nl/actief-in-de-kerk/kerkorde/kerkorde-en-ordinanties.

services and administering the sacraments, under supervision of a minister as designated."

*2009–2013: Evaluation*

The decision of three synods in 2003 to accept the new church order had included that after five years a thorough evaluation of its functioning would take place. In 2009, a special committee was appointed to lead this process. All kinds of hearings and consultations were held, and a website for suggestions from grass-roots level was opened. In a next step, the General Synod gave a list of directives to change the rules, and its church order committee was asked to present proposals for change. These were decided according to the rules, and as of January 2013, quite a few church order changes became law.

From the perspective of this article, some of them are relevant. First, from then on, a preaching license could also be granted to someone registered as church worker if he or she was not really working as such.[7] Second, whereas church workers could not be elders or deacons before 2013, they must now (in principle) be elder or deacon.[8] And third, the classical assembly received a new authorization with regard to church workers working in a congregation "in special circumstances": in addition to a preaching license, the classical assembly could give them "the authority to administer baptism and the Holy Supper, to administer public profession, to confirm office-bearers, to confirm marriages, and to give the benediction."[9] This authorization would only apply to services in that specific congregation. It would be confirmed in a worship service by the act of laying on hands by a minister (!).[10] Church workers who worked as chaplains in institutions like hospitals could receive the same authorization.[11]

So, again a wider circle of people had been granted the authority to administer the sacraments. Finally, the missional character of the church was strengthened by the introduction of "missionary congregations," and "extraordinary congregations."[12] The former are in fact missionary satellites of existing congregations with a certain degree of independence, the latter are groups of Christians—for instance, free

[7]   Ordinance 3-12-10.
[8]   Ordinance 3-12-6.
[9]   Ordinance 3-12-11.
[10]   Ordinance 3-12-12.
[11]   Ordinance 3-13-5.
[12]   See ordinance 2-18a and ordinance 2-17a (*Church Order 2013*), respectively.

congregations of ethnic minorities—that want to become part of the Protestant Church in the Netherlands and can do so under special conditions.

### 2009: Start of Pioneer Spots

As of 2009, "pioneer spots" (*pioniersplekken*) were introduced in the Protestant Church in the Netherlands. As we will see below (p. 191), no church order rules were made to provide for such missionary projects. However, in April 2014, the General Synod took a decision to stretch the scope of the church order regulation regarding congregations in "special missionary, diaconal and pastoral circumstances."[13] It gave a general approval that a classical assembly, within certain procedural limitations, could consider a congregation with a pioneer spot linked to it as a congregation meant in ord 2-18. In fact, this made it possible to grant the authority to administer sacraments to pioneers as well. One could argue that the General Synod was not able to do what it did without changing the church order itself, but no opposition was heard.

### 2016: 'Church 2025'

In 2015, another major operation was initiated. At the initiative of its board, the General Synod started a series of discussions regarding the mid-term future of the church against the background of developments in society. Main issues to be dealt with were: the tendency toward a more and more secular and plural society, individualization, the development toward a network society, digitalization and globalization. The process started with an exploratory report, "Church Towards 2025," and was later commonly called "Church 2025." Its main thrust was presented in the report "Church 2025: Where There is a Word, There is a Way" in early 2016, which was followed by "Church 2025: A Next Step" (April 2016). After that, proposals for church order changes were presented twice a year, either in first or in second reading; in November 2018 the last (minor) steps were taken. Altogether, so many changes were made that it was no longer possible to speak of the Church Order 2004. As of May 1, 2018, the Church Order 2018 is in place.

In the framework of this article, it is not possible to even give a short summary of the changes made. Only a few major renewals can be reported. One of the objectives was to diminish the number of

---

[13]    Ordinance 2-18.

regulations congregations, and particularly church councils, had to deal with; in many cases where, for instance, it had been necessary to ask the classical assembly for permission to act, this rule was canceled. The freedom of the congregations to make their own policies—for instance, regarding cooperation with other congregations—increased. Further, the traditional idea of a "territorial congregation" was left further behind in favor of "congregations by choice." A large impact was the decision to reduce the number of classical assemblies from 74 to 11; as of 2018, congregations are no longer directly represented in the classical assembly, but church councils can nominate office-bearers and then elect some representatives from their region. Finally, also new is the possibility to close down a congregation, if—in terms of membership and resources—it is no longer possible to continue its existence. The legal duty to merge with another congregation in such a case is no longer there.

No new rules were set regarding the authority to administer the sacraments. In some cases, new wordings (e.g., ord 2-18, now 2-6) were adopted, but the content did not change. However, maybe the most significant change was in the area of ministry. In the church order, the office of "classical minister" (*classispredikant*) was introduced; each classical assembly called a minister to serve in this office. His or her task is partly like that of a visitator (traditional visitation by a couple of visitors is abolished): to visit the congregations, the ministers, and the church workers regularly; and to advise and help them out where necessary and possible. In some cases, the classispredikant can provisionally exercise the responsibilities of the classical assembly in order to prevent a crisis from getting worse, for instance by giving a minister a temporary leave of absence. If necessary, the board of the classical assembly can revoke such a ruling within a few weeks. The main goal is that the classispredikant serves as a *pastor pastorum*. Synod considered to give this function the name of "bishop" but decided not to do so because of major objections in the more conservative part of the church and because of the not-very-positive image that (Roman Catholic) bishops have in Dutch society. The opportunity to present another kind of bishop to society was not seized.

Also, no rules were adopted with a view to pioneer spots, and deliberately so. The idea was that new forms should not be unnecessarily burdened with existing habits, structures, and organization of the church; they should get the opportunity to grow in a way that does justice to those who participate. So until now, there is no church order regulation explicitly applicable to such projects.

## A Mosaic of "Church Spots"

### Background

I already referred to the fact that, in 2009, a project of the Protestant Church in the Netherlands was initiated with the goal to start a number of "pioneer spots." Local initiatives could apply for support in terms of advice and resources from the national church. The idea is that the traditional form of congregations—although still valuable for many members of the church—does not sufficiently appeal to the religious and spiritual needs of people in Dutch society. New forms of community and communication are to be found in order to restore contact with society. In 2013, the General Synod set the goal of 100 new pioneer spots nationwide. Different initiatives were recognized, like "messy churches" (regular meetings of children and adults, together working creatively on biblical stories), pub churches, and monastic initiatives, including new forms of community life.[14] A pioneer spot is described as a new form of church for people that do not go to church. All kinds of forms can apply. Tuning to the context, working from a shared faith within the pioneering team, and the building of sustainable communities are all important. These pioneer spots, or "church spots" (*kerkplekken*), have become the object of intensive synodical discussion from 2017.

### January 2017: Inventorization

After eight years of pioneering, an inventory of developments, experiences, lessons learned, and challenges was made early 2017. Before 2013, there were seven pioneer spots, highly subsidized by the national church and with professional staff. From 2013, when the goal of 100 new spots was set, 84 new initiatives were registered with lower budgets and mainly relying on volunteers. Altogether, about 10,000 people were involved, half of them not belonging to a church. Theologians played a role in five out of six projects, most of them academics but also many with a professional training. In nearly 70 percent of the pioneer spots, some form of worship service had a place; in nearly as many spots, some form of communal meals played a role as well. These developments are regarded a spiritual blessing. Theological questions arise as well: How do we understand ministry in this context? What does salvation mean?

---

[14] See: "Mozaïek van kerkplekken" https://www.protestantsekerk.nl/themas/missionair-werk/mozaiek-van-kerkplekken.

Can a church do without professionals? To what extent can baptism and the Holy Supper be contextualized? What is the relevance of a form of membership? Such questions bring us back to the roots of what it means to be church, and they require further research and theological reflection. In 2017, intensive consultations were held in order to get more grip on the matter before involving the General Synod.

*February 2018: Between Uncontrolled Proliferation and Renewal*

A first report to the General Synod reflected on these findings, and particularly on the connection of such new church spots with the church as such. Its title was "Between Uncontrolled Proliferation and Renewal."[15]

The report deals with three fields: (1) community building, networking, and membership; (2) offices, sacraments, and the role of ministers; and (3) organization, decision making, and church government. In the second field, it refers to the decision of the General Synod of April 2014 to give pioneers room to accomplish all tasks normally done by ministers but only within that particular context and under supervision of a minister. Theological education is not required. The number of such pioneers has grown and is expected to continue to grow. Ever more volunteers get involved, like theater makers, teachers, and entrepreneurs. It is recognized as self-evident that in new faith communities the need for rituals like the sacraments, blessings, et cetera will grow.

However, the report raises some fundamental questions:

- Quite a few church spots function without any office-bearer. Should new church spots grow towards a "complete" ministerial structure including the traditional three offices? Should they get the usual place of a congregation within the organizational structure of the Protestant Church in the Netherlands? Should there be at least one office-bearer on every team? Would it be wise to develop a new office, like evangelist? How does this relate to the traditional presbyterial-synodical set-up of the church?
- The size and resources of most new church spots make it impossible to call a (part-time) minister. In many cases, theological training is not seen as very relevant; other leadership qualities are regarded as more important. Is it all right when, in

---

[15] *Tussen wildgroei en vernieuwing*, Protestantse Kerk, February 1, 2018, https://www.protestantsekerk.nl/download7252/Startpaper%20-%20Tussen%20wildgroei%20en%20vernieuwing.pdf, 6.

many places, sacraments will soon be administered by people without a substantial theological training? What impact does this have on "traditional" ministers?

· If so, what are the implications for ministers who somehow may assist church spots? Will they be coaches, or supervisors, taking care of quality? Or won't they play any role at all in such church spots?

· Should someone with a recognized theological training always be involved?

· Do we need to develop lighter versions of theological training?

In terms of organization (field 3), the question of the juridical status of the church spots is pointed out. Should they fit in the traditional structures, or is it possible to create a kind of "deregulated zone" for them with a minimum of organization and consultation?

### May 2018: Elasticity and Tension

A second report was published a few months afterwards. Its title might be translated as "Elasticity and Tension."[16] It is a research report based on a survey about relations between traditional congregations and new church spots.

The report shows that, despite good intentions, it is difficult in pratice to connect a new church spot with an existing congregation. The existing rules and structures simply don't fit, and sometimes there is open competition. The survey further says that 65 percent of those involved (both from traditional congregations and from new church spots) don't see elders and deacons as necessary for new church spots, and even 75 percent say so about ministers. Seventy-one percent of the respondents accept that sacraments can be administered by those without a theological education. However, for most respondents, a theological training is more important than the incorporation in ecclesial structures of office. Supervision by regular ministers is well appreciated. There is some concern about the quality of the sermons of lay leaders. Would not the same apply for "regular" congregations? Fifty-two percent of the respondents are positive about the possibility for non-theologians to lead worship services in such congregations, but 40 percent are negative.

---

[16]   *Over speelruimte en spanning: praktijkonderzoek naar de relatie tussen bestaande en nieuwe kerkplekken*, Protestantse Kerk, May 2018, https://www.protestantsekerk. nl/download8129/Onderzoeksrapport%20-%20Over%20speelruimte%20en%20 spanning.pdf.

Regarding (ordained) ministry, different views are being expressed, but the main tendency is a relativization of traditional office, particularly with those involved in new church spots. It is not seen as very relevant if quality is guaranteed. Fifty-one percent of the respondents would be in favor of an additional, new office for new church spots. Ordained office is not seen as a condition for the authority to administer baptism; basically, the community itself should be able to decide on who might have that authority. In fact, the same goes for the authority to administer the Holy Supper, but here other questions arise as well. The context of the Holy Supper at new church spots is quite different from that of regular congregations. The diverse composition of the group of participants and sometimes the fact that the Holy Supper is celebrated as part of a normal meal foster unrestricted participation of those attending. For many, inviting a minister from "outside" to administer the Holy Supper is artificial. The report concludes that the main challenge is to revisit the theological principles behind (ordained) ministry and church membership and to create more room for different practical forms.

Regarding the relation between traditional structures and new church spots, the report sketches four scenarios. The first is a complete embedding of new church spots in traditional structures (only one percent in favor). The second regards the adaptation of the existing organization to make room for new church spots (31 percent). A third option would be to create a separate "order" for new church spots (with two pioneer ministers taking full responsibility for all new church spots), loosely linked with the traditional structures (49 percent); here, order is not meant as a set of regulations but as a grouping more or less comparable with the religious orders in the Roman Catholic Church. And the final option is to maintain the movement as it is, without any—old or new—framework (16 percent).

*November 2018: A Mosaic of Church Spots*

In the second half of 2018, again, consultations were held in order to share the theological questions at stake with all kinds of people. Based on these discussions, a third (provisional) report was presented to the General Synod in its session of November 2018, "A Mosaic of Church Spots."[17] The introduction speaks of altogether about 250 new initiatives since 2005.

[17]    *Voorproefje: Mozaïek van kerkplekken. Over verbinding tussen bestaande en nieuwe vormen van kerk-zijn.*

What are the minimum requirements to qualify as a church spot? The report suggests the following criteria:

a) There is a group of people who want to live out of God's grace in Jesus Christ,

b) who meet regularly and publicly around Word and sacraments,

c) who want to build a stabile faith community together,

d) that commits itself to the world, in mission and diaconate, and starting from its own context,

e) that exists of at least ten adults that use their gifts for this church spot,

f) under the leadership of a "church spot council," including at least three members of the Protestant Church in the Netherlands that serve in an office in the church,

g) and with in this council at least one (ordained?) person with the ministry of Word and sacraments,

h) and connected with the Protestant Church in the Netherlands as such by participating on a yearly basis in an order for new church spots, and by building good relationships with congregations nearby,

i) taking responsibility for its policies and finances itself,

J) and cooperating with the church regarding oversight and dealing with complaints and conflicts.[18]

The idea is that this might provide an acceptable balance between the necessary room for new church spots and the concreteness required. In an (unpublished) discussion paper that was used in the process of preparing this report, it is stated that every faith community needs some form of office. However, the priesthood or office of all believers is fundamental, and office is always embedded in a collectivity. The form office takes can vary, and spiritual leadership is a matter of organic growth. The paper refers to Article V of the Constitution of the Protestant Church in the Netherlands: "To focus the congregation on salvation and to keep it to its call in the world the public office of Word and Sacrament was given on the part of Christ. With a view to this ministry, the church distinguishes the office of minister, the office of elder, the office of deacon as well as other ministries in church and congregation." The distinction made between the gift of the public

---

[18] *Voorproefje: Mozaïek van kerkplekken,* Protestantse Kerk, https://www.protestantsekerk. nl/download7065/Voorproefje%20rapport%20'Moza%C3%Afek%20van%20 kerkplekken'.pdf, 18.

office of Word and sacrament on the one hand and the differentiation in three offices (and other ministries) by the church on the other hand opens ways for the contextualization of the public office of Word and sacrament in new circumstances. Spiritual leadership can be given new forms in order to do justice to the informal character of most new church spots without neglecting the fundamental orientation of the community toward Jesus Christ.

Recent discussions within the Protestant Church in the Nether-lands have made it clear that there are quite different views about the issue of (ordained) ministry: there is a mix of "high church" and "low church" ideas. Often, office-bearers are reluctant to understand their office in classical terms like vocation, sacrifice, or supervision and rather characterize their responsibility in terms of guiding or facilitating. Nevertheless, they see their role as more than just a function: the church is not an association but a faith community, and that makes a difference.

## Theological Considerations

What can we learn from these developments in the Netherlands, and how can we deal with them with a view to a truly Reformed and ecumenical understanding of ordained ministry?

### A Reformed Perspective on Ordination

"The Church: Towards a Common Vision" does not speak about the ordination as such in detail. In this respect, it implicitly confirms what was already said in the Ministry part of the Faith and Order report on "Baptism, Eucharist and Ministry" (1982). It reads,

> A long and early Christian tradition places ordination in the context of worship and especially of the eucharist. Such a place for the service of ordination preserves the understanding of ordination as an act of the whole community, and not of a certain order within it or of the individual ordained. The act of ordination by the laying on of hands of those appointed to do so is at one and the same time invocation of the Holy Spirit (*epiklesis*); sacramental sign; acknowledgment of gifts and commitment.[19]

---

[19]   *Baptism, Eucharist and Ministry*, Faith and Order Paper No. 111 (Geneva: World Council of Churches, 1982), Ministry (BEM/M), § 41.

In the following paragraphs, these three aspects are further elaborated. Ordination is

> (a) an invocation to God that the new minister be given the power of the Holy Spirit in the new relation which is established between this minister and the local Christian community and, by intention, the Church universal ... (b) ... a sign of the granting of this prayer by the Lord who gives the gift of the ordained ministry ... (c) ... an acknowledgment by the Church of the gifts of the Spirit in the one ordained, and a commitment by both the Church and the ordinand to the new relationship .... [20]

"The Church: Towards a Common Vision" discerns three main responsibilities of ordained ministers: they assemble and build up the Body of Christ by (1) proclaiming and teaching the Word of God, by (2) celebrating the sacraments, and by (3) guiding the life of the community in its worship, its mission, and its caring ministry. It is not difficult to recognize the connection with the Reformed confessional tradition regarding the "true church," as, for instance, expressed in Article 29 of the Belgic Confession. What makes a church really "church," from a theological perspective, is the pure proclamation of the gospel, the pure administration of the sacraments in accordance with Holy Scripture, and the maintenance of church discipline. In other words: what ecumenical dialogue qualifies as the core of ordained ministry (proclamation, celebration, and guidance, or spiritual leadership) reflects what the Reformed tradition understands as the core of being church (proclamation, administration of sacraments, and church discipline). So from a Reformed ecclesiological perspective, there may be good reasons to stipulate a difference between the ministry of Word and sacraments (as vital to the being of the church) and other ministries that contribute to the well-being of the church, like the offices of elder and deacon. In my view, the point of departure should be that the three aspects mentioned belong together in ordained ministry: the administration of the sacraments is a self-evident extension of the proclamation of the gospel, and there we find also the roots of spiritual leadership.

Therefore, someone who has a license to preach should normally also be licensed to administer the sacraments. The same persons should also be involved in spiritual leadership, exercised in a collegial and

---

[20]    BEM/M, §§ 42–44.

communal way, together with others, and they may have a special role in that regard. Exceptions in both respects are possible, for instance in the case of students who, as part of their theological training, have a preaching license for a limited period, but indeed this is an exception. The rule should be that a license is a full license, indeed.

It should not be difficult for churches like the Protestant Church in the Netherlands, with its strong roots in the Reformed tradition, to recognize that the church needs a form of ordained ministry as understood in ecumenical dialogue in order to be fully church. The church needs people who accept and exercise the threefold responsibility of ordained ministry. All those who do so should be ordained, irrespective of the exact nomenclature; they may be called ministers, priests, teaching elders, or whatever seems suitable, as long as it is clear that they are recognized as ordained ministers. And, from the opposite perspective, all those who are ordained (under whatever title) should have the authority linked with this threefold responsibility.

In practice, this implies that the tasks that the church order of the Protestant Church in the Netherlands attributes to elders and deacons, like many other Reformed church orders, do not qualify them for ordination. Characteristic of these offices is that their authority is limited to the congregation of which they are part. Therefore, elders and deacons cannot serve in presbyteries or synods if they are not delegated by their local church council. And they cannot serve in another congregation without the approval of the same church council and that of the receiving congregation (if at all).

Those who are ordained don't have their legitimation from the local congregation. They come "from outside" and are called by and received in the congregation. By virtue of their office, they can serve in other congregations, if invited. In my view, their authorization to preach and to administer sacraments cannot be limited in terms of locality, but it is possible to set limitations to their eligibility for a call, for instance in terms of specific gifts needed or special circumstances. In principle, an ordained minister is eligible beyond denominational boundaries: ordination has an ecumenical impact.

### A Threefold Ordained Ministry

The BEM report suggests that "the threefold ministry of bishop, presbyter and deacon may serve today as an expression of the unity we seek and also as a means for achieving it. ... In the fulfillment of their mission and service the churches need people who in different ways express and perform the tasks of the ordained ministry in its diaconal, presbyteral and episcopal aspects and functions."[21] It seems to me that the Protestant Church in the Netherlands is developing into that direction of a threefold diversification of *ordained* ministry, different from (or in addition to) the traditional Reformed three offices of minister, elder, and deacon.

The episcopal aspect and function of ordained ministry has become visible in the new position of the classispredikant, who is called to serve the unity of the church, acting as a pastor pastorum and supervisor. BEM's description of the office of bishops may not fit completely to their task, but it does so to a high extent:

> Bishops preach the Word, preside at the sacraments, and ad-
> minister discipline in such a way as to be representative pastoral
> ministers of oversight, continuity and unity in the Church. They
> have pastoral oversight of the area to which they are called. They
> serve the apostolicity and unity of the Church's teaching, worship
> and sacramental life. They have responsibility for leadership in
> the Church's mission. They relate the Christian community in
> their area to the wider Church, and the universal Church to their
> community. They, in communion with the presbyters and deacons
> and the whole community, are responsible for the orderly transfer
> of ministerial authority in the Church.[22]

The local minister stands for the presbyteral aspect and function of ordained ministry; what BEM says about this office could easily be accepted in a Reformed church order as a description of the office of the local minister:

> Presbyters serve as pastoral ministers of Word and sacraments in
> a local eucharistic community. They are preachers and teachers
> of the faith, exercise pastoral care, and bear responsibility for
> the discipline of the congregation to the end that the world
> may believe and that the entire membership of the Church may
> be renewed, strengthened and equipped in ministry. Presbyters
> have particular responsibility for the preparation of members for
> Christian life and ministry.[23]

Their ministry focuses on the existing congregations, and they are called by a congregation.

[21] BEM/M, § 22.
[22] BEM/M, § 29.
[23] BEM/M, § 30.

An embryonal form of the diaconal aspect and function of ordained ministry is visible in the new function of the pioneer. BEM says:

> Deacons represent to the Church its calling as servant in the world. By struggling in Christ's name with the myriad needs of societies and persons, deacons exemplify the interdependence of worship and service in the Church's life. They exercise responsibility in the worship of the congregation: for example by reading the Scriptures, preaching and leading the people in prayer. They help in the teaching of the congregation. They exercise a ministry of love within the community. They fulfil certain administrative tasks and may be elected to responsibilities for governance.[24]

This description takes its starting point in the orientation of the deacon toward the world, and I think that we could and should read the rest from that very perspective, although it seems to focus more on internal responsibilities. Unfortunately, in the Roman Catholic Church, the deacon has often lost this external orientation and has rather become an assistant priest. The Protestant deacon has better maintained this external orientation of this office, but he or she does not preach or teach. The pioneers may become a better example of what BEM intends: oriented toward the world, their role in worship (preaching, teaching, and praying) concerns the building of new communities. Although BEM does not explicitly mention the sacraments in this context, it seems to me self-evident that they can also baptize and administer the Holy Supper. In principle, pioneers are not necessarily *called* by an existing congregation, but they are *sent* by the church to their pioneer spot. In fact, it is very much like the missionary we know from our mission history.

### No Hierarchy

Intuitively, such a structure may be understood as incompatible with what has often been the "golden rule" of Reformed Church polity, as expressed in the famous words of the first article of the Church Order of the Synod of Emden (1571): "No church shall lord it over another church, no minister of the Word, no elder or deacon shall lord it over another, but each one shall guard him against all suspicion and enticement to lord it over others." A kind of hierarchy in the relation

---

[24]    BEM/M, § 31.

between classispredikant, minister, and pioneer might seem to be hardly evitable. But that fully depends on the way the competencies, in terms of government and leadership, are divided among them. If decision making is basically attributed to assemblies (synods, classical assemblies, church councils, and church spot councils), and if in all cases an appeal against decisions of individual office-bearers is possible, the risk of hierarchical behavior is limited. By the way, the Belgic Confession does not speak of the same power and authority for all office-bearers: *"As for the ministers of the Word,* they all have the same power and authority, no matter where they may be, since they are all servants of Jesus Christ."[25] This makes perfect sense: in their shared responsibility to interpret situations in the light of Scripture, no one can claim any priority over others.

The core of Reformed polity is not that the three offices are equal but that they are equivalent; it is collegiality and communality (in ecumenical terms, conciliarity) than can prevent hierarchy. There is no reason at all to exclude elders and deacons (or other non-ordained officers) from church government. "Guiding the life of the community in its worship, its mission and its caring ministry" is not the same as church government. [26] Rather, it points toward the specific role of ordained ministers within the governing bodies: by virtue of their office, they have a special responsibility to contribute to the discussion from the perspective of their office as "ministers of the Word." Their authority should reside in the convincing power of their arguments and nowhere else. Of course, this does not exclude other office-bearers from the possibility and duty to understand how to govern the church in accordance with Scripture.

What I suggest here is in no way an underestimation or depreciation of the office of elders or deacons. In his first letter to the Corinthians, Paul deals with the issue of unity and distinction: "And if the ear should say, 'Because I am not an eye, I do not belong to the body,' that would not make it any less a part of the body. If the whole body were an eye, where would the hearing be? ... As it is, there are many members, yet one body. The eye cannot say to the hand, 'I have no need of you,' nor again the head to the feet, 'I have no need of you.'"[27] Not the whole body can be eye, but the eye is needed anyhow. It is not my eye that sees; it is me. The body is more than the total sum of its parts.

---

[25]　Article 31, emphasis added.
[26]　*The Church*, § 19.
[27]　1 Corinthians 12:16-22.

*A Way Forward?*

It seems to me that in fact two arguments play a dominant role in excluding pioneers (and church workers) from ordained ministry and in the emergency solution of giving them the authority to administer sacraments anyhow. One has to do with theological education and the other with financial arrangements.

Pioneers do not always have an academic theological training. There is a fear that including them in ordained ministry would, in the long run, make academic theological education less attractive and would open more doors for ministers, also in existing congregations, without such education.[28] This would not only damage the interests of the Protestant Theological University, the one and only institute for ministerial training in the Protestant Church in the Netherlands; it might also have consequences in terms of the role of ministers in modern culture with its emphasis on intellectual debate. These are real concerns, but they cannot convince me as arguments against ordaining pioneers. Of course, the church should seriously consider what kind of theological training is needed for the respective categories of ministers of the Word in the context of secular society. That is already the case in, for instance, a special theological training trajectory for chaplaincy in hospitals, prisons, et cetera.

The financial argument concerns the position of ministers in terms of labor law. The salary of ministers is related to their academic training, and congregations are obliged to pay a salary according to directives made under the responsibility of the General Synod. Usually, people with a non-academic training get lower wages than those with academic training; this goes for pioneers as well as church workers. This might increase pressure from the side of (small) congregations to make it possible to call pioneers and church workers as "normal" ministers. It will take quite some deliberations how to manage such developments. I don't see a fundamental theological reason why someone with a non-academic professional training could not serve an existing congregation as an ordained minister, but the church can have good reasons to regulate this in terms of teamwork and supervision.

Whatever decisions will be necessary in terms of theological training and finances, I plead in favor of changing the nomenclature in

---

[28]    In my view, there is no valid theological reason not to ordain church workers who are granted the license to preach. In my systematics, they would also be fully licensed ministers (as *predikanten*, see next footnote) although may be limited in terms of eligibility.

the church order of the Protestant Church in the Netherlands as far as it concerns the ministers. In the church order, the ministers are called *predikanten* (preachers) as equivalent to "minister of the Word," a term used only once in the church order.[29] The latter term could, however, serve as an overarching category for those who are ordained, i.e., both predikanten (serving within the traditional structures of the church) and pioneers (serving in a missional context). It would not require far-reaching church order changes. It would be important to introduce the terminology of ordaining and ordination into the church order as distinguished from "confirming'" and "confirmation." The former would be applied to "ministers of the Word" and the latter to elders and deacons. From a historical perspective, this would in fact be the re-introduction of a distinction that was used in the Lutheran church order before 2004.

---

[29]   Cf. ordinance 3-5-2: "the freedom of the minister (*predikant*) as minister of the Word (*dienaar des Woords*)."

CHAPTER 12

# A Theologian's "Novel" Guide
# to Growing Old in Christ

## Carol M. Bechtel

Theologians worth their salt will not wake up the day after they pick up their last paycheck and say, "Okay, I'm done being a theologian now."

Stanley Hauerwas points this out and raises the broader question of whether "retirement" is a relevant concept for Christians. He writes,

> I think it quite fascinating that there is nothing in the New Testament about retirement. It surely never occurred to Paul to think, "I've done the best I can but I am never going to get those Christians in Corinth to straighten out. I am tired of traveling and controversy. I think it is time for me to retire." Nowhere in the New Testament is there a hint that the early Christians think there is a time when they might retire as Christians or from being Christians. I do not think this was only due to the early death of many Christians. Rather I believe Christians could not conceive how their lives could make sense if they did not assume they had particular responsibilities and obligations as they grew old in Christ.[1]

---

[1] Stanley Hauerwas, "How to (Not) Retire Theologically" in *Reflections of Theological and Ethical Inquiry from Yale Divinity School* (New Haven: Yale University, 2013). See

So, perhaps we should leave off thinking in terms of retirement and proceed instead under the rubric of growing old in Christ. Then it will be possible to explore what "particular responsibilities and obligations" a theologian might have in this work of theirs that is—happily—never done.

Of all the pursuits that might clamber for position on such a list, it strikes me that there is one that could plead priority: to become a deeper person. Preacher, pastor, and theologian Doug Nelson once winked conspiratorially at me in the midst of a conversation about the book of Job. "Never pray to become a deeper person," he warned. "It's way too dangerous."

He was right, of course. A safer approach might be to pray, "Gracious God, in whatever trials you should send my way—and don't feel you need to send any at all—help me to process them in such a way as to become a deeper person." This more moderate prayer has much to commend it, especially since aging comes with its own formidable set of challenges. Why ask for more? Still, if the prayer Nelson warned against was overly courageous, then this one could be accused of being too cowardly. Safety, after all, does not seem to be the primary consideration for a people called to take up their cross.

There must be a more excellent way, or at least, a more practical way. Time is short, after all. What if we were to allow God to write whatever prescription God deems appropriate by way of depth-inducing trials? (God will undoubtedly do this with or without our permission.) In the meantime, there *is* one relatively safe way to become a deeper person, and the beauty of it is that, now that you have quit your day job, you may have more time for it.

This depth-inducing activity is: reading novels.

Novels are sometimes shunned as "mere" escapism. To this one could respond: "And what's wrong with a little escapism? It's good for one's blood pressure!" Be that as it may, the novel's ability to invite us to use our God-given imagination is both overlooked and underrated.

For example, a recent edition of the journal *Scientific American* breathlessly announced that reading literary fiction can improve one's empathy.[2] Anyone who has read more than a page and a half of a Jane Austen novel could have told us that. Still, I suppose we should be glad they have found a way to scientifically demonstrate this.

---

also the essays in Stanley Hauerwas, Carole Bailey Stoneking, Keith Meador, and David Cloutier, eds., *Growing Old in Christ* (Grand Rapids: Eerdmans, 2003).

[2]    Julianne Chiaet, "Novel Finding: Reading Literary Fiction Improves Empathy," *Scientific American* (October 4, 2013).

A good novel excavates the heart and the world in a way that we simply don't have the skills or the time for as we're hurtling through it ourselves. And if it is *imitatio Dei* you are after, then novelists lead the way by creating new worlds for the rest of us to explore.

In what follows, I will suggest some novels that show particular promise for increasing empathy, activating imagination, and well helping their readers to become deeper people. The list is neither exhaustive nor, I hope, exhausting. But it is a good place to start. And at the end of the day, it's a much safer way to become a deeper person than just offering up the "blank check" prayer that Doug Nelson warned about.

**Dara Horn's *The World to Come***

Let's start with a novel by contemporary Jewish author, Dara Horn.

I suggested a moment ago that novels create new worlds for us to explore. One of these worlds that has given me much delight is the one created by Horn in *The World to Come*.[3] There are all sorts of reasons to love this novel, especially if you like suspense, art, ethics, history, and comparative literature. But it will also answer questions you may never have considered. Questions like: Where does that little ridge under our noses come from? What are babies doing before they are born? What do our dead relatives do in the afterlife? For lovers of the Hebrew Bible (Old Testament), however, there are treats on almost every page.

My favorite among favorites in this category is Horn's description of the Hebrew Bible as a wine list. Genesis, the sommelier informs the young character, Daniel, should be drunk very slowly since, "A lot of people just chug it down and miss the whole point."[4]

Daniel begins by taking tentative sips but soon mutters, "This is *very good*." Soon he begins "drinking directly from the bottle, curling up with it like [a baby], dreaming sweet drunken dreams of eleven stars and sheaves of grain bowing down before him. A hint of flint again as jealous siblings attacked on his tongue; then a soft note, later of sour grapes."[5]

When Daniel samples Ecclesiastes—notable for its "peculiarly balanced sweet-and-sour flavor"—he encounters a residue at the bottom of the bottle. He finds this "particularly hard to swallow" since it hints that

---

[3]    Dara Horn, *The World to Come* (New York: Norton, 2006).
[4]    Horn, 296.
[5]    Horn, 297.

"of the making of many books there is no end, and that much study is wearying of the flesh." He judges the vintage, at last, "a little too heavy," and admits that it makes him "thirsty for something simpler." So he reaches for the bottle of Psalms.

"Want a new glass?" the sommelier asks.

"Renew it as in days of old," Daniel says, and hiccups. Then, before he knows it, "his cup had runneth over."[6]

### Marilynne Robinson's *Gilead*

John Ames is the elderly Congregationalist pastor and leading voice in Marilynne Robinson's Pulitzer Prize-winning novel, *Gilead*.[7] Ames would appreciate these words about the early Christians, again, from Stanley Hauerwas:

> In particular those who were lucky enough to "grow old in Christ" had as one of their responsibilities to share the vulnerability of the body with their brothers and sisters in Christ. They well understood that we are creatures whose lives move always toward death. Accordingly, to grow old does not grant permission to be free of responsibility. Rather it obligates the elderly to live lives shaped by their baptism so they might help those who are not yet old learn how to grow old and even die.[8]

Ames feels this responsibility keenly, especially as it pertains to his young son. The child is the product of a late but happy marriage, and Ames's words throughout the novel are framed as an epistle for his son to read after Ames is dead.

Yet Ames's sense of baptismal calling and responsibility extends well beyond his son. The following passage could be read as a kind of love letter to his parishioners and neighbors:

> In those days, as I have said, I might spend most of a night reading. Then, if I woke up still in my armchair, and if the clock said four or five, I'd think how pleasant it was to walk through the streets in the dark. ...
> ...People are always up in the night, with their colicky babies and their sick children, or fighting or worrying or full of guilt. ... Sometimes when I walked past the house of one of my own

6   Horn, selected and adapted from 297–298.
7   Marilynne Robinson, *Gilead* (New York: Farrar, Straus and Giroux, 2004).
8   Hauerwas, "How to (Not) Retire Theologically."

families and saw lights on, I'd think maybe I should stop and see if there was a problem I could help with, but then I'd decide it might be an intrusion and I'd go on. ...

... It was on the nights I didn't sleep at all and I didn't feel like reading that I'd walk through town at one or two o-clock. In the old days I could walk down every single street, past every house, in about an hour. I'd try to remember the people who lived in each one, and whatever I knew about them, which was often quite a lot ... I'd pray for them. And I'd imagine peace they didn't expect and couldn't account for descending on their illness or their quarreling or their dreams. Then I'd go into the church and pray some more and wait for daylight. I've often been sorry to see a night end, even while I have loved seeing the dawn come.[9]

The following passage fairly shimmers with the theme of living a life shaped by baptism:

The mention of Feuerbach and joy reminded me of something I saw early one morning a few years ago, as I was walking up to the church. There was a young couple strolling along half a block ahead of me. The sun had come up brilliantly after a heavy rain, and the trees were glistening and very wet. On some impulse, plain exuberance, I suppose, the fellow jumped up and caught hold of a branch, and a storm of luminous water came pouring down on the two of them, and they laughed and took off running, the girl sweeping water off her hair and her dress as if she were a little bit disgusted, but she wasn't. It was a beautiful thing to see, like something from a myth. I don't know why I thought of that now, except perhaps because it is easy to believe in such moments that water was made primarily for blessings, and only secondarily for growing vegetables or doing the wash. I wish I had paid more attention to it. My list of regrets may seem unusual, but who can know that they are, really. This is an interesting planet. It deserves all the attention you can give it.[10]

One would think that passages like these would assuage one's soul-thirst for a while, but to be honest, they leave me greedy for more. The good news is *Gilead* has two sequels, so we can guzzle to our heart's content—or at least as long as it takes us to finish the next two novels.[11]

---

[9]  Robinson, 70–71.
[10]  Robinson, 28.
[11]  The sequels to *Gilead* are *Home* (2008) and *Lila* (2015).

**Alexander McCall Smith's *The No. 1 Ladies"Detective Agency***

Moving from the sublime to the sublimely ridiculous, don't overlook *The No. 1 Ladies' Detective Agency* series by Alexander McCall Smith. One quote from the first book of the same name as the subsequent series will be enough to whet your appetite. (Although when you read the quote, you may feel that to be an unfortunate metaphor.) Still, since the subject is relevant for both aging and current events, it's worth the risk of offending sensitive readers.

In the quote, the main character and founder of the No. 1 Ladies' Detective Agency, Mma Precious Ramotswe, muses about a sensitive subject:

> Now constipation was quite a different matter. It would be dreadful for the whole world to know about troubles of that nature. She felt terribly sorry for people who suffered from constipation, and she knew that there were many who did. There were probably enough of them for a political party—with a chance of government perhaps—what would such a party do if it was in power? Nothing, she imagined. It would try to pass legislation, but would fail.[12]

Moving right along ...

**Chimamanda Ngozi Adichie's *Purple Hibiscus***

On a day when the sun is shining brightly and all is as right as one can reasonably expect it to be with one's world, pick up Chimamanda Ngozi Adichie's debut novel, *Purple Hibiscus*.[13] The sunny day suggestion is a prophylactic against the often depressing subject matter of the book: abuse. But this is abuse on both an intimate and international scale.

Set in post-colonial Nigeria during the civil war of the 1960s, *Purple Hibiscus* invites us to see the world from the perspective of a 15-year-old girl named Kambili. That invitation is not always easy to accept. The world close to home for Kambili, her brother Jaja, and their mother is tightly and sadistically controlled by the family's patriarch, Eugene. "Papa" is a leading light in the community and the local church. He *does* have some genuinely admirable characteristics. It is hard to remember

[12]  Alexander McCall Smith, *The No. 1 Ladies' Detective Agency* (New York: Anchor Books, 2002), 195.
[13]  Chimamanda Ngozi Adichie, *Purple Hibiscus* (Chapel Hill: Algonquin, 2003).

what they are, however, when we meet him at home. A couple of quotes will suffice to indicate the essence of what his family has to contend with. Kambili confides,

> Things started to fall apart at home when my brother, Jaja, did not go to communion and Papa flung his heavy missal across the room and broke the figurines on the etagere ...[14] I meant to say I am sorry Papa broke your figurines, but the words that came out were, "I'm sorry your figurines broke, Mama."[15]

The book would be worth reading if "all" it did was to give us a cringe-worthy education about the inner dynamics of an abusive home. But the brilliance of the novel is the way the rings expand outward from this central situation. Adichie deftly helps us to recognize abusive dynamics in faith as well as family. Finally, the rings spread all the way across cultures and continents. After all, in which of those concentric circles would the following observation *not* fit?

> We did that often, asking each other questions whose answers we already knew. Perhaps it was so that we would not ask the other questions, the ones whose answers we did not want to know.[16]

This novel calls us to confess our sins on several levels, but Holy Week is followed by its own kind of Easter. This springs from both a plot twist (which I will leave you discover for yourself) and from the resilience, nobility, and integrity of the suffering servants at the heart of the story.

**George Eliot's *Adam Bede***

If *Purple Hibiscus* is the anatomy of abuse, then *Adam Bede* is the anatomy of temptation.

Written in 1859 by Mary Ann Evans under the pseudonym George Eliot, this novel is remarkable for any number of reasons—not least because of its sympathetic portrait of one of its main characters, Dinah Morris—a lay Methodist preacher in the late 1700s.

At the heart of the novel, however, is the triangle formed by carpenter Adam Bede, the young squire Arthur Donnithorne, and mild maid Hetty Sorrel. Adam has his heart set on Hetty and has some reason

---

[14]   Adichie, 3.
[15]   Adichie, 10.
[16]   Adichie, 23.

to expect that she may agree to be his wife. He has no reason to expect that his friend and benefactor, Arthur, will betray him by seducing Hetty.

Arthur knows he is in the wrong—or at least, he knows it on his best days. But like most of us, he finds it very easy to make excuses for himself. And as Eliot drolly points out, "It is possible ... to have very erroneous theories and very sublime feelings."[17]

Listen in to this conversation between Arthur and clergyman, Rev. Irwine. It takes place after flirtation but prior to seduction. Hiding the particulars of his own temptation by speaking safely in the abstract, Arthur asks his pastor,

> "But surely you don't think a man who struggles against a temptation into which he falls at last, as bad as the man who never struggles at all?"
>
> [Irwine responds] "No, my boy, I pity him, in proportion to his struggles, for they foreshadow the inward suffering which is the worst form of Nemesis. Consequences are unpitying. Our deeds carry their terrible consequences, quite apart from any fluctuations that went before—consequences that are hardly ever confined to ourselves."[18]

Rev. Irwine's words take on the full weight of prophecy as the story winds its painful way toward tragedy. One particularly memorable milestone on that road is the one where Adam confronts Arthur with what he has done. To Arthur's credit, he does not deny the indictment. But the impact of Adam's accusation is crushing.

> The words of hatred and contempt—the first he had ever heard in his life—seemed like scorching missiles that were making ineffaceable scars on him. All screening self-excuse, which rarely falls quite away while others respect us, forsook him for an instant, and he stood face to face with the first great irrevocable evil he had ever committed.[19]

One might think Eliot would end the story here, but in fact, she is just getting started. In what follows, she lavishes as much attention on the themes of justice and forgiveness as was previously given to temptation.

[17]    George Eliot, *Adam Bede* (Oxford World Classics Penguin paperback edition, 2008), 35.
[18]    Eliot, 156.
[19]    Eliot, 271.
[20]    Eliot, 475.

At the risk of giving too much away, consider this quote. It acknowledges the depth and beauty of the relationship that eventually develops between an older, wiser Adam and Dinah Morris.

> What greater thing is there for two human souls, than to feel that they are joined for life—to strengthen each other in all labour, to rest on each other in all sorrow, to minister to each other in all pain, to be one with each other in silent unspeakable memories at the moment of the last parting?[20]

## Wendell Berry's *Jayber Crow*

Let's skip across the centuries, now, to another author who writes compellingly about human community. All of Wendell Berry's novels take up this theme, but he introduces us to the fictional—yet achingly real—community of Port William in *Jayber Crow*.

There are many unforgettable passages one could quote from this book, but I think I will limit myself to one excerpt about that very thing: memory. Listen for the ways Berry braids various strands of memory together. It refers to the time before Jayber Crow returns to the community of his birth, but the telling of that tale is from some more distant vantage point after he has lived most of his life within the embrace of Port William.

> After I quit waking up afraid, feeling that I might be nowhere, I began getting used to the place. I began to take for granted that I was somewhere, and somewhere that I knew, but I never quite felt that I was somewhere I wanted to be. Where I wanted to be, always, day in and day out, year in and year out, was Squires Landing and all that fall of country between Port William up on the ridge and the river between Sand Ripple and Willow Run. When I heard or read the word home, that patch of country was what I thought of. ...
>
> ... Lying in bed in the dark before I went to sleep, I would picture myself coming up the hill to the house at Squires Landing. I would go around through the kitchen door. I would go through the house slowly, room by room, looking at everything: the kitchen table with three places set and covered with a cloth, the skillet and the pots and the kettle on the stove. ...
>
> ... Of course, what I wasn't telling myself, and maybe was trying not to know (though I did know), was that at Squires Landing ... things were already changed. The things I was remembering were gone from everywhere except my mind. ...

... And so there would always be more to remember that could no longer be seen. This is one of the things I can tell you that I have learned: our life here is in some way marginal to our own doings, and our doings are marginal to the greater forces that are always at work. Our history is always returning to a little patch of weeds and saplings with an old chimney sticking up by itself. And I can tell you a further thing that I have learned, and here I look ahead to the resting of my case: I love the house that belonged to the chimney, holding it bright in memory, and I love the saplings and the weeds.[21]

## Frederick Buechner's *Godric*

Jayber's character could have fallen quite easily into conversation with the eleventh-century Godric and his companion, Cuthbert. Cuthbert turns out to be St. Cuthbert, but we shouldn't hold that against him. Destined for reluctant sainthood himself, Godric gives his companion a pass by allowing that, "Since holiness was all he knew, I think he did not know his own."[22]

If Jayber Crow could somehow join these characters from Frederick Buechner's masterpiece, *Godric*, he might particularly appreciate what Cuthbert tells Godric about the subject of home. "When a man leaves home," Cuthbert confides, "he leaves some scrap of his heart."

But Cuthbert is not content to leave Godric looking back. He nudges him ahead toward the future by pointing out that "It's the same with a place a man is going to ... only then he sends a scrap of his heart ahead."[23]

Godric does indeed send a scrap of his heart ahead, and it lands on the banks of the river Wear.

Looking ahead may not be something we do very eagerly as we age. Still, Godric finds a great deal to celebrate as he goes for his daily dip in the frigid waters of the river Wear. "Praise, praise" he croaks ...

Praise God for all that's holy, cold, and dark. Praise him for all we lose, for all the river of the years bears off. Praise him for stillness in the wake of pain. Praise him for emptiness. And as you race to

---

[21]   Wendell Berry, *Jayber Crow* (New York: Counterpoint, 2000), selected quotes from 36–38.
[22]   Frederick Buechner, *Godric* (San Francisco: Harper and Row, 1980), 38.
[23]   Buechner, 37.

spill into the sea, praise him yourself, old Wear. Praise him for dying and the peace of death.[24]

Sometimes Godric sees a star winking at him from the depths of the Wear. He winks back. "The secret that we share," he says, "I cannot tell in full. But this much I will tell. What's lost is nothing to what's found, and all the death that ever was, set next to life, would scarcely fill a cup."[25]

Even if he were not submerged in the river Wear, it would be hard to miss the ways Godric lives a life "shaped by baptism." And these last words, especially, seem designed to "help those who are not yet old learn how to grow old and even die."[26]

At the very least, I know I am a deeper person for having read them. And that is no small thing for all of us "growing old in Christ."

[24]  Buechner, 96.
[25]  Buechner, 96.
[26]  Hauerwas.

# CHAPTER 13

# A Compendium of Conversations

## Paul Janssen

What do two brothers—eldest and youngest sons of a long-time stated clerk of Pleasant Prairie Classis—chat about when they sit across from each other during family visits? Lots of things, certainly, but when comes the time for shop talk, they talk about polity. Al Janssen is a genuine pastor-scholar with an international reputation on the subject; this writer is a mere practitioner. Nonetheless, both of us have served our own classes as clerks and have served the Reformed Church in America (RCA) in different capacities that deal with church order (counsel, Commission on Judicial Business, commissions on order or administration, and the like).

Over the years, therefore, most of the foundational ideas I have learned about polity have come from Al's interpretation of the way it is practiced in the RCA. I hesitate to call these foundational ideas "principles," because the RCA tends not to think in principles. That is to say, the RCA has conducted matters of order more in the direction of commensality than statutory coherency. We are much better versed—and more comfortable—in a dining room (or at coffee time) than we are in a classroom or a courtroom.

It must be said at the outset that this compendium is *my* take on the conversations Al and I have had. He would no doubt differ on several points to come. But as pastors in whom not only familial but also RCA DNA runs deep, such differences would not break relationship. We would —and will—continue to sit at one another's kitchen tables, and more importantly, around our Table, embraced in a love that is higher than whatever small squabbles may divide us.

Allan Janssen was born in 1948, the first of the six children of John and Joy (Rozendaal) Janssen. The year of his birth landed his college education squarely in the tumultuous years of 1966–1970, which he spent as a Rolscreen scholar at Central College in Pella, Iowa. During his freshman year at Central, the college welcomed Dr. Martin Luther King, Jr., who addressed a packed gymnasium and spoke (according to Donald Kaul, then a reporter for the *Des Moines Register*) on the issues of "The Negro in America: Slavery, emancipation, the liberating decisions of the Supreme Court, the civil rights legislation. Also the lynchings, the high unemployment and infant mortality rates; the low wages and inadequate educational systems."[1] By his senior year, Allan had become deeply involved in student government and helped "break in" the college's new president, Dr. Kenneth Weller, as Central joined the national movement in protesting the Vietnam War and the moratorium of October 1969. That Al became, early on, a kind of "drum major for justice" during his time at Central will not surprise those who have tracked his ministerial career.

Indeed, the activism whose seeds had been planted at Central continued during Al's years in seminary, or perhaps one should say, seminaries. In the late sixties and early seventies, the General Synod of the RCA experimented with the idea of consolidating its two seminaries, New Brunswick in New Jersey and Western in Holland, Michigan. The consolidation proved to be too high a wall for the General Synod to climb, but it entered into an experimental program called the Bi-Level Multi Site (BLMS) program, in which students spent a part of their academic career in each of the two seminaries. The spirit of innovation was in the air, and faculties adopted interdisciplinary approaches to instruction, spending a good deal of class time focusing on the relationship of the church to the turmoil of the American cultural

---

[1]    Jenni Hodges, "Featured: What Martin Luther King Jr. Was Here" *Central College News*, March 14, 2017, https://news.central.edu/2017/03/mlk-50/

landscape, and the students observed the constitutional crises of the Nixon/Watergate years with keen interest.

What was happening "out there" in the culture was not, however, merely "out there." What roiled society found place in the church. One of the strategic turning points of the Reformed Church in America took place during Al's formative years of higher education. The 1969 meeting of the General Synod took place while he was attending Central College. Our father (at the time the stated clerk the Classis of Pleasant Prairie) was present at that synod and returned home more discouraged about the future of the church than we ever saw him before or since.[2]

Al graduated from Western Theological Seminary in 1973. Soon he would be sitting on the General Synod's Commission on Christian Action, advising the General Synod on topics such as immigration and refugee policy, racism, economic justice, human rights and its impact on denominational investment policy, the AIDS epidemic, poverty and unemployment, "English only" movements, and more. It was, however, in 1978 that his influence on the denomination began to take shape. The story of the ordination of women to the office of minister of Word and sacrament is fully told elsewhere.[3] Al served with colleagues in a pivotal role as counsel in one of the judicial cases that made its way to the General Synod of 1979, at which the General Synod approved the authority of individual classes to ordain women to the office of minister of Word and sacrament.[4]

The records of Dr. Janssen's service as counsel for various causes could fill a small volume on their own. As a frequent counsel, as well as his tenure as stated clerk of the Classis of Albany, Al developed a keen eye both for rules and for the larger matter of polity as they reflect the theological matter of the nature and purpose of the church. The name "Janssen" rose to the stature of "Demarest" upon the completion of his 2001 work *Constitutional Theology*. Due to his interest and ability in polity and ecclesiology, he developed significant worldwide contacts through the International Reformed Theological Institute (IRTI). Relationships nurtured in that context drew Al into the early development of the Uniting Reformed Church in South Africa (URCSA), and he was among

---

[2]   For a synopsis of what occurred at that synod, see Lynn Japinga, *Loyalty and Loss* (Grand Rapids: Eerdmans, 2013). See especially chapter 5, "Breaking Up Is Hard to Do."

[3]   See Renée House and John Coakley, eds., *Patterns and Portraits: Women in the History of the Reformed Church in America* (Grand Rapids: Eerdmans, 2002).

[4]   The specific history of the rulings that constituted "approval" is complex and may be found in the 1979 *Minutes of General Synod* (MSG 1979), 64–69.

the RCA's representatives present at the founding of the post-apartheid denomination.

The controversy that has spanned more of Al's career than any other, however, has revolved around matters of human sexuality, particularly regarding same-sex attraction. The discussion is so multivalent that it is difficult to avoid the temptation for dialogues to go several ways at once, with the result that they often go nowhere at all. Beginning in the early eighties, movements were afoot to have the RCA declare itself *in statu confessionis* over the issue, but the church has remained too divided to come to that point. Absent a consensus, the issue has arisen year after year, either directly by means of reports of the Commission on Theology (1978, 1979, 1990, 1994, and 2015) or somewhat indirectly (1998, 2004, 2005, 2012, 2013, 2016, 2017, and 2018). Concerns regarding human sexuality surfaced in other areas as well, particularly in discussions of the RCA's ecumenical posture, as one by one, partners in the (1997) Formula of Agreement adopted policies that opened ordination, or marriage, or both to persons who are in committed same-sex relationships.

In nearly all of these discussions, Al has been present at the table, advocating for honest and healthy conversation as a respected voice on matters of theology, order, ecumenical relationships, the conduct of General Synod meetings, and the import of the General Synod's statements.

What follows is a compendium of many years of different conversations regarding polity as practiced in the RCA.

1. Church polity is, to use the metaphor of A.A. van Ruler, "the rafters in the cathedral of love."[5] It is not the cathedral itself. Nor is it what happens within the cathedral. It is, instead, a superstructure that creates habitable space within which the people of God encounter—and are encountered by—the triune God in the person of the Lord Jesus by the power of the Spirit.

   To draw out the metaphor (as Van Ruler may not have intended, and for which I beg his forgiveness), I would add that I am assuming the rafters constructed in post-and-beam construction, not the prefabricated rafters of modern construction. Such rafters require the most skillful of crafters,

---

[5]   Allan J. Janssen, *Kingdom, Office, and Church: A Study of A.A. van Ruler's Doctrine of Ecclesiastical Office* (Grand Rapids: Eerdmans, 2000), 286.

as, with as elegant and spare a structure as possible, they perform a number of functions simultaneously. On the one hand, they hold the roof up, and the roof keeps the outside of a building out; it keeps its inhabitants dry and shelters them from sun. To function properly, the pitch of the rafters needs to be calculated carefully, not only for the sake of run-off of rainwater or melting snow but also because rafters exercise both a downward and outward stress on the walls that bear them. Rafters that are too heavy and push outward too forcefully may cause the building to collapse. Rafters that are too light will be too weak to hold the roof up. Thus, rafters are not built simply of two diagonal members that meet at the peak of the roof. At or near the bottom of the rafters are joists that span the width of the building and exert a force that holds the outward thrust of the rafters toward center so that the outward thrust is not transferred to the vertical walls, which would push them out of plumb. In addition, easing the stresses that occur parallel to the roofline are underpurlins— horizontal members that both pull the rafters together and, just as importantly, keep them from "racking," or collapsing, domino-like, onto each other during a tempest.

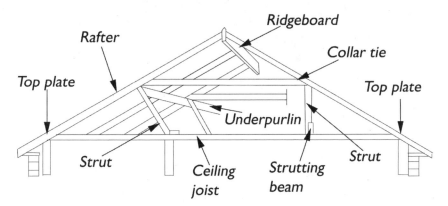

Per the diagram, rafter construction is more complex than I have outlined, but the point of the exercise is to indicate that the overhead construction of a building—generically called "the rafters"—are a delicate balance of forces, such that the removal of some member or the substitution of one material for another can (over time or under sufficient stress) cause the whole structure to collapse. Not only that, but if the householder decides to alter the construction of the rafters (by cutting slots in the critical members for any number of reasons), the structure not only becomes weaker than originally constructed; before long, the esthetic quality of rafters is simply a mess. A collapse may not occur on a sunny day when all seems right with the world. But when winds arise, and rains fall, and the structure is tested, a roof whose rafters are inadequate or compromised will eventually give way.

That is why the metaphor is apt for adequate church polity: polity balances forces that push outward, downward, and sideways in tension (sometimes even in torsion). It pulls varying forces inward, toward the stable center.

Here, then, is an attempt at a "definition" (though I prefer the term "sense") of polity: church polity is the superstructure of the church that balances countervailing forces in order to enable the people of God to live fully into the presence of divine grace.

But since not every church's polity is the same, just as rafters are custom engineered and crafted for the stresses of the buildings they serve, varying polities display different characteristics. The next few items will speak of broadly Reformed commitments in the area of polity. They have the character of standing in several different locations and looking up at the rafters from different angles, noticing differences in how they function.

2. Inasmuch as a functioning polity enables the people of God to live fully into the presence of divine grace, polity is about more than comity (courteous and considerate behavior). What is at stake in polity is not just how genial people can best get along with one another. On an *observable* level, Reformed polity intends to preserve the ability of the people of God to make use of the visible means of grace that Christ instituted for the benefit of the believing community, i.e., *Word and sacrament*. The rafters protect the foci of the cathedral of love: pulpit, font, and Table. These are the gifts God has given to communicate with God's people: preaching, baptism, and the Lord's Supper.

That said, the "profile" of polity rises above the province of mere wonks who enjoy arguments about articles and sections and paragraphs of a church's book of government. A "good" polity, practiced wisely, serves the communication of God's grace; without ever looking up at the rafters (say, without ever reading the *Book of Church Order*), one may be moved to say, "surely the Lord was in this place, and I did not know it." A "poor" polity, on the other hand, may well hinder such communication by allowing sermons to become rambles of somewhat entertaining tropes; baptism, to become either a quaint family ceremony or an act of individual personal testimony; or the Lord's Supper, to devolve into a mere visual aid.

3.  At the same time, on a *conceptual* level, a functioning polity makes way for the presence of God in *Word and Spirit*. As the Confession of Belhar puts it, "We believe in the triune God, Father, Son and Holy Spirit, who gathers, protects and cares for the church *through Word and Spirit*." Here we are referring to the *source* of the church's life, not its practices. Thus in this use of the term, "Word" is not preaching but is Christ, and Spirit is the Holy Spirit who offers inner testimony that preaching, baptism, and the Holy Supper are what God intends them to be: means of grace.

    Thus the church is not only *creatura verbi*; it is *creatura verbi et spiritus*. Word and Spirit are never separable. A church characterized by a mere babble of words, no matter how well intentioned or biblical-sounding, is untethered from its Lord unless the Holy Spirit is present, bringing to remembrance all that Christ taught. Baptism in such a church is being washed in sand; the Supper is a feast of corrugated cardboard and fetid water. Likewise, a church possessed of what appears to be great spirit may well manifest all sort of enthusiasm, but insofar as that enthusiasm is humanly generated, baptism becomes (rather than a means of divine grace) a personal testimony. The Supper—if practiced at all—becomes a mere pedagogical tool that points to a Christ who remains a figure of long ago and far away but who does not "come to us" in the sharing of the bread and cup.

    The implication for polity is that we must be more specific than to define it as merely a superstructure that balances countervailing forces. Polity that functions well is an *elegant* superstructure, one that uses as few members as possible to order a space within which the people of God receive the means of grace, i.e., to encounter the living God in Word and

Spirit. It serves its purpose, but it does not call attention to itself.

4.  To this point, I have been addressing polity as a superstructure of the church that enables the people of God to live fully into the presence of divine grace. What specifically does this have to do with the persons of God, i.e., not for the body as a whole, but for individual believers? How might polity hit home for the ordinary believer?

    By making way for Word and Spirit to be present in Word and sacrament, the rafters of polity offer the believer freedom to be enveloped in the embrace of her Lord, to contemplate the beauty and complexity of her relationship with Christ, to enjoy companionship with him, to take the towel and basin and serve, and to die and be raised with him; in other words, to experience the *unio mystica cum Christi*.

    Thus, when polity is working well, these are the sorts of things that happen: believers receive their new identity in Christ and receive forgiveness and new life through the Spirit. They self-consciously abide in the Vine. They know themselves as sinners adopted into the household of God as coheirs with Christ. God's Spirit is making the life and teaching of Jesus real to the church.[6] To use old-school terms, the gospel is being preached in its purity, the sacraments are being practiced faithfully, and discipline is taking place pastorally.

    From a pastoral perspective, it is sadly all too easy to detect when polity is not working well. Consistory members spend more time consulting the rule books than having conversations. Assemblies are consumed with an agenda of avoidance. Table fellowship is suspended as individuals absent themselves from sharing with those whom they have labeled as "other." The common baptism—and relationship with the Lord Jesus—is denied. Believers construct their identity as "of a different spirit." Christ is crowded out, and the believer experiences neither union with Christ nor an integrated sense of faith and life.

5.  To close the discussion of commonly shared convictions among those who practice Reformed polity, the intent of a

---

[6]    Based on J. Todd. Billings, *Union with Christ: Reframing Theology and Ministry for the Church* (Grand Rapids: Baker Academic, 2011), Introduction.

shared polity *as it serves assemblies* is to allow assemblies to hold large scale conversations (even when they are contentious and last for decades) and to maintain relationship despite disagreement. Polity at work allows the church to discern what seems "good to the Holy Spirit and to us"[7] in assemblies and judicatories ranging from the governing body of a local congregation to the broadest assemblies. It does not necessarily, however, give time tables or mechanisms for the closure of discernment. To many, this can be problematic. Within the Reformed family, there are forms of polity that allow for and encourage the closure of conversations by means of authoritative interpretations of the Scriptures by the broadest possible representative body, but not all Reformed polities operate in the same way. Conflicts arise when assemblies are composed of office bearers who are committed to more open- and to more closed-ended polities. Absent a shared polity, delegates to assemblies focus on disagreements, retreat to their own (metaphorical) houses, and, if they are dissenters, attempt to remake the rafters of the house in which they are living now to look and function like the rafters of another, preferred house.

Thus, to cite an example of the difference in one Reformed body, in debates regarding same-sex attraction within the RCA, assumptions about polity have been at issue during the 40-year discussion. Opponents of a more inclusive stance have repeatedly requested the General Synod of the RCA to develop changes to its Constitution (for example, to have a specific liturgy included in the Constitution, or to grant the General Synod an authority it does not have, i.e., to make authoritative interpretations of the Scriptures)—in effect, to end the conversation by shifting to a non-conversational form of polity. "No more kicking the can down the road!" means, "Let's end this conversation! No more talking!" These voices desire a polity of closure—a polity more commonly found in other Reformed assemblies—that the RCA does not possess.

Proponents of a more inclusive stance have assumed a peculiarly "RCA" shared polity. The rafters they assume to be holding the structure up (one might say, fighting cultural

---

[7]   Acts 15:28.

gravity) place limits on the scope and the binding ability of statements of General Synods, because "authoritative interpretations" close down conversation rather than enable it. Likewise, in part because cross-classis discipline would encourage a denomination-wide shouting match, shared polity, as it currently exists, sees such a change as both practically and ecclesiologically impossible. Because marriage has not been regarded as a sacrament, is not thereby a means of grace, and is therefore not a core gospel matter, the RCA does not have a constitutional position on marriage of any kind, much less same-sex marriage. In other words, it hasn't closed a conversation for which its polity does not demand closure.

6.   Reformed polity as practiced in the RCA reflects an irenic, Heidelberg value set, in distinction from a polity that reflects a confession formed during conflict. Daniel Meeter's brilliant article on Heidelberg and Westminster, at long last published in this festschrift, offers several pertinent observations to that end. First, whereas Westminister, formed as it was "against the royal interests," spoke in a polemical tone of voice, Heidelberg, written under the protection of Elector Frederick, spoke in a manner that is "as practical as it was pacific." Second, while the Westminster spends the bulk of its ink on *duty* (what must we do to glorify God and enjoy God forever?), the Heidelberg focuses on *comfort* and *benefits*, i.e., on how the actions of God accrue to the believer. Third, while (per Meeter) the Westminster "lacks a positive ecclesiology," the Heidelberg speaks fulsomely of the Son of God "gather[ing], protect[ing] and preserv[ing] for himself a community chosen for eternal life, and united in true faith." Direct implications on polity are no doubt speculative, but I speculate nevertheless that, in the first instance, a Heidelberg-shaped polity may function well only in an atmosphere that seeks authentic long-term conversation and comity rather than seeking to bring matters to a head and settle them once and for all by means of new rules. In the second, the RCA has been remarkably wary of defining both duties (in a positive sense) and sins (in a negative) within its order, inasmuch as the proper place to discuss such things is the same place where one receives comfort and grace from the Lord, i.e., at the local level where one sits at the table.

Thirdly, a polity that assumes Heidelberg sensitivities will see the gathering, protection, and preservation of the church as the work of the Holy Spirit who works faith in our hearts "through the preaching of the holy gospel and ... strengthens it through the use of the holy sacraments." And now we have circled around to the second point in this compendium—the argument that the "point" of polity is not that people may get along swimmingly with one another but that believers might partake of the means of grace in the communion of the faithful; in other words, that they might encounter the living God and not be consumed.

7.   Reformed polity as practiced in the RCA is a commensal polity. I have referred above to the way that the rafters make space for the people of God to gather around the Lord's Table, to taste and see that the Lord is good. It is meant for hospitality, therefore. It allows room for dispute but bids dispute be set aside when it's time to eat. It sees the Supper principally as supper, (albeit with the overriding tone of eucharist) as a meal shared together with our Lord as the host. While it asks of members to seek the things that make for unity, purity, and peace, it does not demand that all have attained a monolithic standard of credal unity, a narrowly-defined measure of personal ethical purity, or that sort of peace that puts aside all differences before they can come to the Table. It makes space for people who are *simil iustus et peccator* to come and eat together, not because they are on a single mind but because they are all invited by the one Lord. Hence, though it is quite common for RCA General Synod meetings to erupt—albeit in a rather mild and stylized way—into something that approximates conflict in which bright lines are drawn between "sides," each meeting of the General Synod concludes at the Table. It is common, as well, for those who have battled matters out on the close quarters of the General Synod plenary (fewer than 250 delegates are seated) to stand together in line as they approach the Table or to receive the elements from a fellow delegate with whom they have had the most severe differences. Here, the commensal polity does not smooth over the differences; rather, it submits them to one Lord and bids the participants partake in a common humility. Who knows how many times an analogous experience has taken place at

the level of the local congregation, where neighbors dwell under the same roof and rafters and agree to sit together at the table even while they maintain deep disagreement about the life of the congregation or an interpersonal conflict?

8.   Reformed polity as practiced in the RCA manifests a particular of set of convictions about the offices in the church. Aside from its preservation of the office of the General Synod professor of theology, RCA polity maintains the offices of minister of Word and sacrament, elder, and deacon, which act together as the pastorate in the local congregation. The Order for Ordination and Installation of Elder and Deacon makes clear that no office can function at the congregational level completely independently from the other two offices. Deacons may meet separately from elders, but they regularly meet together with the pastor or teacher present, and this body is the consistory of the church. A consistory, as a portion of its responsibilities as a legal corporation, may act as a board of trustees (or directors), but consistories and boards of trustees are two fundamentally different things. Although many of the functions of a board will appear quite similar, the difference has to do with the direction of representation. A consistory, composed as it is of gathered office-bearers elected by the people of God and ordained by God to serve the church, represents Christ to the congregation. It is not, at least in Reformed polity, a group of persons who represent the voices of several caucuses or constituencies to a large-group meeting. Because Christ is the head of the church and the consistory represents Christ to the congregation, the consistory is that body of which the local church consists. "The congregation" receives little mention in RCA polity, in contrast to the polities of congregationally-driven churches.

Further, no office is ontologically "higher" than any other. Although one (minister of Word and sacrament) is far more highly regulated and requires a significant regimen of education, all three offices at the local level are bound together in ministry and mutuality. But they do focus in different ways on the life of the church as expressed in Word and sacrament. Elders are responsible for admitting those who apply for baptism; deacons are charged with helping the baptized live out their call to confess Christ to their lives"ends. Elders are given the task of discerning who may come to be fed at the Table, while deacons have the responsibility for those who have been fed to be about the Christian exercises of compassion in the world. And elders see to the proper preaching of the gospel so that the people of God can clearly hear the compassionate and challenging Word of God; deacons provide frameworks for the concrete living out of that Word in the world.

Allan Janssen has written extensively on the nature of office in reformed polity,[8] though he has not gathered his own theology of office into one volume. His thoughts follow van Ruler's closely; I refer you to his dissertation[9] for a vision of this critical matter in the life of the church.

9.  Related to my fifth point above, because polity as in the RCA provides a forum for long-term discernment (that, along with the pernicious presence of sin), the decisions of assemblies come with an important limitation: assemblies make mistakes. As they search the Scriptures, assemblies attempt to discern the will of the Spirit, but their results are tentative. In practical terms, the statements of assemblies (I am using the term "assembly" intentionally here rather than "judicatory"—see my tenth point below) speak *to* the narrower assemblies; they do not speak *for* them in a final, "authoritative" manner. Thus, the RCA does not have a place in its order for "authoritative interpretations" of the Scriptures. Broader assemblies offer words of counsel and encouragement; their power to instruct extends to those bodies that work for them (executive committees, staff members, and the like).

    The Preamble to the *Book of Church Order* lines the limitation in this way: "Jesus Christ is the only Head of his church.... As the church's true Head, he has complete authority over its life, and therefore the church must ever yield to him a ready obedience and faithfulness." The church is a creature of the Word—of Jesus Christ—and the Word always remains the final word. No assembly may ever arrogate to itself the authority of the Word. The church knows but one Lord.

---

8   See "Office as an Instrument of Unity," in Eduardus Van der Borght, ed., *The Unity of the Church* (Leiden: Brill, 2010); and "Minister as Witness," in E. Van der Borght and van Geest, eds., *Strangers and Pilgrims on Earth* (Leiden: Brill, 2012).

9   Janssen, *Kingdom.*

Some may point to the statement: "The church shall declare what is in the Word and act upon it, and may not properly go beyond this"[10] to make the case that the General Synod is charged with making authoritative interpretations. However, on the one hand the statement says "the church," not "the General Synod" shall declare what is in the Word; and further, the latter half of the statement indicates that the intent of the statement is to delimit the declarative authority of the church to govern its own life and activity, not to broaden the church's authority to every social and cultural cause that may arise.

10. Assemblies are assemblies; judicatories are judicatories. While they may consist of the same persons, the distinction matters. To use spatial metaphors, the four assemblies of the RCA expand in breadth as they go from consistory to classis to regional synod to General Synod. A consistory governs the life of a congregation, a classis is a gathering of delegates from consistories, and a regional synod consists of delegates from classes. The next broader step, however is not that the General Synod is made up of delegates from regional synods. The General Synod consists (principally) of delegates from classes. It is the broadest body to which classes—which hold consistories to account for the conduct of the means of grace where they are located—send representatives. (Regional synods as well as the professorate are also represented at the General Synod, but the overwhelming majority of its members are delegates from classes.) In this way, the broadest assembly of the RCA maintains deep consciousness of how local consistories are hearing the needs of their communities and what the local contexts are demanding to hear of the gospel.

That said, there is a sense in which the classis is "higher than" the consistory, the regional synod is "higher than" the classis, and the General Synod is "higher than" the regional synod. Verticality (as opposed to breadth) is a characteristic of the disciplinary and judicial procedures in the RCA. A church member who feels that her local consistory has violated the government or the Scriptures may complain the action in question to the classis, and the classis has the

---

[10]    RCA *Book of Church Order (BCO)*, 2018 edition, Preamble, 2.

authority to decide the matter. It is, in a sense, a "higher" authority: consistories are accountable to classes. Classes are not, however, the final authority. If that member believes she has just cause to appeal the action of the lower judicatory (in this case, the classis), she may lodge and appeal with the next highest judicatory: the regional synod. Judicial matters that arise in local congregations may (unless they are disciplinary matters first heard by a board of elders) eventually "rise" to the level of the General Synod.

Hence, in the RCA, we speak of "broader" assemblies and "higher" judicatories, and it is helpful to keep the distinction in mind. Especially when the matter of boundaries arises (for example, what can the classis "make" a consistory do?), one notes that classes and regional synods are limited by the provision that any bodies they create to do ministry in the church "do not infringe upon the prerogatives of other classes, consistories, or synods." A classis, as a broader body, creates ministries and agencies that assist several consistories to work more effectively in their local contexts; however, a classis is not authorized to run roughshod over the prerogatives of the consistory to provide for the ministry that is occurring in a local congregation.

11. It has become *de rigueur* for corporate bodies these days to speak of boundaries: establishing them, maintaining them, honoring them. One such boundary that is often ignored is the boundary between church *per se* on one hand and, on the other, the programs that the church carries out in the performance of "all Christian good works."

Although the polity of the church intends to enable the people of God to live fully into the presence of divine grace by means of Word and sacrament, at every level of polity, from narrowest to broadest, it is common for members to desire more than Word and sacrament. At the local level, church members want programs that run the gamut from ministry to young families, to Bible studies, to youth programs, to financial advice seminars, to hunting fellowships, to after-school tutoring, et cetera. By and large, there is no fault to be found with such programs. But while they may have some relationship to "Christian good works" (sometimes the relationship strains the imagination), they have little to do with encountering the living God at pulpit, font, and Table. The encounter comes at God's initiative through the offices (see my eighth point above). Commenting on Van Ruler's theocentric vision of office, Al writes: "If it is clear that certain ministries come *to* the church, entire varieties of ministries can emerge *from* the church without the burden of having to constitute the church."[11]

At the classis level, the RCA's *Book of Church Order* maintains a tight focus on the supervision of churches and supervision of ministry (from training students to supervising active ministers), but classis agendas are peppered with church planting, program, development, foundations, multicultural committees, administration, et cetera. Again, many functions need to be carried out at the classis level, but the government is clear that the core functions of the classis have to do with the living proclamation and celebration at the level of the congregation. While the classis *may* perform several other tasks, it *must* be the body to which consistories and ministers are accountable, because consistories and ministers have Word and sacrament as their core ministries. (Though classes sometimes celebrate the Lord's Supper, they are not eucharistic bodies in the same way that local congregations are.)

Regional and General Synods face the same tension. In a sense, they serve the church as deliberative assemblies and judicatories; in that sense, they are, in a way, just as much "the church" as the classis and congregation. But inasmuch as they engage in activities that the narrower assemblies are unable to perform on their own (camps and conference centers, ministries to the aging, non-specific congregational support programs, et cetera), they tend to operate quite differently from the way congregations or classes operate. The parachurch ministries they operate require special expertise and are hence "staff-driven." At the same time, even the church-focused ministries carried out by regional and General Synods (agencies that train ministers, commissions that study issues, and offices that carry forward synodical initiatives) are ordinarily carried out (or at least "staffed") by paid personnel

[11]  Janssen, *Kingdom*, 283.

whose responsibilities are delegated to them by the body of the church that hires them to work on its behalf. To put it another way, the staff of these broadest bodies are given the task of helping the church carry out the decisions that the church, in its gatherings of offices, has made. They overstep their bounds when they decide to drive the church in a direction of their own choosing, when they mistake "program" for "church" and invert the relationship between church and parachurch.

12. Every form of polity has its advantages and disadvantages. While, in theory, polity in the RCA is intended to enable the people of God to live fully into the presence of God, in fairness, on a practical level the manner in which the polity is practiced may (to borrow from Orwell) enable some to live in God's presence "more fully" than others.

    The RCA continues to maintain the tradition of annual General Synod meetings and annual regional synod meetings (though the shapes of these are vastly different from region to region). Classes meet as seldom as semi-annually (this is largely a function of geography), while most consistories meet monthly. When men and women meet that regularly, they form relationships. Since at the narrowest levels of governance committee meetings are held between plenaries, those relationships are even longer lasting and more intense. People become friends (or enemies) with such extensive face-to-face contact. Even the annual General Synod meeting has frequently been called the RCA's annual "coffee break," with breakfast, coffee, lunch, coffee, dinner, and receptions barely interrupted by assembly or judicatory business.

    This kinship manner of practicing polity has the advantage of certain types of efficiencies. The RCA is small enough that, when one wants to get something done, one pulls out the thin denominational directory, calls the person in charge, introduces oneself as affiliated with an RCA congregation, and the service provided is usually delivered quickly. For those who are in the know, and more importantly "in the network," this is all to the good.

    However, in a denomination in which the term "Dutch Bingo" is still a fairly well-known term (it refers to the practice of church members—especially in the midwestern

RCA—visiting one another after Sunday evening worship, trading stories about relatives and generations past, until supposedly unrelated persons find a common ancestor, at which point comes the metaphorical "Bingo!"), a polity whose practice is in many ways framed by kinship has the effect of marginalizing those who are not by ancestry or length of association (or, frankly, by interest) "kin." Phrases such as "the New York mafia" or "the Michigan Mafia"—with apologies to the seldom-told story of Italians in the RCA—spoke of a reality that left broad swaths of the RCA outside the circles of power. Thus, if the metaphor of "rafters" applies here—i.e., if polity is "the superstructure that balances countervailing forces," it is legitimate to ask whether the composition of the rafters is sufficient to withhold the forces of racism, sexism, ageism, regionalism, classism, and homophobia that have beset the church from generation to generation. Those who find the RCA's affiliation-based polity to be endearing need to consider who is being "affiliated in" and who is being "affiliated out."

13. For some time, commentators have noted that the entire government of the RCA can fit inside a rather small and unimpressive three-ring binder. Even if one were to incorporate the entire Constitution (the Doctrinal Standards—the Belgic Confession of Faith, the Heidelberg Catechism with its Compendium, the Canons of the Synod of Dort, and the Belhar Confession—the Liturgy with the Directory for Worship, the Government of the Reformed Church in America, the Disciplinary and Judicial Procedures, This Preamble, and the Formularies) into a single document, they could still be bound in a relatively small volume.

Because the Constitution of the RCA is relatively compact,[12] some have mistaken it as being easy to amend. This is incorrect in two senses. First, amendments are not *made* by General Synods. They are *proposed* by General Synods—proposed to the classes, which must agree to amendments (by a two-thirds majority of classes) before they can be sent back to a General Synod for a declarative resolution. More

---

[12]   The importance of having a constitution is ably defined in Daniel Meeter's book, *Meeting Each Other in Doctrine, Liturgy, and Government* (Grand Rapids: Eerdmans, 1993).

importantly, however, is the deliberation required to "tweak" the government here and there to conform to current practices in the church. Of late, General Synod watchers have noted that those who wish to introduce a new form (of ministry, for example) into the life of the church will hastily and without extensive theological or ecclesiological study bring proposed amendments to the floor of the General Synod. The expectation is that the form will be approved and that the General Synod will instruct its Commission on Church Order to write amendments for the next General Synod to consider. At worst, such actions are taken lightly on the deliberative floor of the General Synod with just a few moments"consideration.

Al served the Commission on Church Order for several years, and when he was not actively serving on the commission, he was regularly consulted for wisdom. Early on in his service in this capacity, he learned that ostensibly small changes in polity actually have extensive consequences in both space and time. In space—because changes that are made to address a situation in one region of the church will be interpreted in a different way by assemblies in other regions of the church—the government, which is meant to have something of a unifying force, ends up diverging more and more. This happen over time, as, at first, a provision of the government affects only a few, but as the years go on, that provision affects more and more until the church's self-understanding has changed.

This yields two insights into the polity. First, it is best that changes happen slowly. Consequences of proposed changes need time to be considered, and the church trusts the men and women who are charged with altering the order to be careful. Second, there are times that General Synods make unwise decisions (see my ninth point above) and asks its commissions to perform actions that are contrary to the polity and the nature of the church. In such situations, it is not only advisory, but it is incumbent on a commission to respond to a General Synod with a clear but direct "no." The more delegates mistake "polity" for "rules," the more likely it is that the body charged with safeguarding the church's order will have to offer such a response to the General Synod.

There is much more that could be said (anyone who expects a Janssen to write a compendium that is actually brief has made a categorical mistake of a sort), but it will be left to others, such as the editor of this volume, who is one of the next generation of scholars of order who have learned much from Al and his cohort. I conclude with a few provocative questions for them to consider as they don the mantle of my elder brother.

If, as my sixth point above contends, RCA polity has operated with deep Heidelbergian assumptions, will such a polity continue to function in a church that continues to become more diverse, not only racially, ethnically, and geographically, but even theologically and ecclesiologically? Aside from any forces "outside" the church that may cause the roof to fall in, has the RCA become so diverse that we may cut into the joists, ties, and underpurlins to such an extent that we will pull it down on ourselves?

Can the RCA any longer expect its polity to exert a protective force? The divergence between those who seek "unity in truth" (i.e., a polity that offers authoritative interpretations of the Scriptures) and those who seek "truth in unity" (i.e., a polity that allows persons who may not agree on specific issues to nevertheless encounter the living Christ as he continues to speak to and in the church by the power of the Spirit) continues to widen. Are the rafters strong enough to balance those countervailing forces?

Does polity such as it has evolved in the RCA serve the cause of responding to the commissions of Christ? The Scriptures bear witness to at least four such commissions (Matthew 28:16-20; Luke 24:45-49; John 20:19-23; John 21:15-19; though there may well be others). Is it time to reexamine the extent to which the polity, developed in the sixteenth and seventeenth centuries and since, continues to address the current situation of the church and its mission? Does polity of the RCA reflect a Christendom vision of the nature of the church? Is it time to ask that question deeply and critically, and—especially if some form of the RCA ends up being reconstituted in the near future—is it time to renew its governing compact?

# Index

# Publications in the Historical Series of the Reformed Church in America

The following Historical Series publications may be ordered easily through the Faith Alive web site at www.faithaliveresources.org

The home page has a search the site box. Either enter the specific title or author, or enter "Historical Series" to search for all volumes available. Titles will appear with the option of adding to cart. Books may also be ordered through your local bookstore.

You may also see the full list of titles on the RCA website at:

www.rca.org/series

1.  *Ecumenism in the Reformed Church in America*, by Herman Harmelink III (1968)
2.  *The Americanization of a Congregation*, by Elton J. Bruins (1970)
3.  *Pioneers in the Arab World*, by Dorothy F. Van Ess (1974)
4.  *Piety and Patriotism*, edited by James W. Van Hoeven (1976)
5.  *The Dutch Reformed Church in the American Colonies*, by Gerald F. De Jong (1978)
6.  *Historical Directory of the Reformed Church in America, 1628-1978*, by Peter N. VandenBerge (1978)
7.  *Digest and Index of the Minutes of General Synod, 1958-1977*, by Mildred W. Schuppert (1979)
8.  *Digest and Index of the Minutes of General Synod, 1906-1957*, by Mildred W. Schuppert (1982)
9.  *From Strength to Strength*, by Gerald F. De Jong (1982)
10. *"B. D."*, by D. Ivan Dykstra (1982)
11. *Sharifa*, by Cornelia Dalenburg (1983)
12. *Vision From the Hill*, edited by John W. Beardslee III (1984)
13. *Two Centuries Plus*, by Howard G. Hageman (1984)
14. *Structures for Mission*, by Marvin D. Hoff (1985)

15. *The Church Speaks,* edited by James I. Cook (1985)
16. *Word and World,* edited by James W. Van Hoeven (1986)
17. *Sources of Secession: The Netherlands Hervormde Kerk on the Eve of the Dutch Immigration to the Midwest,* by Gerrit J. tenZythoff (1987)
18. *Vision for a Christian College,* by Gordon J. Van Wylen (1988)
19. *Servant Gladly,* edited by Jack D. Klunder and Russell L. Gasero (1989)
20. *Grace in the Gulf,* by Jeanette Boersma (1991)
21. *Ecumenical Testimony,* by Arie R. Brouwer (1991)
22. *The Reformed Church in China, 1842-1951,* by Gerald F. De Jong (1992)
23. *Historical Directory of the Reformed Church in America, 1628-1992,* by Russell L. Gasero (1992)
24. *Meeting Each Other in Doctrine, Liturgy, and Government,* by Daniel J. Meeter (1993)
25. *Gathered at Albany,* by Allan J. Janssen (1995)
26. *The Americanization of a Congregation,* 2nd ed., by Elton J. Bruins (1995)
27. *In Remembrance and Hope: The Ministry and Vision of Howard G. Hageman,* by Gregg A. Mast (1998)
28. *Deacons' Accounts, 1652-1674, First Dutch Reformed Church of Beverwyck/Albany,* trans. & edited by Janny Venema (1998)
29. *The Call of Africa,* by Morrill F. Swart (1998)
30. *The Arabian Mission's Story: In Search of Abraham's Other Son,* by Lewis R. Scudder III (1998)
31. *Patterns and Portraits: Women in the History of the Reformed Church in America,* edited by Renée S. House and John W. Coakley (1999)
32. *Family Quarrels in the Dutch Reformed Churches in the Nineteenth Century,* by Elton J. Bruins & Robert P. Swierenga (1999)
33. *Constitutional Theology: Notes on the Book of Church Order of the Reformed Church In America,* by Allan J. Janssen (2000)
34. *Raising the Dead: Sermons of Howard G. Hageman,* edited by Gregg A. Mast (2000)
35. *Equipping the Saints: The Synod of New York, 1800-2000,* edited by James Hart Brumm (2000)
36. *Forerunner of the Great Awakening,* edited by Joel R. Beeke (2000)
37. *Historical Directory of the Reformed Church in America, 1628-2000,* by Russell L. Gasero (2001)
38. *From Mission to Church: The Reformed Church in America in India,* by Eugene Heideman (2001)
39. *Our School: Calvin College and the Christian Reformed Church,* by Harry Boonstra (2001)

"Beginning with Donald Bruggink's own notion that 'history is a tool for understanding,' the dozen essays in this volume are tools for understanding four areas of his life and his fifty-five years of ministry. While all the contributors to this volume have benefited from Bruggink's friendship, teaching, and ministry, the first and last essays are by the contributors he has known longest, who had a formative role in his life"

— Eugene Heideman and I. John Hesselink.

61. *Chinese Theological Education*, edited by Marvin D. Hoff (2009) 470 pp. ISBN: 978-0-8028-6480-2

This book offers insight into the emergence of the Christian church after Mao's Cultural Revolution. While reports of Communist oppression have dominated American perceptions of church and state in China, this is an increasingly dangerous view as China changes. Dr. Marvin D. Hoff, as executive director for the Foundation for Theological Education in Southeast Asia, traveled at least annually to China for the period covered by this book. The original reports of his encounters with Chinese Christians, especially those involved in theological education, are a historic record of the church's growth—and growing freedom. Interspersed with Hoff's accounts are reports of essays by Chinese and other Asian Christians. Introductory essays are provided by Charles W. Forman of Yale Divinity School, Daniel B. Hays of Calvin College, and Donald J. Bruggink of Western Theological Seminary.

62. *Liber A*, edited by Frank Sypher (2009) 442 pp. ISBN: 978-0-8028-6509-0

*Liber A* of the Collegiate Church archives contains detailed seventeenth-century records of the Reformed Dutch Church of the City of New York, including correspondence, texts of legal documents, and lists of names of consistory members. Especially significant are records pertaining to the granting in 1696 of the royal charter of incorporation of the Church, and records relating to donations for, and construction of the church building on Garden Street. The full Dutch texts have never before been published.

63. *Aunt Tena, Called to Serve: Journals and Letters of Tena A. Huizenga, Missionary Nurse to Nigeria*, edited by Jacob A. Nyenhuis, Robert P. Swierenga, and Lauren M. Berka (2009) 980 pp. ISBN: 978-0-8028-6515-1

When Tena Huizenga felt the call to serve as a missionary nurse to Africa, she followed that call and served seventeen years at Lupwe, Nigeria, during a pivotal era in world missions. As she ministered to the natives, she recorded her thoughts and feelings in a diary and in countless letters to family and friends--over 350 in her first year alone. Through her eyes, we see the Lupwe mission, Tena's colleagues, and the many native helpers. Aunt Tena (Nigerians called all female missionaries

"Aunt") tells this profoundly human story. Interesting in its own right, the book will also prove invaluable to historians, sociologists, and genealogists as they mine this rich resource.

The extensive letters from Tena's brother Pete offer marvelous insights into the Dutch Reformed subculture of Chicago's West Side. Because his scavenger company later evolved into Waste Management Inc., those letters are especially valuable. Pete's winsome descriptions and witty dialogue with his sister add a Chicago flavor to this book.

64. *The Practice of Piety: The Theology of the Midwestern Reformed Church in America, 1866-1966,* by Eugene P. Heideman (2009)  286 pp. ISBN: 978-0-8028-6551-9

"With the instincts of a historian and the affection of a child of the RCA, Gene Heideman has accessed both Dutch and English sources in order to introduce us to the unique theology and piety of the Midwestern section of our denomination from 1866 to 1966. Through the words of pastors, professors, and parishioners, he has fleshed out the Dutch pilgrims of the 19th century who found their roots in the Netherlands but their fruit in America. Accessing the Dutch language newspaper *De Hope,* and the writings and lectures of a century of Western Seminary professors, the history of the RCA in the Midwest has come alive. This book is a gracious and winsome invitation to its readers and other scholars to dig deeper and understand more fully the theological and ethnic heritage of those who have helped ground our past and thus form our future."

— Gregg A. Mast, president, New Brunswick Theological Seminary

65. *Freedom on the Horizon: Dutch Immigration to America, 1840 to 1940,* by Hans Krabbendam (2009)  432 pp. ISBN: 978-0-8028-6545-8

"It's been eighty years since the last comprehensive study of the Dutch immigrant experience by a Netherlands scholar—Jacob Van Hinte's magisterial *Netherlanders in America* (1928, English translation 1985). It was worth the wait! Krabbendam has a firmer grasp of American history and culture than his predecessor, who spent only seven weeks on a whirlwind tour of a half-dozen Dutch 'colonies' in 1921. Krabbendam earned an M.A. degree in the USA, is widely traveled, versed in American religious culture, and has written the definitive biography of Edward W. Box (2001). *Freedom on the Horizon* focuses on the ultimate meaning of immigration—the process by which one's inherited culture is reshaped into a new Dutch-American identity. 'Only the steeple was retained,'

Krabbendam notes in his tale of a congregation that tore down its historic church edifice in favor of a modern new one. This is a metaphor of the Dutch immigrant experience writ large, as told here in a masterful way."

— Robert D. Swierenga, Kent State University

66.  *A Collegial Bishop? Classis and Presbytery at Issue*, edited by Allan Janssen and Leon Vanden Broek (2010) 176 pp. ISBN: 978-0-8028-6585-4

In *A Collegial Bishop?* classis and presbytery are considered from a cross-cultural, indeed cross-national, perspective of the inheritors of Geneva and Edinburgh in their contemporary contexts in the Netherlands, South Africa, and the United States.

"Dutch theologian A. A. van Ruler compares church order to the rafters of a church building. Church order sustains the space within which the church is met by God, where it engages in its plan with God (liturgy), and where it is used by God in its mission in and to God's world. Presbyterian church order intends to be faithful to its root in God's Word, as it is shaped around the office of elder and governed through a series of councils of the church."

Alan Janssen

— Pastor, Community Church of Glen Rock, NJ

67.  *The Church Under the Cross*, by Wendell Karssen (2010) 454 pp. ISBN: 978-0-8028-6614-1

*The Church Under the Cross: Mission in Asia in Times of Turmoil* is the illustrated two-volume account of Wendell Paul Karsen's more than three decades of cross-cultural missionary work in East Asia.

In one sense a missionary memoir of Karsen's life and ministry in Taiwan, Hong Kong, China, and Indonesia, the work also chronicles the inspiring story of the Christian communities Karsen served—churches which struggled to grow and witness under adverse circumstances throughout years of political turbulence and social upheaval.

68.  *Supporting Asian Christianity's Transition from Mission to Church: A History of the Foundation for Theological Education in Southeast Asia*, edited by Samuel C. Pearson (2010) 464 pp. ISBN: 978-0-8028-6622-6

"This volume, telling the story of how one North American ecumenical foundation learned to move from a 'missions' stance to one of 'partnership,' is at once informative, intriguing, and instructive for anyone curious about or interested in the development of contextual theological education and scholarship in China and Southeast Asia. It traces the efforts of Protestant churches and educational institutions emerging from World War II, revolution, and colonization to train an indigenous leadership and to nurture theological scholars for the political, cultural, and religious realities in which these ecclesial bodies find themselves."

— Greer Anne Wenh-In Ng, Professor Emerita, Victoria University in the University of Toronto

69. *The American Diary of Jacob Van Hinte,* edited by Peter Ester, Nella Kennedy, Earl Wm. Kennedy (2010) 210 pp. ISBN: 978-0-8028-6661-5

"This is a charming translation, scrupulously annotated, of the long-lost travel diary of Jacob Van Hinte (1889–1948), author of the monumental Netherlanders in America. Van Hinte's energetic five-week sprint in the summer of 1921 from "Dutch" Hoboken up the river by dayliner to Albany and on to the Dutch-settled towns and cities in the Midwest convinced him that the "migration to America had been a blessing" to the Dutch. But in his brief sojourn among the descendants of the immigrant generation, he also became aware of the "tales of misery" and the "noble struggles" of the settlers that will put readers of all ethnic backgrounds to wondering about their own poignant histories."

— Firth Fabend, author of Zion on the Hudson: Dutch new York and the New Jersey in the Age of Revivals

70. *A New Way of Belonging: Covenant Theology, China and the Christian Reformed Church, 1921-1951,* by Kurt Selles (2011) 288 pp. ISBN: 978-0-8028-6662-2

"As someone who spent much of my childhood on the mission field described in this book, I anticipated having my early memories refreshed by reading it. I did indeed find the book to be an accurate and thorough account of the work of the CRC China Mission as I remember it, but—more surprising—I also learned a good deal of new information. Kurt Selles has performed an important service for the history of missions by uncovering so much new information and doing such impressive research under difficult circumstances. Although the events took place more than a half-century ago, Selles has been able to retrieve a vast amount of detail. His analysis of the cross-cultural dynamics of this work is insightful. Anyone interested in the successes and failures of Christian mission should find this study interesting and informative."

— J. William Smit, professor of sociology, Calvin College, child of CRC China missionary Albert Smit

71.  *Envisioning Hope College: Letters Written by Albertus C. Van Raalte to Philip Phelps, Jr., 1857-1875*, edited by Elton J. Bruins and Karen G. Schakel (2011) 556 pp. ISBN: 978-0-8028-6688-2

These letters between the colony's leader and the first president of Hope College in Holland, Michigan, are sequentially placed in historical context and richly footnoted. They offer an intimate view of Van Raalte as he seeks funding for his college from the Dutch Reformed Church in the east, as well as insights into his pioneer community in the midst of conflagration and war.

72.  *Ministry Among the Maya*, by Dorothy Dickens Meyerink (Dec. 2011) 434 pp. ISBN: 978-0-8028-6744-5

Dorothy Meyerink entered her ministry among the Maya of Chiapas, Mexico, in 1956, and spent her entire service there. *Ministry Among the Maya* is an exciting account of persecution and success, relating the story of how, through the faithful witness of the laity and the early ordination of Mayan ministers, a strong, large, indigenous church was established and continues to flourish. Meyerink interweaves her personal experiences and the history of the church with reflections on the effective application of church growth principles.

73.  *The Church Under the Cross, Vol. 2*, by Wendell Karsen (Dec. 2011) 802 pp. ISBN: 978-0-8028-6760-5

See volume 67.

74.  *Sing to the Lord a New Song: Choirs in the Worship and Culture of the Dutch Reformed Church in America, 1785-1860*, by David M. Tripold (2012) 304 pp. ISBN: 978-0-8028-6874-9

As their privileged status evaporated in America's melting pot, the Dutch Reformed Church was forced to compete with a host of rising Protestant denominations in the New World. Survival became linked to assimilating within a new American way of life, with its own distinct language, culture, and religious practices. Gradually, organs, hymns and institutional church choirs were added to the traditional singing of the Psalter—innovations that altered the very fabric of Dutch Reformed religious life in America.

Sing to the Lord a New Song examines how choirs in particular revolutionized the Dutch Reformed Church in the nineteenth century, transforming the church's very nature in terms of worship, ecclesiastical life, institutional structures, and even social, fiscal, and moral practices. Moreover, the book examines how choirs helped break social barriers, particularly those regarding the status and role of women in the church.

Includes audio CD.

75. *Pioneers to Partners, The Reformed Church in America and Christian Mission to the Japanese,* by Gordon Laman (2012) ISBN: 978-0-8028-6965-4

Beginning with Japan's early exposure to Christianity by the very successful Roman Catholic mission to Japan in the sixteenth and seventeenth centuries, and the resultant persecution and prohibition of Christianity, Laman lays the groundwork for understanding the experience of nineteenth-century Protestant missionaries, among whom those of the Reformed Church in America were in the forefront. The early efforts of the Browns, Verbecks, Ballaghs, and Stouts, their failures and successes, are recounted within the cultural and political context of the anti-Western, anti-Christian Japan of the time.

Verbeck's service to the government helped bring about gradual change. The first Protestant church was organized with a vision for ecumenical mission, and during several promising years, churches and mission schools were organized. Reformed Church missionaries encouraged and trained Japanese leaders from the beginning, the first Japanese ministers were ordained in 1877, and the Japanese church soon exhibited a spirit of independence, ushering in an era of growing missionary/Japanese partnership.

The rise of the Japanese empire, a reinvigorated nationalism, and its progression to militarist ultranationalism brought on a renewed anti-Western, anti-Christian reaction and new challenges to both mission and church. With the outbreak of World War II, the Japanese government consolidated all Protestant churches into the Kyodan to facilitate control.

Laman continues the account of Reformed Church partners in mission in Japan in the midst of post-war devastation and subsequent social and political tensions. The ecumenical involvement and continued clarification of mutual mission finds the Reformed Church a full participant with a mature Japanese church.

76.  *Transatlantic Pieties*, ed by Hans Krabbendam, Leon van den Broeke, and Dirk Mouw (2012) 359 pp. ISBN: 978-0-8028-6972-2

*Transatlantic Pieties: Dutch Clergy in Colonial America* explores the ways in which the lives and careers of fourteen Dutch Reformed ministers illuminate important aspects of European and American colonial society of their times. Based on primary sources, this collection reexamines some of the movers and shakers over the course of 250 years. The essays shed light on the high and low tides, the promises and disappointments, and the factors within and beyond the control of a new society in the making. The portraits humanize and contextualize the lives of these men who served not only as religious leaders and cultural mediators in colonial communities, but also as important connective tissue in the Dutch Atlantic world.

77.  *Loyalty and Loss, the Reformed Church in America, 1945-1994*, by Lynn Japinga (2013) ISBN: 978-0-8028-7068-1

Offering a meticulously researched yet also deeply personal history of the Reformed Church in America throughout much of the twentieth century, Lynn Japinga's *Loyalty and Loss* will be of intense interest to the members of the RCA, reminding them of where they have come from, of the bonds that have held them together, and of the many conflicts and challenges that they have together faced and ultimately surmounted.

For those outside the RCA the questions of identity raised by this book will often sound very familiar, especially, perhaps, in its account of the church's struggle throughout recent decades to reconcile the persistently ecumenical spirit of many of its members with the desire of others within the denomination to preserve a real or imagined conservative exclusivity. Others may find the conflicts within the RCA reflective of their own experiences, especially as they relate to such issues as denominational mergers, abortion, the Viet Nam war, and women's ordination.

78.  *Oepke Noordmans: Theologian of the Holy Spirit*, Karel Blei (tran. By Allan Janssen) (2013) ISBN: 978-0-8028-7085-8

Oepke Noordmans was one of the major Dutch theologians of

the twentieth century, whose recovery of a vital doctrine of the Holy Spirit placed him at the center of thought on the nature of the church and its ministry.

In this volume Karel Blei, himself a theological voice of note, has provided a lucid introduction to and summary of Noordmans's thought and contextual impact. The book also includes substantial excerpts of Noordmans's writing in translation, offering a compact representation of his work to an English-speaking audience.

79. *The Not-So-Promised Land, The Dutch in Amelia County, Virginia, 1868-1880*, by Janet Sjaarda Sheeres (2013) 248 pp. ISBN: 978-0-8028-7156-5

*The sad story of a little-known, short-lived Dutch immigrant settlement.*

After establishing a successful Dutch colony in Holland, Michigan, in 1847, Albertus Van Raalte turned his attention to the warmer climes of Amelia County, Virginia, where he attempted to establish a second colony. This volume by Janet Sheeres presents a carefully researched account of that colonization attempt with a thorough analysis of why it failed. Providing insights into the risks of new settlements that books on successful colonies overlook, this is the first major study of the Amelia settlement.

A well-told tale of high hopes but eventual failure, *The Not-So-Promised Land* concludes with a 73-page genealogy of everyone involved in the settlement, including their origins, marriages, births, deaths, denominations, occupations, and post-Amelia destinations.

80. *Holland Michigan, From Dutch Colony to Dynamic City* (3 volumes), by Robert P. Swierenga (2013) ISBN: 978-0-8028-7137-4

*Holland Michigan: From Dutch Colony to Dynamic City* is a fresh and comprehensive history of the city of Holland from its beginnings to the increasingly diverse community it is today.

The three volumes that comprise this monumental work discuss such topics as the coming of the Dutch, the Americans who chose to live among them, schools, grassroots politics, the effects of the world wars and the Great Depression, city institutions, downtown renewal, and social and cultural life in Holland. Robert Swierenga also draws attention to founder Albertus Van Raalte's particular role in forming the city—everything from planning streets to establishing churches and schools, nurturing industry, and encouraging entrepreneurs.

Lavishly illustrated with nine hundred photographs and based on meticulous research, this book offers the most detailed history of Holland, Michigan, in print.

The volume received the Historical Society of Michigan 2014 State History Award in the Books, University and Commercial Press category

81. *The Enduring Legacy of Albertus C. Van Raalte as Leader and Liaison*, edited by Jacob E. Nyenhuis and George Harinck (2013) 560 pp. ISBN: 978-0-8028-7215-9

The celebration of the bicentennial of the birth of Albertus C. Van Raalte in October 2011 provided a distinct opportunity to evaluate the enduring legacy of one of the best-known Dutch immigrants of the nineteenth century. This book of essays demonstrates his unique role not only in the narrative of the migration to America but also in the foundation of theological education for Seceders (Afgescheidenen) prior to his emigration. These essays were all presented at an international conference held in Holland, Michigan, and Ommen, Overijssel, the Netherlands, with the conference theme of "Albertus C. Van Raalte: Leader and Liaison." Three broad categories serve as the organizing principle for this book: biographical essays, thematic essays, and reception studies.

Van Raalte began to emerge as a leader within the Seceder Church (Christelijk Afgescheidene Gereformeerde Kerk) in the Netherlands, but his leadership abilities were both tested and strengthened through leading a group of Dutch citizens to the United States in 1846. In his role as leader, moreover, he served as liaison to the Reformed Protestant Dutch Church in America in the eastern United States (renamed the Reformed Church in America in 1867) to the Seceder Church in the Netherlands, and to the civil authorities in the United States, as well as between business and their employees.

These fifteen essays illuminate the many facets of this energetic, multi-talented founder of the Holland kolonie. This collection further enhances and strengthens our knowledge of both Van Raalte and his Separatist compatriots.

82. *Minutes of the Christian Reformed Church, Classical Assembly, 1857-1870, General Assembly, 1867-79, and Synodical Assembly, 1880*, edited and annotated by Janet Sjaarda Sheeres (2014) 668 pp. ISBN: 978-0-8028-7253-1

"Janet Sheeres, noted scholar of the Dutch in North America, here turns her skill to the early years of the Christian Reformed Church in North America. She has painstakingly researched all the individuals who attended denominational leadership gatherings and the issues discussed and debated at these meetings. Her extensive annotations to a new translation of the minutes provides unprecedented and cogent insight into the early years of the denomination and the larger Dutch trans-Appalachian immigration of the nineteenth century. The annotations reflect Sheeres's characteristically detailed research in both Dutch and English. Scholars of immigration, religion, Dutch-American immigrants, and the Christian Reformed Church will benefit from data in this book, and the appendix of biographical data will be invaluable to those interested in family research."

— Richard Harms, archivist of the Christian Reformed Church

83  *New Brunswick Theological Seminary: an Illustrated History, 1784-2014.* John W. Coakley (2014) ISBN: 978-0-8028-7296-8

This volume marks the 230th anniversary of New Brunswick Theological Seminary and the reconfiguring of its campus by retelling the school's history in text and pictures. John Coakley, teacher of church history at the seminary for thirty years, examines how the mission of the school has evolved over the course of the seminary's history, focusing on its changing relationship to the community of faith it has served in preparing men and women for ministry.

In four chapters representing four significant eras in the seminary's history, Coakley traces the relationship between the seminary in New Brunswick and the Reformed Church in America, showing that both the seminary and the RCA have changed dramatically over the years but have never lost each other along the way.

84. *Hendrik P. Scholte: His Legacy in the Netherlands and in America.* Eugene P. Heideman (2015) 314 pp. ISBN: 978-0-8028-7352-1

This book offers a careful contextual theological analysis of a nineteenth-century schismatic with twenty-first-century ecumenical intent.

Hendrik P. Scholte (1803-1868) was the intellectual leader and catalyst of a separation from the Nederlandse Hervormde Kerk. Leaving the state church meant being separated from its deacon's funds, conflict with the laws of the state, and social ostracism. Due to poverty, Scholte emigrated with a group that settled Pella, Iowa. Schismatic tendencies continued in this and other nineteenth-century Dutch settlements with the most notable division being between those who joined the

Reformed Church in America and those who became the Christian Reformed Church in North America.

As Heideman says: "Although this book concentrates on what happened in the past, it is written with the hope that knowledge of the past will contribute to the faithfulness and unity of the church in the future."

85. *Liber A:1628-1700 of the Collegiate Churches of New York, Part 2,* translated, annotated, and edited by Frank J. Sypher, Jr. (2015) 911 pp. ISBN: 978-0-8028-7341-5

See volume 62.

86. *KEMP: The Story of John R. and Mabel Kempers, Founders of the Reformed Church in America Mission in Chiapas, Mexico,* by Pablo A. Deiros. 558 pp. ISBN 978-0-8028-7354-5

"This faithful story reveals God's power to transform thousands of people's lives through a couple committed to spreading God's message of love and devotion. The Kempers' commitment to their slogan "Chiapas para Cristo" was evidenced in all that they did. They were our surrogate parents, mission colleagues, and mentors."

— Sam and Helen Hofman, career RCA missionaries in Chiapas, Mexico.

"Employing a creative narrative style, Pablo Deiros has fashioned a fully documented biography into a compelling story of the lives and witness of John and Mabel Kempers. *Kemp* is a must read for those who are interested in the intersection of the Christian Church and the social revolution in Mexico during the twentieth century, the struggles of Maya cultures in Chiapas, and the transformative impact of the gospel of Jesus Christ among the people of Chiapas. *Kemp* is an inspiring and engaging history."

— Dennis N. Voskuil, Director, Van Raalte Institute

87. *Yes! Well...Exploring the Past, Present, and Future of the Church: Essays in Honor of John W. Coakley,* edited by James Hart Brumm. 324pp. ISBN: 978-0-8028-7479-5

In this volume, authors from around the world present essays in honor of John W. Coakley, L. Russell Feakes Memorial Professor Emeritus of Church History at New Brunswick Theological Seminary in

New Jersey. Following the pattern of Coakley's teaching, the contributors push readers to think about aspects of the church in new ways.

Contributors include: Thomas A. Boogart, James Hart Brumm, Kathleen Hart Brumm, Jaeseung Cha, James F. Coakley, Sarah Coakley. Matthew Gasero, Russell Gasero, Allan Janssen, Lynn Japinga, Mary L. Kansfield, Norman J. Kansfield, James Jinhong Kim, Gregg A. Mast, Dirk Mouw, Ondrea Murphy, Mark V. C. Taylor, and David W. Waanders

88. *Elephant Baseball: A Missionary Kids Tale*, by Paul Heusinkveld. 282 pp. ISBN: 978-0-8028-7550-1

This fascinating book recounts the up-and-down experiences of a missionary kid growing up overseas away from home in the 1960s. A sensitive autobiographical exploration of the universal trials of adolescence, Paul Heusinkveld's *Elephant Baseball* luxuriates in narrative fluidity—truly a riveting read.

89. *Growing Pains: How Racial Struggles Changed a Church and a School*, by Christopher H. Meehan. 240 pp. ISBN: 978-0-80287-570-9

In the 1960s, black parents from Lawndale Christian Reformed Church in Chicago tried to enroll their children in an all-white Christian school in the suburb of Cicero. A power struggle ensued, taking the matter to synod and inspiring the creation of the Office of Race Relations.

90. *A Ministry of Reconciliation: Essays in Honor of Gregg Mast*, edited by Allan J. Janssen. 272 pp. ISBN: 978-0-80287-598-3

Respect and affection for Gregg Mast permeates this volume of essays written by his colleagues across the fruitful years of his ministry. He certainly has much to show for his years of labor; the list of his accomplishments is long. But it is his heart that impresses me the most. I consider it a privilege to number myself as one of his colleagues, and I can attest, along with many others, to his generosity of spirit, kindness of speech, and faithful persistence of character. This book is a fitting tribute to his impact, and I warmly commend it to a wide readership.

Leanne Van Dyk
President and Professor of Theology
Columbia Theological Seminary
Decatur, Georgia

91. *For Better, For Worse: Stories of the Wives of Early Pastors of the Christian Reformed Church*, by Janet Sjaarda Sheeres. 224 pp. ISBN: 978-0-80287-625-6

In *For Better, for Worse*, Janet Sjaarda Sheeres highlights the lives of the wives of the first ten pastors of the Christian Reformed Church. Beginning in 1857, when the CRC was founded, Sheeres proceeds in the order in which the first ten pastors joined the church.

Drawing on genealogical and census data, church records from congregations their husbands served, and historical information about the position of women at the time, Sheeres brings the untold stories of these women's lives to light.

92. *In Peril on the Sea: The Forgotten Story of the William & Mary Shipwreck*, by Kenneth A. Schaaf. 382 pp. ISBN: 978-0-98914-696-8

"Historian Ken Schaaf has mined the rich holdings of the Library of Congress, the National Archives, and research facilities on both sides of the Atlantic to uncover the amazing story of the eighty-six Frisians who boarded the William & Mary en route to America. After weeks of sailing, they found themselves abandoned at sea by captain and crew aboard their sinking vessel. Readers interested in transatlantic passages under sail will not be able to put this book down. The story grabs the emotions and will not let go."
    —Robert P. Swierenga, Senior Research Fellow,
        Van Raalte Institute

93. *Jack: A Compassionate Compendium: A Tribute to Dr. Jacob E. Nyenhuis, Scholar, Servant, Leader*, edited by Donald A. Luidens and JoHannah M. Smith. 366 pp. ISBN: 978-0-98914-697-5

A tribute to Dr Jacob E. Nyenhuis, scholar, servant, and leader. Nyenhuis served as a professor of Classics at Hope College (Holland, Michigan) and later served as its Provost, before becoming the director of the Van Raalte Institute.

94. *A Commentary on the Minutes of the Classis of Holland, 1848-1876: A Detailed Record of Persons and Issues, Civil and Religious, in the Dutch Colony of Holland, Michigan*, edited by Earl William Kennedy (three volumes). 2,080 pp. ISBN: 978-0-98914-695-1

"This much-anticipated, annotated edition in English of the Dutch-language minutes of the Classis of Holland (Michigan)-- the seminal regional assembly of Dutch Reformed immigrants in the Midwest--is extraordinary for its scope and detail. Every substantive theological and ecclesiastical issue, whether Netherlandic or American in origin, is rooted in the foundational Synod of Dort (1618-19) and the Later (Nadere) Reformation. In addition, Kennedy provides biographical sketches of virtually every ministerial and elder delegate, likely hundreds of churchmen. Only a scholar grounded in Reformed theological and ecclesiastical history, fluent in languages, and skilled in genealogical search engines could have written such an extensive work. This multivolume sourcebook will be indispensable to anyone interested in Reformed church history."

—Robert P Swierenga, Research Professor, A. C. Van Raalte Institute, Hope College

95. *Hope College at 150: Anchored in Faith, Educating for Leadership and Service in a Global Society*, Jacob Nyenhuis et alii (two volumes).1,414pp. ISBN: 978-1-950572-00-7

A comprehensive survey and history of 150 years of Hope College, edited by Jack Nyenhuis with contributions by James C. Kennedy, Dennis N. Voskuil, Robert P. Swierenga, Alfredo M. Gonzales, John E. Jobson, Michael J. Douma, Thomas L. Renner, and Scott Travis. The two volume set includes many full-color images of the buildings on the campus and the history of Hope's architecture as well as lists of alumni, faculty, enrollment data, summaries of student life and housing, ending with a plan for the future.